INTRODUCTION TO SATIRE

INTRODUCTION TO
SATIRE

BY *Leonard Feinberg*

THE IOWA STATE UNIVERSITY PRESS
Ames, Iowa

LEONARD FEINBERG, professor of English at Iowa State University, was named Professor of the Year in the College of Sciences and Humanities in 1964. He has done a series of educational television lectures on satire entitled "Man and Laughter" and has had radio plays produced on NBC. A Fulbright lecturer in American Literature at the University of Ceylon in 1957–1958, he has also lectured at universities in India, Hong Kong, and Saigon. Articles written by him have appeared in *Atlantic, College English, Satire Newsletter,* and other periodicals. The author received his Ph.D. degree from the University of Illinois in 1946. With his wife he is coauthor of an English handbook-workbook (Oxford University Press) and is author of *The Satirist* (Iowa State University Press, 1963, Citadel Press, 1965).

© 1967 The Iowa State University Press
Ames, Iowa, U.S.A. All rights reserved

Composed and printed by
The Iowa State University Press
Stock #1378

First edition, 1967
Second printing, 1968
Third printing, 1968

Library of Congress Catalog Card Number: 67–12134

For Lilian

Preface

A GREAT MANY PEOPLE who realize that there are "satiric" elements in the books they read, the plays they see, and other arts to which they are exposed are curious about the implications of the term. In this book I have tried to satisfy that curiosity by showing what satire is and how it works.

The plan of the book deserves an explanation. Satire is such a protean species of art that no two scholars use the same definition or the same outline of ingredients. My arrangement is, admittedly, arbitrary. It is easier to discuss one component at a time than to deal with all aspects of satire simultaneously, so I have divided the material into four parts: nature, content, technique, and results. All four parts overlap, and even within each category the separate ingredients display related qualities and could as reasonably be classified under one heading as another. That is what satire is, a heterogeneous mixture of incongruous elements which simply cannot be satisfactorily classified, except for the purpose of focusing discussion.

Part One outlines the characteristics of satire. Part Two examines the content of satiric literature.

Part Three explains the general theory of satiric technique, demonstrates how the basic techniques of humor are used for satiric purposes, and analyzes the structure of satiric fiction. Part Four discusses the effects and limitations of satire.

This book would have taken longer to complete if Professor Albert Walker, Chairman of the English Department, Dean Chalmer Roy, and the administration at Iowa State University had not been considerate enough to provide time for my research. I am grateful to Professors Albert Walker and Keith Huntress for reading the manuscript. Edna Henry did her usual conscientious job of typing and Susan North helped check bibliography. Among colleagues from whose comments I have benefited are Norris Yates, Will Jumper, John Stroupe, David Bruner, James Lowrie, and Richard Herrnstadt.

No author could ask for more amicable cooperation than I have received from the staff at Iowa State University Press—particularly Nancy Schworm, Robert Campbell, and Merritt Bailey.

LEONARD FEINBERG

Contents

PART ONE: The Nature of Satire
1. Characteristics of Satire, 3

PART TWO: The Material of Satire
2. Sources, 23
3. Image of the World, 44
4. The Bitter and the Sweet, 61

PART THREE: The Technique of Satire
5. Theory of Satiric Technique, 85
6. The Technique of Incongruity, 101
7. The Technique of Surprise, 143
8. The Technique of Pretense, 176
9. The Technique of Superiority, 206
10. Beams and Studs, 226

PART FOUR: The Results of Satire
11. Effects, 253
12. Limitations, 263
Postscript. In Defense of Satire, 273

Notes, 275
Bibliography, 281
Index, 286
Acknowledgments, 293

PART ONE

The Nature of Satire

CHAPTER ONE

Characteristics of Satire

L IKE OTHER ARTS, the best satire is concerned with the nature of reality. Unlike other arts, which emphasize what *is* real, satire emphasizes what *seems* to be real but is not. It ridicules man's naive acceptance of individuals and institutions at face value. That ridicule may be expressed in amused or in bitter terms, but the essence of satire is revelation of the contrast between reality and pretense. La Rochefoucauld says, "We all have sufficient strength to bear up under the misfortunes of others."

Like the fable and allegory, satire almost always pretends to be something other than what it really is. (Sometimes it succeeds so well that readers miss the satiric intention entirely, as children do reading *Gulliver's Travels.*) But unlike the fable and allegory, satire does not always teach a moral lesson or offer a desirable alternative to the condition it criticizes. Readers sometimes assume that the satirist is offering a positive solution, in the form of behavior which is exactly opposite to that displayed in his satire, but this rarely proves to be true when one gets to know the satirist. And even direct satire, in the form of expository prose, is a pose: the satirist pretends to be giving objective, factual information but actually he is exaggerating and distorting facts.

Although satire often contains both humor and criticism, attempts to find the precise amount of each are not particularly useful. In Juvenalian satire there is likely to be a minimum of humor, and in Horatian satire a minimum of criticism. But though in theory the humor can be separated from the criticism, in practice comic devices are constantly used in order to criticize. Perhaps the best way to determine, in each case, whether humor or satire is being used is to evaluate the intention. "The laughter of comedy is relatively purposeless," David Worcester suggests. "The laughter of satire is directed toward an end."[1] The closeness with which the satirist pursues the object of his satire may help distinguish the satiric from the purely comic, as in Will Rogers' report from a disarmament conference: "Every time we sink a battle-ship, the Japs tear up a blue-print."

It is generally assumed that satire appeals primarily to the intellect. But the mechanism of satire is not that simple. The intellect seeks order. But the basic technique of satire is distortion, usually in the form of exaggeration, understatement, and pretense; and distortion implies disorder. A popular satiric method of achieving distortion is incongruity, which also results in disorder. Reason, then, is used to create unreason; logic is used to create illogic. Schopenhauer called humor an escape from "the tyranny of reason," yet humor is an appeal *to* reason. Bergson was so convinced that satire (and all other humor) should appeal only to the intellect that he required for its presence "an anesthesia of the heart." But most of the great satirists are anti-intellectual, distrustful of logically reached generalizations, and skeptical about the validity of all dogmas concerning men and institutions.[2] "The only way to get rid of a temptation," says Oscar Wilde, "is to yield to it."

There are several reasons why satirists distrust theory. For one thing, being inconsistent human beings themselves, they are painfully aware of the contradictions between logic and fact. For another, most satirists suspect that people choose a philosophy and an ethic not to redirect their lives to nobler ends, but to justify the kind of life they are already leading. Also, satirists know that almost all absolute generalizations about men and institutions are inaccurate; almost always there are exceptions to the rule, deviations from the generalization, contradictions to the theory. Satirists appreciate Schopenhauer's story of the minister who was preaching about man being made in God's image, while the village idiot walked by.

 ## *Pleasures of Satire*

SATIRE OFFERS the reader the pleasures of superiority and safe release of aggressions. Both of these

pleasures often involve derision, and some de-
fenders of satire have denied that so ungentlemanly
a quality could be characteristic of satire. One
scholar, for example, insists that the motivating
spirit of satire is not derision but a noble "moral
indignation."[3] Professor Bredvold's gesture is well
meant but futile. Satire does deal in derision, and
man enjoys derision as long as it is not directed at
himself. There is nothing cynical in this admission and nothing harmful to satire. Anyone whose
pleasure in satiric writing could be spoiled by
acknowledgment of its derisive spirit will not be
mollified by a satirist's pretense of moral indignation. And no one honest enough to admit that he
is delighted by vigorous ridicule needs any euphemisms to justify his pleasure. Most people find
pleasure in derision and satirists have made the
most of it, as when Heinrich Heine said of Alfred
de Musset, "yes, vanity is one of his four Achilles'
heels."

The excesses that we laugh at are usually inferior excesses; the fat man, not the strong man;
the fool, not the genius; greed, not philanthropy.
Literature of strife, discord, and attack has always
been more popular than the literature of praise
and agreement, and Paradises Lost have always appealed to more readers than Paradises Regained.
For the satirist, attack is likely to result in a stimulating piece of writing; defense and praise are
likely to be dull, even when they are justified. But
this aggression must be controlled. It rarely can be
expressed in the form of vituperation, because un-

dissembled anger is an unpleasant emotion to observe or read about.

We read satire because it gives us pleasure; but scholars disagree about the *kind* of pleasure it gives us. Some critics suggest that the pleasure is a moral one, the identification of a "good" reader with a "good" satirist, both of whom are indignant at a miscarriage of justice. This ethical satisfaction may be one of the pleasures involved in the satiric experience, but there are many, many others. One of the reasons why we get more pleasure from satire than from a sermon, even when the satire is making exactly the same point as the sermon, is that we have an uncomfortable feeling that the minister expects us to do something about it. We enjoy the satire because we know that nobody really expects us to do anything about it, and that we have no real intention of ever doing anything about it. It may not be a moral reaction, but for most human beings it *is* the reaction.

John Dryden preferred Juvenal to Horace because the former gave him more pleasure, although Horace gave him more instruction. "Pleasure, though but the second in degree is the first in favor. And who would not choose to be loved better, rather than to be more esteemed?"[4] Dryden was right. The appeal of satiric literature lies in the pleasure it gives the reader. It is not read for moral instruction. It is not a substitute for a sermon and is certainly not approached in the hope of getting a lesson in ethics. Satire may criticize evil but the didactic elements are incidental, not primary. The essential quality is entertainment. Satire must please the reader by imaginative richness as in *Gulliver's Travels* and *Brave New World,* or by vigor of invective as in Juvenal and Rabelais, or by sustained mockery as in *Candide.* Satire may offer other gratifications, but some pleasure it must give in order to hold the reader. That pleasure may come from the incongruity of Swift's Lilliputians or Anatole France's penguins, or the characters in "Li'l Abner" and "Peanuts." It may come from an avoidance of the censor, as in *A Modest Proposal* and *Jurgen,* or in jokes about bosses and officials, or in the retorts of Groucho Marx. It may consist of the pleasure in recognizing the contrast between the real and the pretended, as the social satires of Voltaire and Sinclair Lewis and Bernard Shaw reveal that contrast.

The appeal of satire lies in its literary merit: brilliance, wit, humor, freshness. But its longevity depends on the material to which these techniques have been applied. Because we have been conditioned by our society, we usually do not find entertaining that which seriously opposes what we have come to believe is socially appropriate behavior. The satire that survives uses material that continues to be significant, and issues that remain relevant, long after the time when the satire was written.

THE ASSUMPTION that satire relies on moral norms is so widely accepted that one hesitates to challenge it. But moral norms are not easy to define. Many satirists consider their work moral even when it contradicts the satire of other writers who also call themselves moralists. The same milieu produced the bohemian satire of Oscar Wilde, the socialist satire of Bernard Shaw, and the Catholic satire of Gilbert Chesterton; the conflicting satires of Dryden, Andrew Marvell, and Lord Rochester; Samuel Johnson and Charles Churchill; Roy Campbell and W. H. Auden. If moral norms were the criteria, readers would not enjoy satire based on the amoral or immoral norms of H. L. Mencken, Norman Douglas, Luigi Pirandello, Samuel Beckett, William Wycherley, James Joyce, Wilde, Bernard Mandeville, Machiavelli, and Jean Genêt.

Before accepting the morality theory, we might ask: *Whose* moral norms is satire based on? A universal norm? It is hard to prove that one exists, except in such vague terms that even bitterly opposing satirists claim simultaneously that they adhere to it. A democratic norm? There has also been satire on behalf of communism, fascism, and aristocracy. A Christian norm? Satire appears in every society, including atheistic Russia and skeptical China. Some readers approve only of didactic satire, Thomist or humanist or Marxist. But others, quite as well informed, prefer destructive satire which provides what Robert Brustein calls a "purely purgative function, relieving the spectator of his outrage and frustration."

In the middle of the twentieth century no one has the right to set up his own preferences as absolute moral norms. Thousands of intelligent and sophisticated readers and spectators find a great deal of pleasure in the satire of Nathanael West, Book IV of *Gulliver's Travels, Catch-22, Jonathan Wild,* Restoration dramatists, Jules Feiffer, James Joyce, *Waiting for Godot,* Eugene Ionesco, and *Dr. Strangelove.* This audience finds critical humor, entertaining exposé, or playfully critical distortion in these works. No critic is eminent enough to tell these readers and viewers that they are all, regrettably, mistaken, that these works are not satire because the critic prefers to rely on some traditional moral norm.

Satire appeals strongly to a feeling of superiority and a desire for censor-evasion on the part of the audience. Is that moral or immoral? Psychoanalysts who have written on the subject say that in comedy the audience always identifies with the aggressor, and in Molière and Ben Jonson we laugh at the victim. Is that moral? If hypocrisy is a prime source of satiric material, is our pleasure at the unmasking of the hypocrite moral or merely sadistic? And is it the immorality of the hypocrite or simply the exposure that entertains us? If distortion is the basic technique of satire, how does morality justify the use of such an unfair method? If morality is the norm, why do even such "moralists" as Shaw and Mark Twain and Henrik Ibsen spend so much time attacking conventional morality? If, as some scholars believe, the pleasure of satire comes from identifying with a strong personality (Swift, Rabelais, Johnson, Voltaire), what does this have to do with morality? And what of satire which ridicules excessive morality, such as the rigid honesty of Molière's Alceste?

Finally, what of the objects of satire? Parody provides much of the satirist's material, but it concerns itself with such technical elements as style, manner, and diction. *The Pooh Perplex* is delightful satire, but what is immoral about the idiosyncrasies of literary critics? Fools have often been victims of satirists, especially of such self-proclaimed moralists as Alexander Pope. Is being a fool immoral? Naiveté, idealism, ignorance, and incompetence are popular subjects for satiric attack. Are these qualities immoral?

Of course satire relies on norms. The moment one criticizes and says that something has been done in the wrong way, he is implying that there is a right way to do it. The "right" way has been interpreted by some to mean the moral way, but that is only one of the possible criteria. In actual practice, satirists usually apply a standard not of morality but of appropriateness—in other words, a *social* norm. It is a norm concerned not with ethics but with customs, not with morals but with mores; and it may be accepted by an entire society, or only one class in that society, or just a small coterie. The more exclusive the norm, the less likely the satire is to have wide appeal. Still, works complying with specialized tastes do provide satire for audiences which share those tastes. The Reverend Sydney Smith said there are three sexes: "men, women and clergymen."

It is also true that what is called "great" satire, satire which achieves lasting acceptance, is likely to depend on norms that seem to be universal, values that transcend their own time and locale. In that sense social norms tend to overlap with widely accepted moral norms; from that gray area of semantics comes the confusion over norms in satire. But satire ranges over the entire field of human activities and relies on standards which may be metaphysical or social or moral.

The satirist is motivated by the aesthetic desire for self-expression far more than by the ethical desire for reform. He is stimulated by the incongruities in society, he is infuriated or amused by them, and he ridicules them. Later, because men are expected to justify their actions, he rationalizes that his purpose was noble and virtuous. It is an understandable rationalization and a pardonable one. But there is not much valuable morality in *Jurgen, Penguin Island, Candide,* or *Brave New World.* Unless one postulates that any attitude toward life is "moral," it is hard to show high ethical purpose in James Cabell's paean to disillusionment, Anatole France's attack on religion, Voltaire's burlesque of Leibnitz, or Aldous Huxley's *reductio ad absurdum* of scientific planning. It seems likely that the subjects appealed to the authors, as material might strike the fancy of any artist, and that they worked with those subjects to produce art. Having the attitude of satirists, and using the devices most adaptable to satire, they produced the kind of books they did, not to teach a better way of life but primarily to satisfy a creative drive. Satire may be moral, as in Samuel Johnson, amoral as in Mencken, or immoral as in Machiavelli's *Mandragola.*[5]

 ## *Unfairness of Satire*

SATIRE IS UNFAIR. There is no denying this fact, and no need to deny it. The satirist is trying to arouse the attention of men, some of whom are hostile to him and most of whom are completely indifferent. In every society it is the business of established institutions to justify, defend, and glorify the functions of that society. Schools, churches, and governments insist that the society of which they are parts is superior to other societies, that its faults are at worst venial, and that its way of life is an excellent one. Popular literature helps to foster the optimistic concept that life is good, cheerful, and rewarding. Some men accept this doctrine. Most men attain, instead, a dull stolidity, a placid acceptance of things as they are, a conviction that reforms or changes are not likely to affect them. Nothing that fails to concern them personally has any perceptible effect on them.

They cannot be stirred by imagination or moved by protest, and they make the satirist's task a difficult one.

The satirist, then, has to exaggerate because he is facing formidable opposition: an audience indifferent to expression of unpleasant truths, and a throng of teachers, officials, and writers who insist that these truths do not exist. The modern satirist has to fight the propaganda of television, movies, radio, books, comic strips, newspapers, and popular magazines, all of which, even in democracies, misrepresent reality. *Satire is always unfair.* Byron, Mencken, Rabelais, Juvenal, Pope, Voltaire exaggerate shamelessly. There is no room for fairness in so unequal a struggle as the satirist's against the affectations of orthodoxy. In minimizing goodness, the satirist is no more guilty than the orthodox writers who minimize evil.

The satirist has another good reason for not being fair. To examine carefully the position of one's opponent is to develop a sympathy for him. Since very little in society is all good or all bad, the satirist would find extenuating circumstances in his opponent's situation. To know all is to forgive all. But to be sympathetic is to stop being a satirist. Effective satire cannot be fair and permit Samuel Beckett to describe life as a progression from "the spermarium to the crematorium."

One of the frequent, and absurd, charges made against satire is that it fails to offer satisfactory alternatives for the conditions it criticizes. Why it should be expected to offer these alternatives is dif-

ficult to see. On the assumption that only constructive criticism is valuable, no one but a fireman
would inform people that a house was burning; no
one but a doctor would announce an illness. The
mind which sees the faults in society is rarely the
kind of mind which visualizes adequate solutions.
There is no reason why it should possess two gifts
instead of one. It is sufficient to point out faults
and let others correct them. A satirist should no
more be expected to provide the world with a satisfying way of life than a detective or an extermi-
nator. "My business," said Mencken, "is diagnosis,
not therapeutics." He was right. When satirists
try to offer alternatives, they usually fail miserably.
Both Aldous Huxley and Sinclair Lewis suffer when
they imply solutions, the former becoming mys-
tical and the latter banal. The satirist has work to
do but planning the ideal society is not part of that
work.

Freshness of Satire

PERHAPS the most striking quality of satiric literature is its freshness, its originality of perspective.
We are shown old things in a new way. Satire
rarely offers original ideas. Instead, it presents the
familiar in a new form. Satirists do not offer the
world new philosophies. What they do is look at
familiar conditions from a perspective which makes
these conditions seem foolish, harmful, or affected.
Satire jars us out of complacence into a pleasantly

shocked realization that many of the values we unquestioningly accept are false. *Don Quixote* makes chivalry seem absurd; *Brave New World* ridicules the pretensions of science; *A Modest Proposal* dramatizes starvation by advocating cannibalism. None of these ideas is original. Chivalry was suspect before Cervantes, humanists objected to the claims of pure science before Aldous Huxley, and Englishmen were aware of famine in Ireland before Swift. It was not the originality of the idea that made these satires popular. It was the manner of expression, the satiric method, which made them interesting and entertaining. Satires are read because they are aesthetically satisfying as works of art, not because they are (as they may be) morally wholesome or ethically instructive. They are stimulating and refreshing because with common-sense briskness they brush away illusions and second-hand opinions. With spontaneous irreverence, satire rearranges perspectives, scrambles familiar objects into incongruous juxtaposition, and speaks in a personal idiom instead of abstract platitude. The vision of life it gives may be unfair but it is fresh and diverting, as when Mencken says, "Posterity is the penalty of a faulty technique" and Nietzsche mentions "two great European narcotics, alcohol and Christianity."

Satire exists because there is need for it. It has lived because men appreciate a refreshing stimulus, an irreverent reminder that they live in a world of platitudinous thinking, cheap moralizing, and foolish philosophy. Satire serves to prod men into an awareness of truth, though rarely to any action on behalf of truth. Satire tends to remind men that most of what they see, hear, and read in popular media of communication is sanctimonious, sentimental, and only partially true. Life resembles in only a slight degree the popular image of it. Soldiers rarely hold the ideals that movies attribute to them, nor do ordinary men devote their lives to unselfish service of mankind. Intelligent men know these things but tend to forget them when they do not hear them expressed. Satire expresses them in a form pleasant and memorable. "Englishmen," says Shaw, "will never be slaves; they are free to do whatever the government and public opinion allow them to do."

Satire is not the greatest form of literature but it is a necessary one. It serves a function that the realist and romantic do not fulfill, by dramatizing and exaggerating objectionable qualities in man and society. It does not, and does not try to, give the kind of insight into personality that Dostoevsky, Rolland, Tolstoy, and Mann have achieved. A man whose reading was limited to satire would have a perverted vision of life. But so would a man who read only romance or philosophy. It has always been the misfortune of satire to be criticized for failing to do things which it had no intention of doing. No one asks lyric poetry to give a realistic picture of society. No one asks comedy to be introspective. No one requires of the novel that it reform society. Yet all of these demands are made of satire. Sinclair Lewis, a satirist who uses exaggeration for comic effects, is criticized for not giving a wholly realistic portrayal of society. Molière is belittled because his characters do not show the depth and subtlety of William Shakespeare's. Critics repeatedly demand that satire justify its existence by serving a moral purpose. Why should it, any more than any other form of literature? The test for satire is its success within its prescribed sphere. That sphere is criticism of man and society, a criticism made entertaining by humor and moving by irony and invective.

Satire is such an amorphous genre that no two scholars define it in the same words. No less an authority than Professor Robert C. Elliott comes to the reluctant conclusion that no satisfactory definition is possible. The best we can do, he suggests, is to look at a number of works traditionally accepted as satires and compare the new work with these examples. If the work we are considering has a reasonable number of resemblances to accepted satires, we are justified in calling it a satiric work. But we should never demand complete conformity to a particular type, and we should accept numerous deviations from familiar practice.[6]

This is a reasonable suggestion. The more one studies satire the more likely he is to permit the widest possible latitude in defining terms. But for purposes of discussing the subject in this book I use this working definition: Satire is a playfully critical distortion of the familiar.

PART TWO

The Material of Satire

CHAPTER TWO

Sources

DISSIMULATION is the richest source of satire. Pretense and hypocrisy permeate satiric literature because pretense and hypocrisy are, as teen-aged Holden Caulfield learns, inescapable attributes of man and of society. The necessity for pretending increases as civilization develops, and dissimulation becomes not only socially acceptable but socially indispensable. The idealism of man makes constant pretense an unavoidable characteristic of his institutions; the nature of man makes pretense a frequent characteristic of individuals.

Dissimulation comes from man's pretense that he is always motivated by the ideal, the moral, the good, never by the actual, the immoral, the evil. He tries to avoid admitting the validity of amoral or immoral motivation, by pretending either that what seems to be evil is merely the temporary absence of good, or that the unpleasant elements of life are transitions to eventual happiness. Man has a definite preference for believing what is consoling.

Out of this conflict between the ideal and the practical has grown the necessity for falsifying, to some degree, almost all human values. Because of this discrepancy between the desirable and the actual, there exists a double standard in the structure of society. We really do know that life is a struggle for survival, that the fittest tend to survive longest, and that this fitness consists only to a limited degree of the qualities which conventional morality calls "good." Honesty, piety, humility, hard work, sacrifice, altruism, and love of labor are all meritorious qualities. But even a cursory examination reveals that the successful men in our society (successful in the sense that they have power, money, or other socially desirable possessions) have achieved their objectives by using capacities which are irrelevant to morality; ability, ambition, shrewdness, energy, and sometimes unscrupulousness and selfishness result in material success. In the very primary activities of life we pretend to accept one standard; we practice another. This is of course elementary, and this double standard in society is the fundamental source of satire.

 The Individual

MODERN PSYCHOLOGY IMPLIES not only that conscious man is a dissembler but that even subconscious man may be called a hypocrite. The important part played in man's life by psychological mechanisms is evidence of pretense, conscious or unconscious. Sublimation, rationalization, compensation, repression—all are means of avoiding honest self-appraisal. With sublimation the satirist would have no quarrel, if it were admitted as such. But, instead, man pretends; he makes a noble virtue of necessity; and it is in pretense itself, in the attempt to misrepresent, that the satirist finds his material. He is delighted to hear one social psychologist say, "The fanaticism of the religious bigot is often a compensation for lack of the very qualities which he finds in others";[1] and another: "A 'martyr complex' may show itself as courageous liberalism. Feelings of hostility and fear toward all that is unfamiliar (for instance, foreigners) may disguise themselves as patriotic emotions."[2]

Writers have been aware of camouflaged motivation long before Freudian terminology made it popular. Tolstoy, Shakespeare, and Dostoevsky recognized the real causes of aberrations; and satirists like Aristophanes, Ben Jonson, and Molière concentrated on duplicity and hypocrisy in their characterizations. Because they emphasize disproportionately a single weakness, satirists are often accused of creating caricatures instead of characters.

The technique we call Socratic irony (a form of satire) is based on Socrates' demonstration that although everyone pretends to accept the virtues which his society commends, in some specific instances almost everyone fails to practice those virtues. What made Socrates' method especially effective was his feigned surprise at the contrast between man's pretense and man's action. It is a surprise that many satirists have since simulated.

Most people first respond to stimuli emotionally, then try to justify those responses by rationalizing. Because the incidents of life are so varied, because stimuli are so different, because individual conditioning has made each man a unique person, it is almost impossible to react with complete consistency to one's professed philosophy or religion. As a result we find devout parishioners defending gambling at their church carnival, and American Communists supporting imperialist wars. Few people can pass an objective snobbery test. What interests the satirist is not these actions themselves but the hypocritical justifications which are offered for them. In fiction the works of satirists like Bernard Shaw and Sinclair Lewis and Mark Twain are full of such examples. And in life the last words of Captain Kidd before he was hanged were, "This is a very fickle and faithless generation."

There is, then, dissimulation in man's adaptations. This dissimulation may be ethically defensible and socially beneficial, but the satirist limits his interest simply to the fact that dissimulation exists. Obviously, hypocrisy is not the only object of the satirist's attack; he also criticizes vice, sentimentality, folly, and other qualities regarded as socially undesirable.

The reason that hypocrisy provides so large a part of the satirist's material is that vice, vanity, and folly rarely dare admit their true nature. In a society committed to praise of goodness, it is not politic to proclaim one's viciousness. In a society which admires intelligence, it is deplorable to be stupid. These values are sometimes reversed. In

Stalin's Russia loyalty to the state superseded loyalty to the family; the inclination under such cultural pressure was to disguise a strong family affection under the pretense of indifference. In general, whatever the society, the tendency is to try to camouflage socially objectionable qualities under socially approved labels. Thus selfishness may pose as devotion, folly as joviality, pugnacity as patriotism. As a result, in addition to being evil or foolish, these qualities tend to partake of dissimulation. The satirist has a twofold source for satire, as George Orwell demonstrates in *1984* and Eugene Zamiatin in *We*.

The more interdependent men are, the less possibility there exists for what Stuart Chase calls the "luxury of integrity." In such societies the dependence of most individuals on other people breeds an artificiality of relationship, a need to be polite and agreeable and fawning, not out of personal conviction but as a matter of social necessity. It is not wise to object openly to a superior's taste, or a boss's politics, or a potential customer's eccentricity. Withdrawal is one of the few alternatives to the artificialities of cooperative living, and it is more than a century since Thoreau left Walden Pond. The unavoidable hypocrisy of yes-men, salesmen, junior executives, and ambitious men in every competitive enterprise has been portrayed by such contemporary satirists as Jean Giradoux, J. P. Marquand, Giovanni Guareschi, Sinclair Lewis, Kingsley Amis, and Joseph Heller.

Conformity, security, self-protection, tradition,

and manners frequently require a behavior which is hypocritical. T. S. Eliot referred to the need to "put on a face to meet a face." Anne Lindbergh speaks of the exhaustion brought on by social life, which requires constant insincerity. In *The Great God Brown,* Eugene O'Neill has people wear masks to indicate when the "social" rather than the "real" person is speaking. Even at the level of television comedy, this condition is sometimes recognized: Comedian Red Buttons has just saved a man from capture and given him a bag of money; the man says, "I'll never forget what you did for me." Red says, "You'll forget. It's human nature."

Part of the hypocrisy of society comes from the nature of individual drives. The "pecking order" among chickens prescribes that in every group of chickens one is the boss, a second can peck all but the first, a third is superior to all except the top two, and so on, down to the very lowest chicken who can peck no one. A similar relationship exists among the cormorants trained by Japanese fishermen. If such aggression is present among human beings also (and most psychiatrists think that it is), then many of the good desires of man are constantly being thwarted by aggressive drives. Similarly, the aggressions of children at an age preceding socially conditioned behavior show them to be domineering and selfish—a fact known long before William Golding wrote *Lord of the Flies.* Freud called dreams acts of "inner dishonesty." The contrast between what society regards as ideal and

what man finds possible is frequently startling;
Mencken was amused by the fact that cowardice
exists everywhere, and is everywhere shameful.

Satirists disagree as to whether particular individuals or general types should be the objects of
satire. Aristophanes chose specific men as victims.
So did Lucilius, the first Roman satirist. Ambrose
Bierce, who attacked contemporaries by name in
poems and essays, was contemptuous of writers who
criticize abstract vices and unsatisfactory conditions
without naming the individuals concerned. H. L.
Mencken also insisted that the men attacked be
clearly identified. On the other hand, Horace pro-
claimed the satirist's mission to be criticism of
foolish customs and wrong ideas rather than particular men. And Pope piously announced that
he accepted Horace's advice. But in practice both
groups of satirists carried out both objectives.
Horace and Pope attacked particular individuals,
and Aristophanes, Lucilius, Bierce, and Mencken
often satirized ideas and types. Nor is there guarantee of success with either method; when Gilbert
chose Oscar Wilde as his victim in *Patience,* he was
less entertaining than when he chose types to satirize in other plays.

In theory antisocial acts and antisocial individuals should be the objects of satiric attack. But
actually hypocritical deviations and hypocritical
deviants are most likely to be satirized. Although
folly and vice are both supposed to be fair game,

the fact is that they are likely to be attacked by satirists only when folly poses as good sense and vice as goodness. In *The Alchemist* and *Tartuffe* we have not just greed and lust but greed pretending to be generosity and lust pretending to be spirituality.

It is not merely deviation from the norm, social or moral, that qualifies an individual for satiric treatment. Great villains have always been hard to ridicule. Men like Attila and Hitler are antisocial, immoral, monstrous, yet they do not lend themselves to satire until they become hypocritical. The villain who openly admits both his villainy and his motivation may be horrible but he is not entertaining. When he tries to seem noble, he invites satiric treatment. By pretending to be something he is not, he becomes a hypocrite; and hypocrisy is an inferiority that we can laugh at, feel contempt for, and enjoy. The sincere fanatic, the frank brute, may be wrong and dangerous but he gains a certain stature from his frankness, his failure to pretend that he is more conventional or more moral than he really is. Also, satire requires a certain detachment which is almost impossible to achieve toward someone whom we genuinely fear or hate.

The satirist uses individuals as sources for satiric material in two ways: He may select an identifiable person and put him into a satiric work, or he may create characters who reveal human weaknesses in a convincing manner.

The list of actual human beings attacked by

satirists is too large to be compiled even by earnest graduate students. Robert Walpole was satirized by Swift, Gay, and Fielding, among others. Dryden attacked Buckingham and Shadwell; Pope ridiculed Addison; Byron named King George III, Southey, Castlereagh, and literary critics; both Browning and Swift castigated contemporary fortune-tellers. Huxley satirized Middleton Murry, D. H. Lawrence, and a number of other acquaintances in *Point Counterpoint.* Juvenal and Dante identified their victims with considerable venom. Waugh has been suspected of distorting live models, particularly in *Decline and Fall,* and Koestler used Stalin as an object of hatred in *Age of Longing.* Maugham satirized Hugh Walpole in *Cakes and Ale.* Aristophanes named generals, philosophers, politicians, poets, and actors in his plays. Twain and Mencken did the same in essays.

The other method of satirizing individual human beings is to create believable characters whose behavior exposes their pretenses. In a charming way this is what Charlie Brown and the other characters in the cartoon strip "Peanuts" achieve. In more biting fashion this is also what the characters of Ring Lardner, Sinclair Lewis, Aldous Huxley, Vladimir Nabokov, Gogol, Thackeray, Dickens, Meredith, Jane Austen, and many other satirists do. Thurber's bumbling Walter Mitty, Marquand's frustrated George Apley, Maugham's lusting clergyman in *Rain,* Twain's bombastic Beriah Sellers in *The Gilded Age,* all are examples of this technique.

INSTITUTIONS, like individuals, practice dissimulation. Having developed out of necessity, often harsh necessity, established institutions tend to deny the original reasons for their existence and sanctimoniously assume noble virtues. Government, having sprung from man's insecurity, minimizes its paternalism and stresses its benevolence. Communism, crushing individuality and repressing criticism, chatters pompously of humanitarianism and freedom. Altruism—never economic gain—is the announced purpose of every nation at peace conferences. Religious institutions lay claim to the virtues of benign omniscience. Man accepts for his institutions the obligations of his religious ethics—Christian, Buddhist, Moslem, Hindu, Jewish—which interfere with the successful operation of those institutions. God serves on each nation's side in war, according to each nation's priests. And business always pretends that it is motivated primarily by patriotism.

Since the structure of civilized societies is ostensibly based on ethical systems possible only in utopia, the satirist has an unlimited source of satiric material. Many things once called "sinful" are today called "natural." Whatever the future chooses to call improper (even if it should be the *repression* of aggressive or sexual impulses) will try to conceal its socially disapproved characteristics under the cover of such qualities as the future will consider desirable. A brutal society simply inverts the conventional values and creates a new source of duplicity; in Nazi Germany, for example, gentleness was considered shameful and a kind man had to pretend to be more brutal than he was. But, ironically, hypocritical society laughs contemptuously at unmasked hypocrites.

The satirist, with Martian detachment, points out the inconsistencies of the farmer who demands simultaneous independence and parity payments; the businessman who insists on laissez-faire and a high protective tariff; the labor leader who opposes monopolies except among unions. Poking fun at women pleases men more than it does women; poking fun at men pleases women more than it does men. Ridiculing the upper classes pleases the lower classes more than the upper, and vice versa. The popularity of gossip columnists and "confidential" magazines is due to their revelation of the seamy side of prominent personalities.

Usually it is the violation of *social* norms that arouses the satirist's attack. Because social norms are often similar to moral norms, or identical with them, didactic critics tend to assume that morality is the primary source of criticism. But there is considerable evidence against this assumption.

It is ironic, of course, that the more civilized and idealistic a society becomes, the more hypocritical it is likely to become. Because what we call civilization requires the suppression of aggressions and desires which may harm society, politeness is socially useful but often artificial. It may be a "good" pretense, but pretense it is, and the satirist disregards the extenuating elements and concentrates on the artificiality. The more restraints there are, the more need there is for the civilized individual to pretend to accede to them. The more ethical a society wants to be the more hypocritical it has to be, because the gap between the ideal and the actual continues to widen. An avowedly evil society would have less hypocrisy; it would not be a better place to live in.

Sometimes the irony of history itself amuses us. Müller points out that "Rome made almost all its great contributions to civilization *after* it had become corrupted."[3] The Roman Empire, he says, was "created by force and fraud, like all other empires. . . . They had not consciously set out to rule the world." Bret Harte insisted that vice was responsible for bringing "the graces of civilization so quickly to the Far West." "It is the gamblers who bring the music to California," he said. "It is the prostitute who brings the New York fashions in dress there, and so throughout."[4] The radicalism of one generation becomes the conservatism of the next. English Conservatives and American Republicans retain, when they come to power, the "socialist" legislation of their predecessors. And forty years after the Revolution, four separate classes of service were available on Russian ships.

The satirist is remarkably observant of contemporary ironies. Here, for example, is Heine's comment on racial prejudice: "We saw the bloody parody of this madness at the outbreak of the revolution in San Domingo—where a negro band, devastating the plantations with fire and sword, was led by a black fanatic carrying a huge crucifix and screaming: 'The whites killed Christ, let us kill all the whites.' "[5]

In the same age what seems virtuous to the preacher may seem abnormal to the psychiatrist. Not everything that entertains one culture is amusing to another. One of the popular forms of fun among the Fijians was to put prisoners in heated ovens and howl with laughter when the heat made the victims writhe with pain. A judge who shot three of his four critics in a Mexican tavern was censured by friends—for his poor aim in so small a place. Whittaker tells of a Pueblo artist who, in his first painting, showed an American Indian kneeling before a priest in full vestments; the embroidery on the priest's stole was a dollar sign.[6] Pre-Columbian Indians laughed at puns, mistakes in pronunciation, innuendos, and fools. The American Indians of the Northwest took pride in burning in public objects which symbolized thousands of blankets in order to show their wealth. This seems odd to us. But the things for which we spend millions of dollars must seem odd to the Northwest Indians. The most popular rat poison in Mexico is named "The Last Supper," and the dysentery with which most tourists are afflicted is called "Montezuma's Revenge."

It is hardly necessary to point out that the maneuvering that goes on among ordinary people differs only in degree from the machinations on a higher level of political or economic activity. The fight for power and scheming for favor that everyone can see going on around him are similar to those featured in newspapers and histories. They are obvious to the satirist.

After the crucifixion, a Roman centurion turned to his companion and said, "You've got to admit He was a great teacher." "Yes," said the other, "but what has He published?"

This anecdote, circulating on American campuses in recent years, does more than express the irritation of many professors with the preferential treatment given to research. It illustrates that everything is subject to satire and that Francis Bacon was mistaken when he wrote, "As for jest, there be certain things which ought to be privileged from it: namely, religion, matters of state, great persons, any man's present business of importance, and any case that deserves pity."[7] The fact is that every item Bacon mentions, plus a great many more, has been successfully satirized by practitioners of the craft. No subject seems to be sacred: Nuclear war was satirized in *Dr. Strangelove*, cannibalism and funerals by Evelyn Waugh, God by Mark Twain, and democracy by Mencken.

Molière was much closer to the truth when he made a character say, "The business of comedy is to represent in a general way all the defects of men, and particularly those of our own age."[8] Nor is it surprising that clergyman Swift criticized Christianity, snobbish Evelyn Waugh ridiculed the aristocracy, and socialist Orwell castigated socialism. Successful satire deals with specific individuals in particular situations; it is full of concrete examples and convincing details. To get this kind of information a writer has to be familiar with his subject, and that is why satirists write about, and criticize, the things they know best. When a person gets to know any subject well, he becomes aware of the imperfections beneath its superficial excellences—and it is imperfection which lends itself to satiric treatment.

Politics and religion have long been objects of satiric attack. Emory Storrs felt that "the Democratic party is like a mule—without pride of ancestry or hope of posterity." But William Jennings Bryan, finding no platform at a country meeting, climbed on a manure spreader and said, "Ladies and gentlemen! This is the first time I have addressed an audience from a Republican platform." Oscar Wilde's attitude was more genteel, though hardly more complimentary. In *The Picture of Dorian Gray* he says, "There is hardly a person in the House of Commons worth painting; though many of them would be the better for a little whitewashing."

During a disarmament conference Will Rogers wrote, "The big countries say the trouble with little countries is that they're little." And in 1943 when Germany was threatening to invade England, a bookstore in occupied Holland exhibited a large picture of Hitler in the center of a window—surrounded by copies of a book called *How To Swim.*

According to Bernard Shaw, "No public man in these islands ever believes that the Bible means what it says: he is always convinced that it says what he means."[9] The Reverend Sydney Smith observed, "When a man is a fool, in England we only trust him with the immortal concerns of human beings." Oscar Wilde remarked, "A bishop keeps on saying at the age of eighty what he was told to say when he was a boy of eighteen." And Mark Twain assumed that in heaven wings "ain't to fly with! The wings are for show, not for use."

Sometimes it is religious writers themselves, like Quevedo, Samuel Johnson, St. Jerome, Swift, C. S. Lewis, Hawthorne, and Chesterton, who satirize Christians. It is worth noting that both groups, the skeptics and the devout, criticize religion for failing to practice what it preaches, not for the ideals on which the religion is based. Even the most vehement satirists have usually attacked not Christ but Christianity, not Buddha but Buddhism. Only rarely do satirists attack the spiritual concepts of the major religions.

The law, as a profession and in the person of its representatives, has been satirized by many writers, especially Dickens, Swift, Voltaire, Gogol, Lewis, Carroll, and France. Courtroom procedure is particularly susceptible to satire on the grounds of apparent hypocrisy. In most cases brought to court, two contradicting truths are asserted; two groups of witnesses, experts, and lawyers prove two opposite conclusions to be true. The satirist is unkind enough to assume that at least one of the sides is deliberately lying. This assumption is corroborated, the satirist pretends, by the court's verdict. The liar is thus officially determined. As the satirist sees it, the courts are constantly proving to the world that half the legal profession is dishonest. And since the members of this half are rapidly interchanging, depending on the verdict of the day, a naive observer, or a satirist like Voltaire, might suspect that absolute truth is not the guiding principle of jurisprudence. Juvenal, Genêt, Daumier, and Vercors shared that suspicion.

The Cosmos

IN ADDITION TO the dissimulation of the individual and of society there is another source of satire: cosmic irony, the apparent dissimulation of the universe. One may call it the illogic of the cosmos, or, as Worcester puts it, "an impractical joke." Because man has grown accustomed to a certain order in nature (birth, youth, maturity, death) and has come to expect a certain continuity, sudden reversals and unanticipated events strike him as being ironic. Expecting people to reach old age, he is resentful when someone he loves dies young. Resigned to the normal pattern of nature's activity, he finds hurricanes and earthquakes somehow disorderly. He sees a resemblance between the fickleness of fate and the dissimulation of society; both pretend to do one thing, but do another. This apparent deception on the part of the cosmos is usually called *irony* rather than satire, but cosmic irony is sometimes a form of satire as well as of tragedy.

Because people who die unexpectedly have made plans for at least the immediate future, man is shocked by the irony of those uncompleted preparations. There is cosmic irony in the simultaneous deaths of millionaries and paupers; in failing to get aboard planes which later crash, and in managing unfairly to get aboard planes which later crash; in the fact that many good or great men die early, while evil men live a long time.

When the Russian revolutionary Bestoujeff was being hanged, the rope broke. "Nothing succeeds with me," he said. "Even here I meet with disappointment." One of Charles Addams' cartoons shows a woman walking into a room where her husband is dangling awkwardly from a poorly improvised noose. "Can't you do anything right?" she asks disgustedly.

Cosmic irony is implied in Luke's remark: "Physician, heal thyself." It appears in Pinero's calling one of his plays *The Notorious Mrs. Ebbsmith;* a woman with that name, whom Pinero had never heard of, committed suicide, thinking that her immorality had been exposed. Nathanael West, whose novels are saturated with the irony of purposeless death, died with his wife in an auto accident.

The satirist does not concern himself with the question of whether he has the right to apply human logic to suprahuman levels. Struck by the similarity of cosmic irony to social irony, he uses the cosmos as a source of satiric material.

The irony of fate is sometimes called Sophoclean irony, but it is not limited to the plays of the Greek tragedian. Fate has seemed capricious or indifferent to observers as dissimilar as Omar Khayyam and Dean Inge. There is cosmic irony in calamity which results from apparent good luck, as in W. W. Jacobs' *Monkey's Paw*. There is irony in Thornton Wilder's *Bridge of San Luis Rey,* where an attempt to justify God's action backfires; in Hardy's novels, where petty incidents lead to tragedy; in Sophocles' plays, where men unwittingly bring about their own destruction; in Mark Twain's *Mysterious Stranger,* where Satan suggests that only death or madness can give man happiness. There is irony when people or events turn out better than one expects, as in O. Henry's stories, and when they turn out worse than one expects, as in Somerset Maugham's or Maupassant's.

Heinrich Heine, fascinated by cosmic irony, wrote: " 'Nature,' Hegel told me once, 'is strange and wonderful; it employs the same tools for the most august and the very lowest purposes—for instance, the very member to which the highest mission, the propagation of mankind, is entrusted, serves also. . . .' "[10]

The levels of irony vary considerably. Although the irony of the Greek theater attained immense dignity, Euripides' contemporaries recognized a salient and often infuriating difference between his rationalistic irony and the reverent at-

titudes of Aeschylus and Sophocles. In Faulkner's
Sound and the Fury, Quentin forces himself to
complete the year at Harvard for which his family
has paid, before he commits suicide. And in Beckett's *Waiting for Godot* man anticipates the arrival
of someone who he knows will not come. In
Brecht's *Good Woman of Setzuan,* one of the three
gods is deaf. In much of modern literature, in
Kafka, Pirandello, Sartre, and the theater of the
absurd, cosmic irony is based not on the concept
that the gods play with men's destinies but with
the equally tantalizing idea that men behave as if
there were gods in a godless universe.

Scholars have done a great deal of speculating
about the relationship of satire to society. One of
the areas of controversy is whether satire flourishes
in an unstable, changing society or in a secure,
homogeneous one. Proponents of the former view,
such as Edgar Johnson and Cazamian, cite the success of Voltaire, Cervantes, and Gogol in times of
social change. But other critics, like Evelyn Waugh
and W. H. Auden, point to the achievements of
Molière and Pope in stable societies. Another
source of dispute is the question of censorship: Do
satirists work best in a regimented or free society?
Some scholars think that censorship stimulates a
satirist to imaginative heights and cite Dante,
Swift, Gogol, and Voltaire as examples. But other
scholars believe that a free society nourished the
satire of Shaw, Twain, Anatole France, and Gira-

doux. Still another dispute has been waged over the problem of whether great satire is produced when the writer is in tune with his times, as Taine and Plekhanov insisted, or by writers who are hostile to their environment, such as Aristophanes, Juvenal, Oscar Wilde, and Evelyn Waugh.

The indisputable fact is that significant satire has appeared in all kinds of society, whether they were labeled "stable" (Molière, Swift, Dickens), "unstable" (Gogol, Heine, Voltaire), "renascent" (Rabelais, Jonson), "decadent" (Juvenal, Rochester), "restrictive" (Chaucer, Gogol), or "free" (France, Twain, Shaw).

The *kind* of satirist a man becomes is determined to some extent by his environment—when strict censorship forces him to create ingenious satire to circumvent the authorities or when the development of his craft may offer new, or encourage the use of old, techniques. But for the satirist all times are out of joint. At whatever time he is born he can be a satirist, for society always provides satiric material. The conflict between the ideal and reality always transcends the limited degree of harmony that society may at any particular period temporarily achieve. That degree fluctuates between dissatisfaction and resignation. But even in the most congenial period there is an enormous amount of pretense, hypocrisy, and artificiality in society—and the satirist concentrates on that material.

CHAPTER THREE

Image of the World

THE WORLD is a *madhouse,* some satirists claim. Günter Grass shows atrocities committed by what society considers normal people—the grocer Matzerath, German bourgeoisie, Russian soldiers. The world of *The Tin Drum* is insane, distorted, illogical. Lankes the corporal murders five nuns walking on a beach—simply because his orders are to shoot all dangerous trespassers. Oskar never finds out who his real father was. In a mental hospital Oskar finds refuge from a mad world. There are four characters whom society calls mad—Leo Schugger, who haunts funerals; Fajngold, who thinks his wife is still alive; Herbert, who tries to rape a wooden statue; and Oskar himself—but these mad characters are harmless, while the sane people create the horrors.

The levels of intensity in portraying a mad world vary considerably. At its most playful it is the wonderland of Alice containing the tea party where the Mad Hatter and the Hare and Dormouse offer wine when there is none, shift the conversation inexplicably, reply in *non sequiturs,* ask riddles without answers, indulge in pointless insults, and butter watches. The world is still charming in Gilbert and Sullivan and in *The Importance of*

Being Earnest. But not many satirists work at this level.

More often, the image of a mad world is expressed with such bitterness that the satirist comes dangerously close to sheer vituperation and sometimes crosses the line between art and fury. Book III of *Gulliver's Travels* shows a world of mad scientists, mad rulers, and mad citizens. A number of critics insist that Nathanael West is not a satirist because an implied standard of morality is missing from the grotesque world of brutality, ugliness, hatred, and madness that he creates, and in which his protagonist confuses himself with Jesus. Other critics have made the same objections to Genêt's vision of the world—inverted, grotesque, irrational, mad.

The protagonist in Pirandello's *Henry IV* prefers a world of illusion to the horrors of the real world. In Paul Green's *Johnny Johnson* the only sane man in a warring world is kept in an insane asylum which seems considerably more rational than conventional society. Mad generals run the war of *Johnny Johnson,* mad colonels control lives in *Catch-22,* mad kings rule Gulliver's Europe, and mad dreamers take over the mad world of Genêt's *Balcony.* Bertold Brecht, in *Mother Courage* and *The Good Woman of Setzuan,* creates characters whose "madness" is infinitely preferable to the brutality, hypocrisy, and stupid rigidity of the sane world. And the world of *Dr. Strangelove* permits a mad general and a mad scientist to destroy the sane amid howls of laughter.

Only a grotesque literature can express suitably the mad world we now live in, says Friedrich Duerrenmatt, a world so confused that no one can be charged with guilt for creating the holocaust. Many modern writers agree, as we see in the work of Kafka and Ionesco, Beckett and Adamov, *Lord of the Flies* and *The Madwoman of Chaillot* and the night-town scenes in *Ulysses*.

But the vision of the world as mad is not limited to modern writers. Juvenal gave us some fairly vivid images of approved insanity, Apuleius and Petronius offer glimpses of rather violent misbehavior, and the narrator of Bonaventura's *Nightwatch,* son of the devil and a saint, has a philosophy which is understandably jaundiced. It was Goethe who said, "Looked at from the height of reason, life as a whole seems like a grave disease, and the world like a madhouse."

Satirists sometimes see the world as a ridiculous *puppet show*. Among variations of this view are portrayals of human beings who act like machines, machines which act like human beings (such as temperamental autos), and robots. At more lighthearted levels this is the world of the ventriloquist's dummy, puppets (such as Punch and Judy), and movie cartoons. We are reminded of Bergson's injunction that only the human is funny, and we laugh at things (as we laugh at animals) only when they remind us of human beings.

Many writers about the theater of the absurd are Bergsonians and see in the characteristic qualities of that theater—such as repetition, stereotypes, rigidity—evidence of the "mechanical encrusted on the living." Samuel Beckett's tramp types and reiteration lead to the ultimate in mechanization, which is immobility, in *Endgame, Unnamable,* and *Malone Dies.* A forerunner of the absurd, Alfred Jarry, produced in 1896 the play *Ubu Roi,* described as a "monstrous puppet play, . . . acted by a cast clad in highly stylized, wooden-looking costumes." Another version of the puppet world is Ionesco's theater *(The Bald Soprano, Maid To Marry, Rhinoceros),* where the banal repetition of clichés by indistinguishable conformists emphasizes the machine-like behavior of the bourgeois types the playwright is ridiculing.

But the puppet-world concept is as old as the satiric tradition. Lucian ridiculed Pythagoras' rigidity, and Swift applies the concept in "Mechanical Operation of the Spirit." All stereotypes are a form of mechanical construction, providing the staple form of characterization in satire from Aristophanes to the theater of expressionism, from Plautus to the theater of the absurd. In a sense, Sinclair Lewis' conformists are puppets, and the characters in Huxley's *Brave New World,* Kafka's "Penal Colony," Butler's *Hudibras,* Capek's *R. U. R.,* Rice's *Adding Machine,* E. M. Forster's "Machine Stops," O'Neill's *Hairy Ape,* and the plays of Toller, Wedekind, and Kaiser. Human beings become grotesque mechanisms in the cartoons of pictorial satirists like Tomi Ungerer.

The advantage of using puppets is the same

as that of using animals; the device provides detachment to the spectator and makes it easier for him to observe with guiltless pleasure behavior which, on the part of human beings, would seem revolting or absurd. An increasingly automated world offers a limitless source of this kind of material.

Still another popular image of the world is a *fools' carnival*. Sometimes the identification is so direct that the satirist calls his book *Ship of Fools*, as Sebastian Brant and Katherine Anne Porter did. Or he calls a satiric poem *The Dunciad*, as Pope did. Or he names his novel *Vanity Fair*, as Thackeray did. Or he entitles a lengthy monologue *In Praise of Folly*, as Erasmus did. But the usual method is to introduce fools into the world the satirist has created. These fools are likely to belong in one of two groups: dunces whose stupidity the reader or spectator is expected to laugh at, or individuals whom the other characters regard as fools but in whose statements the audience recognizes forbidden truths.

The first type is more frequent. He provides a butt for society, a symbolic object to which practically everyone can feel superior. We find him in Rabelais, Swift's *Battle of the Books* and *Tale of a Tub*, Rochester's "Tunbridge Wells," Dryden's *MacFlecknoe*, Philip Wylie's *Generation of Vipers*, and Mencken's *Prejudices*. Jane Austen has given us a gallery of foolish characters: Mr. Collins, the pompous fool in *Pride and Prejudice;* Mrs. Jennings, the gossip in *Sense and Sensibility;* Mrs. Allen, the vain chaperone in *Northanger Abbey;* Miss Bates, the foolish chatterer in *Emma.*

Other fools in satire include Aimee Thanotogenos in Waugh's *Loved One,* the writers of letters to West's *Miss Lonelyhearts,* the captain in Heggen's *Mister Roberts,* William Dobbins and Joseph Sedley in *Vanity Fair,* Butler's Hudibras, Oscar Wilde's Miss Prism and Dr. Chasuble, and the fools in *Volpone.* If one stretched a point, he might include certain characters of Theophrastus, such as the Flatterer and the Coward, and even such monomaniacal critics as those parodied by Frederick Crews in *The Pooh Perplex.*

In his anthology of Jewish humor Nathan Ausubel distinguishes between two popular types of fools. The "schlemiel" he identifies as "an awkward, bungling fellow, plagued not only with 'butter-fingers,' but with absolutely no skill in coping with any situation in life." The "schlimazel," on the other hand, fails in everything he attempts not out of stupidity or incompetence but simply because he has no luck. "A schlemiel," says Ausubel, "is a man who spills a bowl of soup on a schlimazel."

But there is another, quite different way in which the satirist uses the fool: to achieve distortion, indirection, and protection from the censor by pretending that it is the fool rather than the satirist speaking. The fool intersperses unpopular and forbidden truths among genuinely foolish remarks. And like the child and clown, who presumably do not know any better, the fool is permitted to express ideas which would be dangerous or vulgar in the mouths of "normal" adults.

The junkman in *The Madwoman of Chaillot* is one example of this kind of fool. Another is Melville's Pierre, "the fool of Truth . . . of Virtue . . . of Fate." Shakespeare used fools in more ways, and in more perceptive ways, than any other writer, as Falstaff, Lear's Fool, Lance, Touchstone, and Feste demonstrate.

A variation of this approach is Samuel Beckett's, many of whose characters behave like grotesque fools. But they are not fools in the conventional sense. Beckett explains what he is trying to do: "I'm working with impotence, ignorance, . . . that whole zone of being that has always been set aside by artists as unusable. . . . I think anyone nowadays who pays the slightest attention to his own experience finds it the experience of a non-knower, a non-can-er."[1]

Often the satirist populates his world not only with fools but also with rogues. It may be true, as Mencken says, that in every conflict between a knave and a fool, the spectator sides with the knave. But wherever the audience's sympathy lies, the spectacle of rogues fleecing dupes has always been a popular element of satiric literature. The picaresque novel exploits this device, built as it is around the adventures of an entertaining rogue, in Apuleius' *Golden Ass,* Quevedo's *Great Rascal,* Nash's *Unfortunate Traveller,* or Gogol's *Dead Souls.*

Rogues abound also in Twain's *Huckleberry Finn* and *Mysterious Stranger* and practically everything else he wrote. Fielding's novels contain rogues ranging from Jonathan Wild to Blifil, Thwackum, and Square. The stereotyped knaves of Molière, Jonson, and Plautus join the more individualized rascals of Restoration comedy, the novels of Dickens and Thackeray, and *Topaze* of Marcel Pagnol. Rascals, amiable or piquant, provide victims for Juvenal, Aristophanes, Samuel Johnson, St. Jerome, Ambrose Bierce, Mencken, and Philip Wylie. They people the poetry of Dryden, Marston, Rochester, Byron, Burns. They throng the fiction of Voltaire, Evelyn Waugh, Anatole France, Rabelais, Smollett, Joyce Cary. And they provide pleasure for viewers of Gay's *Beggar's Opera* and Brecht's *Three-Penny Opera*.

It is rogues and fools who present themselves to Candide and Gulliver and Don Quixote and Pantagruel and Chichikov and Paul Pennyfeather and Huckleberry Finn and MacHeath and Yossarian and Tom Jones and Rasselas and the Citizen of the World and the writer of *Letters From a Persian in England*. It is rogues and fools, wicked institutions and stupid customs, that the protagonists of all successful satires are exposed to.

"The ludicrous," Bergson says "must be human; animals or inanimate objects become laughable only so far as they remind us of something human." Satirists have long known this and used the *animal fable* as a device for criticizing man.

From Aesop, *Jataka Tales,* and *Panchatantra,* through the *fabliaux* of the Middle Ages and Chaucer, to Joel Chandler Harris and Thurber, the behavior of animals has proved for many writers an easy method of parodying the behavior of men. The fables of Aesop and La Fontaine are better known now than the medieval narratives which used the fox, wolf, crow, cock, bear, sheep, and other animals as symbols for human types and human vices.

The satiric fable is more critical, more pointed, and usually more entertaining than the conventional beast fable. It serves the same purpose—making moralizing palatable—but it sometimes gives the impression of being immoral. Bre'r Rabbit and Reynard the Fox are rascals, and they please more by demonstrating the vices and hypocrisies of the world than by defending virtues. The fables of satirists express social criticism and mockery, and sometimes, as in the fables of William March and John Gay, a poignant cynicism. In his most trenchant satire Gay achieves, in Sven Armens' words, "the full extent of this debasement . . . by placing man below the beast, who appears to act only from instincts of mere sensation."[2]

Ambrose Bierce contributed an element of the grotesque, as in "The Lion and the Mouse" and "Man and Bird." William March's *99 Fables* express a concentrated bitterness that is unlikely to make them required reading in Sunday school classes. But James Thurber added sophistication, grace, and a modern touch that make his fables delightful, refreshing, and pungent.

Apart from the animal fable proper, satirists have often made animals serve as symbolic extensions of human beings. Long before the theory of evolution was proposed by scientists, writers found in animals irresistibly tempting symbols for men. Although theoretically these animals need not be used for critical purposes, in a remarkably large number of cases they are.

We do not usually laugh at animals when they do what animals are expected to do; but we laugh at walking dogs, boxing bears, cycling monkeys. Conversely, we enjoy recognizing bovine or equine or porcine or ornithoid characteristics in human faces. It is an unresolved point whether there is a hierarchy of animals in the satiric scale, with those most resembling us providing the greatest amount of entertainment.

Swift uses the virtuous horses as a contrast to contemptible men in Book IV of *Gulliver's Travels*. George Orwell satirizes Communism by letting animals practice it in *Animal Farm*. Aldous Huxley examines man as a conditioned animal in *Brave New World*. Bierce, in the "Civilization of the Monkey," attacks human values. Peacock creates an ape, Sir Oran Haut-ton, to ridicule the concept of the noble savage in *Melincourt*. Aristophanes uses birds and frogs to parody human conduct. Anatole France, in *Penguin Island* and "Pensées de Riguet," makes the actions of animals serve as a burlesque of men's behavior. Clarence Day's *This Simian World* speculates on how the earth would look if the elephant, cat, eagle, or some other animal had gained ascendancy instead of man. And Mark Twain, in "A Dog's Tale," "A Horse's Tail," and other satires, used animals to symbolize—and criticize—men.

Ibsen, Molière, Gogol, and Nathanael West keep comparing people to animals in their plays and novels. In *Dead Souls,* for example, Gogol points out resemblances between his characters and pigs, birds, and flies. West presents brutalized creatures surviving on a subhuman level. Apuleius and Shakespeare change men into donkeys, and Ionesco transforms all of his characters but one into rhinoceroses. Shaw makes effective use of a lion's friendship for Androcles, and Beckett casts man as a beast of burden in *Waiting for Godot.* Kafka's stories contain horses, beetles, apes, mice, cats, and birds, as well as a man called a "hunger artist" displayed in a cage.

Mrozek, the contemporary Polish satirist, exhibits a "liberal" in a living-room cage, and elsewhere chooses an elephant for a satiric symbol. Erih Kos centers his satire of Yugoslavian conformity around the nation's reaction to a dead whale. Capek turns to the nonhuman world for his cast in *The Insect Play* and *War With the Newts.* Instead of using a fox and a fly, Jonson names his characters Volpone and Mosca. Saki introduces a precocious cat, Tobermory, whose ability to speak results in disconcerting mishaps. Don Marquis immortalizes a cockroach and a cat. There is method in the madness of animals whom Alice meets in Wonderland. And an Italian moviemaker created a devastating film, *Mondo Cane,* which does nothing but compare the behavior of dogs and men.

Readers who would resent being told unpleasant truths about themselves seem quite willing to accept the same indictment about donkeys, foxes, pigs, roosters, horses, penguins, wasps, birds, butterflies, beetles, ants, cats, cockroaches, whales, elephants, rhinoceroses, monkeys, and apes. This is the reason for using animals in satire: it is much easier for the reader and spectator to attain detachment—and consequently amusement—toward animals than toward men.

The concept of *utopia* has been perverted by satirists. Every literary utopia is of course an implied criticism of society, but not every literary utopia is satiric. Although no arbitrary line of demarcation can be drawn, there is a clear difference between an idealistic dream of the future, expressing in positive terms the author's vision of the good society (such as Bellamy's *Looking Backward*), and a pseudo utopia which ridicules what the satirist regards as harmful elements of his own society (such as Huxley's *Brave New World*).

Sometimes, of course, the two purposes overlap. Sir Thomas More presents both a vision of an ideal society and philosophic criticism of the existing one in his Utopia. Rabelais offers, in the "Abbey Thélème," his version of an ideal community which compensates somewhat excessively for the shortcomings of Renaissance cloisters. The

Eldorado episode in *Candide* provides both perfection and criticism. But in general the emphasis is positive, idealistic, and earnest in such utopias as Plato's *Republic,* Bacon's *New Atlantis,* William Morris' *News From Nowhere,* Hilton's *Lost Horizon,* H. G. Wells's visions of the future, Campanella's *City of the Sun,* Fénelon's *Telemachus,* and Skinner's *Walden Two.*

But the satirist's utopia is directed toward a different end. Instead of stating what is desirable, he exaggerates the undesirable characteristics of society and pretends that they have produced a satisfying way of life. Thus Huxley's characters in *Brave New World* keep repeating how happy they are in a world where the pretensions of science have reduced men to the level of completely conditioned physiological organisms. The inhabitants of Orwell's totalitarian society reiterate their satisfaction with their miserable lives. Similarly the proletariat in *Animal Farm* is fed inspirational pap. And the citizens of *Erewhon* are quite convinced that the inverted society they have created is a perfect community.

This group rationalization is credible. Sociologists and philosophers offer ample evidence that even imperfect societies try to create the impression that everything is wonderful. Pareto observes that society rationalizes its institutions into dignity, no matter what those institutions actually do. And Sinclair Lewis' Babbitts, with the help of Dale Carnegie and Arthur Murray, cheerfully face a perfect world every morning.

Samuel Butler's device in *Erewhon* is reversal of all accepted values—and the resultant reduction to absurdity. *Erewhon* is a land where physical illness is punished by imprisonment, but crime by psychiatric care; bad luck is a crime, a concept Butler shared with Bernard Shaw; religion is satirized in the form of Musical Banks that distribute useless coins and drafts on the hereafter; Colleges of Unreason educate students in Hypothetical Languages for life in an unreasonable world. Children arrive voluntarily from the World of the Unborn, animals and vegetables demand equal rights, machines are stopped from taking over the nation by outlawing all mechanical progress and using only primitive tools, and conformity is openly encouraged.

Politics is the subject of pseudoutopian satire in works as varied as Gilbert and Sullivan's *Utopia, Ltd.,* Zamiatin's *We,* Pezet's *Aristokia,* Fialko's *New City,* and Ronald Knox's *Memories of the Future.* The emphasis is primarily economic in Don Marquis' *Almost Perfect State* and Archibald Marshall's *Upsidonia.* Society is ridiculed in a pseudoutopian section of France's *Penguin Island,* and higher education is treated with less than reverence in Leacock's *Afternoons in Utopia.*

Other versions of satiric utopia include sections in *Don Quixote,* Book IV of *Gulliver's Travels,* Wood's *Heavenly Discourses,* Montesquieu's *Letters From a Persian in England,* Goldsmith's *Citizen of the World,* Twain's *Connecticut Yan-*

kee and *Report From Paradise,* Aristophanes'
Birds, Bang's *House-boat on the Styx,* Wells's *War
of the Worlds,* Cabell's *Jurgen,* Chaplin's *Modern
Times,* Mayakovsky's *Bedbug,* Connelly's *Green
Pastures,* Douglas' *South Wind,* Goethe's *Faust,*
Flaubert's *Bouvard et Pecuchet,* Morris' *Dream of
John Ball,* Henry Miller's *Air Conditioned Night-
mare,* and Lucian's *True History.*

As is fitting for a great satirist, Swift gives us
the whole range of world images in *Gulliver's
Travels*—puppet show, pseudo utopia, menagerie,
madhouse, a throng of fools and rascals. All significant satirists share one or more of these visions of
the world. All of them base their satire on fact
rather than theory, experience rather than con-
templation, what they see rather than what society says they should see. And what they see, with
most satirists whose work survives, turns out to be
nasty rather than charming. There are good things
in the world, and beauty and courage and loyalty.
But the satirist ignores these and concentrates on
other things which he sees in much greater profusion—hypocrisy, selfishness, brutality, treachery,
and stupidity.

The horrors of the real world do not surprise
satirists. They know what war and discrimination
and sadism and brutality are; and the newest man-
ifestation of an old outrage, the latest demonstration of man's inhumanity to man, does not aston-
ish them. The satirist assumes that the least flatter-

ing motivation of men and institutions is probably the true one. He may laugh at catastrophe; but he is not really amused, even when he suggests, as Bernard Shaw did, that our earth may be another planet's hell. Stalin's concentration camps, Hiroshima, and Hitler's crematoria are not really news to Twain, Voltaire, Swift, Juvenal, and Anatole France. Unlike Browning's Rabbi Ben Ezra, satirists find old age disgusting as in Book III of *Gulliver's Travels,* Juvenal's "Tenth Satire," and Johnson's "Vanity of Human Wishes." Except in parody, satire deals with distasteful matters varying in degree from mere annoyances to insufferable pain. And most satirists share Colonel Sherburn's attitude toward the mob in *Huckleberry Finn:* he tells the men they are cowards, conformists, hypocrites, and scoundrels—and he proves it.

It is this censorious attitude, finally, that provides the one consistent element in all satirists' views of the world. For whatever else they do, they criticize; satire is permeated with disapprobation, complaint, exposé, denunciation, rebuke, condemnation. It is in this sense that satire is unique, its final perspective different from that of every other genre. Comedy is also critical; but comedy ends in a conciliatory mood, having resolved the conflict and pretended that things will be better in the future. Tragedy, like satire, ends in the protagonist's defeat but tries to imply that somehow an inspirational value can be found in his failure. Naturalism, like satire, ends unhappy but resigned—it's too bad but that's the way it goes, the naturalistic writer implies, and all we can do is accept it quietly. But most satires that survive do not accept the inevitable defeat quietly—they gibe at it or insolently expose it—and they offer no solace, no panacea, no positive alternative. They offer only the pleasure of refreshing, vigorous, and entertaining mockery of a world which resembles a madhouse, a puppet show, a menagerie, a horde of fools, a gallery of rogues, a utopia *manqué* and a beguiling mixture of all these images.

CHAPTER FOUR

The Bitter and the Sweet

IN SELECTING his material the satirist of course considers the subjects available to all writers. He finds, after a period of trial and error, that in addition to the sources listed in Chapter Two certain materials are especially suitable for satiric treatment. Among these are grotesqueness, the Devil, sex, sentiment, and realistic details—an incongruous group but one which offers exceptional opportunities for the satirist's purposes.

Pseudo Realism

IN HIS PRETENSE that the scene he describes is an accurate representation of life, the satirist uses an abundance of specific details. Realistic satirists like Sinclair Lewis, Vercors, Guareschi, Marquand, Juvenal, Dickens, and Lardner, utilize their vast firsthand knowledge of the material they describe and their sensitive ear for dialogue to support the illusion of reality. But satirists who use elements of the fanciful or strange—like Swift and Rabelais and Gogol and Orwell and Huxley—are just as careful in providing a detailed illusion of reality;

they support their fantastic deceptions with a profusion of authentic details, specific names, dates, and statistics. They allude to apparently competent authorities for confirmation. They quote witnesses whose names sound vaguely familiar, like the noblemen in Ben Franklin's "Sale of the Hessians."

The principle that specific and concrete details add interest is especially applicable to satire. When a character has been named, described, and located, the reader's interest is to some degree aroused.

The essence of Sinclair Lewis' satire (as contrasted to that of Lewis Carroll, for instance) is exaggeration of material whose components are absolutely genuine and unquestionably authentic. It is not "realism" that Lewis writes, for such devices as the comic monologue and caricature and parody are all distortions of reality; but it is a familiar reality that he and H. G. Wells and John P. Marquand distort. Their pseudo realism sometimes succeeds so well that all three writers have had to protest when attempts were made to identify the actual models for their characters.

Sometimes satirists achieve the illusion of reality by using actual historical characters, such as Shaw's General Burgoyne in *The Devil's Disciple,* John Erskine's bitingly pragmatic *Helen of Troy,* and Mark Twain's King Arthur. Rabelais insists belligerently that every detail in his account of Pantagruel is absolutely true. Capek's manager in *R. U. R.* describes in detail how the robots are manufactured, naming the metals and chemicals used; in *War With the Newts,* Capek presents a great deal of scientific information about newts, material authenticated by biologists. Swift goes to considerable length to concoct latitudes and longitudes, dates and names, proportions and weights—all of them false but immensely credible. The terrifying exposés of science and politics in *Brave New World* and *1984* are meticulously documented. And the grotesque worlds of Nathanael West and Günter Grass are filled with realistic details, spiced in *The Tin Drum* by such slightly offbeat items as miraculous statues and thaumaturgic music.

It is worth mentioning that many satirists believe, or pretend to believe, that they are not satirists at all, but realists. Sinclair Lewis, Bernard Shaw, and Evelyn Waugh all insisted that they were offering an accurate picture of the world to audiences whose vision and judgment had been so perverted by sentimental conditioning that they refused to recognize the unpleasant truth when they were shown it.

The Grotesque

SINCE PSEUDO REALISM is so essential an element of satire it may seem surprising that satirists also use a great deal of grotesque material—material at the other end of the continuum from realistic reproduction of life. The fact is that satirists use anything that helps them satirize—and a number of scholars have observed that humor is sometimes allied to fear. Constance Rourke defined the grotesque as a "median between terror and laughter." "The psychology of the grotesque," suggests psychoanalyst Ernst Kris, is "based largely on the sudden and surprising relief from anxiety which leads to laughter."[1]

It is a well-known fact that the term "funny" has at least two quite different connotations, in continental languages as well as in English: "amusing" or "strange." The definition of "grotesque" in *Webster's Second Unabridged Dictionary* reveals a number of similarities to satire: "representing in the material world a distortion of aesthetic relations, or qualities similar to that of the comic in the mental world. . . . Pertaining to a type of design in which heterogeneous and incongruous details are combined for artistic effect." Of course, not all grotesque material is satiric.

The vehemence of grotesque satire sometimes makes squeamish audiences feel that the satirist is stepping beyond the boundaries of good taste. He often is. One of the reasons for the intensity of his expression is that he sometimes finds the ugliness of the real world so unbearable, the discordance of life so frustrating, that only an excessive reaction seems possible.

Satirists have always used grotesque materials. But Wolfgang Kayser *(The Grotesque in Art and Literature)* offers interesting evidence to explain why three periods in Western history—the sixteenth century, the age preceding eighteenth-cen-

tury Romanticism, and our own day—provide the
greatest amount of grotesque elements in literature. It is Kayser's contention that in times of
skepticism—when man's belief in a logical universe
and a protective deity has been shaken—the grotesque becomes an artistic expression of man's
alienation from a hostile, irrational, and incom-
prehensible world. As typical subject matter of
the grotesque, Kayser lists monsters, insects, sinis-
ter animals (like bats), plant worlds in the shape
of jungles, menacing fish, insane people, and living things confined to rigid movements. Like satire
the grotesque proceeds as if the rational categories
of our world view were no longer applicable. There
is no system, no logical pattern; the world has become absurd.

Freud explains the humor of the gallows in
these terms: Ordinarily the sight of a condemned
criminal would arouse intense pity in us; but when
we realize that the criminal himself—who should
be most concerned—is indifferent to the situation,
we find that the emotional expenditure for pity
which we have already prepared is inapplicable and
we laugh it off. Arthur Koestler extends Freud's
analysis to other forms of gruesome humor and
suggests that they entertain because, far from
being tragic, they are parodies of tragedy; and gruesome humor "debunks its own horrid narrative by
showing that blood, daggers, and hangman's nooses
are merely meant as stage props, while at the same
time admitting a good deal of repressed sadism
into the emotional charge."[2]

Citing as examples of the grotesque the Wife

of Bath, Sir Hudibras in stocks, "Tam O'Shanter," and Swift's detailed description of the imperfections of Brobdingnagian women, Worcester suggests that there is a fascination in the sluttish, the ugly, and the revolting, as used by these satirists. Grotesque art makes the ugly seem fascinating. All these examples are repulsive—yet we enjoy reading them. "Two devices bridge the gap between loathing and liking. These are closeness of vision and detachment."[3] The closeness of vision is provided from an unfamiliar point of view; we see the old things but from a new perspective. The satirist shocks us out of complacency and dullness by showing us a patch of skin under his magnifying glass. The details are shown not for their own sake but to expose the inaccuracy or sentimentality or hypocrisy of the conventional attitude toward these details. And detachment makes the experience amusing rather than repulsive, bearable rather than horrible.

Wilson Mizner's humor has a strong element of grotesqueness, stemming from excessive detachment. Informed that his brother had just been killed in an auto accident, Mizner said, "Why didn't you tell me before I put on a red tie?" When a young woman with whom he had quarrelled jumped out of a twelfth-floor hotel room, Mizner left for the racetrack immediately, convinced that he had been given a lucky number to bet on.

Perhaps the most successful modern exponent of the grotesque as a source of humor in cartoons is Charles Addams. He carries exaggeration and understatement so far that laughter instead of horror results. In one cartoon Addams shows a woman looking up to see an enormous bird carrying away her husband. The woman yells, "Drop the car keys." Addams obtrudes into commonplace twentieth-century America the clothing of giants, the homes of midgets, the footsteps of statues, and the bell ringing of ghosts. He shows a man disconnecting a trailer, with his wife in it, at a railroad crossing. In another cartoon a man cheerfully waves to a motorist, urging him to pass on a mountain curve—where a large truck is approaching. That the instinct for grotesque humor is fairly widespread is indicated by unsolicited suggestions sent to Addams, such as a vampire at a blood bank and a TV antenna on a tombstone.

Another cartoonist using the grotesque for social satire is Tomi Ungerer, whose *Underground Sketchbook* is accurately described in its preface as a chronicle of "automated inhumanity." Men in a conference room are panic-stricken as the carpet gives like quicksand. The upper halves of two lovers keep embracing as they are drawn into a giant meat grinder. A male boxer cringes from the blows of his female opponent in a barbed-wire ring. In France, Sine (Maurice Sinet) is a very popular cartoonist. Among his masterpieces: a wife eating her husband's brains, after having carefully cut the skull apart like a melon. In another drawing Sine shows a Boy Scout thumbing a ride from Christ as the latter bears his cross.

In art the tradition of the grotesque is old

and honorable. From the gargoyles of Europe to distortions in Bangkok temples, satiric sculptors have extended caricature to the point of the grotesque—and beyond. Among the best known practitioners are Hogarth, Brueghel, Velasquez, Bosch, El Greco, Daumier, Cruikshank, Max Ernst, Dali, Chagall, Goya, George Grosz, and Diego Rivera.

Tom Lehrer has contributed as much grotesqueness to the popular song as it is likely to withstand. His parodies of saccharine sentimentality include "I Hold Your Hand in Mine" (in which a lover holds the severed hand of his murdered sweetheart), "Poisoning Pigeons in the Park," "When You Are Old and Gray," and "Wiener Schnitzel Waltz." And Jake Rybakoff, a gangster refusing to tell police who had shot him, said just before he died, "Me mudder did the job."

Modern satire is permeated with the grotesque. Apart from drama—where the theater of expressionism and the theater of the absurd are grotesque by definition—most contemporary satirists turn to the grotesque as spontaneously as earlier writers turned to lyricism. *The Tin Drum* of Günter Grass provides a few examples: A man trying to rape a wooden statue is killed by the statue's ax. Eels are caught by throwing a horse's head into the sea, waiting until eels get inside, then pulling the blood-soaked fish out, one by one. The prolonged vomiting of Oskar's dying mother is described with meticulous and nauseating detail. What the corpse of the grocer looked like after he hanged himself is made quite clear to the reader. Oskar, the protagonist, is a midget with a hump. Like Swift, Grass is obsessed with physically revolting objects and actions.

Nathanael West too has managed to push the grotesque to the point of revulsion. In his four novels he created a gallery of cartoon characters and a basement of fantastic scenes, varying from bitter whimsey in *Balso Snell* to horror in *Day of the Locust*. He calls the posterior opening of the Trojan Horse's alimentary canal "Anus Mirabilis." Grotesque characters crowd his macabre sets: Janey, a paralyzed hunchback; Shrike, a psychotic mocker; the pathetic writers of letters to Miss Lonelyhearts; a paralyzed boy who wants to play the violin; sex-starved wives of crippled husbands.

Corpses and cannibals are casually sprawled through Evelyn Waugh's books. *The Loved One* concerns itself with grotesque funeral parlors— for humans and animals. In *Black Mischief* a British ambassador and his family are eaten by cannibals. At the end of *Handful of Dust* Tony Last is left in a Brazilian jungle, destined to keep reading Dickens aloud to a madman. Aimee kills herself in response to the casual telephone-call advice of a fake guru. And the characters in Waugh's satiric novels, from Mr. Joyboy in *The Loved One* to Captain Grimes in *Decline and Fall*, comprise a zoo of bizarre caricatures.

To use the word "grotesque" in reference to Samuel Beckett's work is to be guilty of understatement. Beckett is obsessed with illness and physical deformity. With loving care he describes the death struggles of Malone and the bedsores of other characters. In *Unnamable* the protagonist is a freak without arms or legs, "planted" in a pot outside a restaurant and serving as an advertisement. Violence dominates Beckett's world: Pozzo whips Lucky, Moran is brutal to his son, Hamm mistreats his ash-can-inhabiting parents. Before his death, Murphy had requested that his ashes be flushed down the toilet of the Abbey Theater. But the executor of the will, Cooper, stops in a pub and after a few drinks throws the packet of ashes at a belligerent drunk. The ashes are scattered all over the floor and swept up the following day with the sand, butts, beer, spit, and vomit. The ultimate grotesquerie in Beckett's world is death and even devotees of offbeat theater have been startled by Beckett's couple in ash cans and half-buried woman.

The reaction to Kafka's work has been described as "horrified laughter" and "rueful humor." His particular quality of grotesqueness, in Heller's *Catch-22* as Kafkaesque nightmares—as indeed the trials of Clevenger and the chaplain are.

All of the great satirists use the grotesque— Rabelais, Juvenal, Aristophanes, Petronius, Voltaire, Cervantes, Gogol, and of course, Swift. "The Metamorphosis," "A Hunger Artist," "The Penal Colony," "The Country Doctor," and the novels, has become an international adjective. We use it casually in describing the trials in

Swift's preoccupation with filth and deformity, excrement and ugliness, is too familiar to require much documentation. His scatological verse, microscopic description of the gigantic Brobdingnagians, cataloguing of the miseries that longevity brought to Struldbrugs, Gulliver's revulsion at the filth and lust of the Yahoos, and the experiments of Laputan scientists, all lead to the suspicion that Swift was not a very delicate satirist. His description of the goddess Criticism in *The Battle of the Books* is a fair example: "She had claws like a cat; her head, and ears, and voice, resembled those of an ass; her teeth fallen out upon herself; her diet was the overflowing of her own gall; her spleen was so large, as to stand prominent . . . nor wanted excrescences in form of teats, at which a crew of ugly monsters were greedily sucking; and, what is wonderful to conceive, the bulk of spleen increased faster than the sucking could diminish it."

Not all satirists are as fascinated by scatology as Swift, Rabelais, West, and Grass; but even the Victorian W. S. Gilbert enjoys ridiculing ugly old women like Katisha, Little Buttercup, and Nursemaid Ruth. Other satirists who make relatively frequent use of grotesque elements are Christian Morgenstern, William Golding, Duerrenmatt, Wilhelm Busch, Grimmelshausen, Pope, Dickens, Edward Lear, and Lewis Carroll. American writers include Stephen Crane, Ambrose Bierce, Mark Twain, and William Faulkner.

Finally, there is some element of the gro-

tesque in Charles Lamb's reply to a gushing
mother who had asked him, "How do you like
children?" "B-boiled, madam," Lamb said.

 ## The Devil

THE DEVIL appears in the work of satirists often
enough to justify an examination of his aesthetic
function. He is a familiar figure in folk humor
because, as Norris Yates observes about the frequent use of the Devil in early American super-
natural tales, his nature offers many possibilities
for sardonic humor.

Psychoanalysts have suggested a close relationship between the Devil and the clown. Like
Luther, who identified clowns with the Devil and
inveighed against both, Dr. Sidney Tarachow
finds that the Devil represents man's forbidden
sexual and aggressive impulses. Clowns and fools,
he claims, have traditionally been used to act out
various attributes of the Devil, genital and hostile.[4]
Another psychoanalyst, W. M. Zucker, elaborates
on Tarachow's theory. He suggests that the Devil,
as clown, serves as "the antagonist of the whole
cosmic order," but he is tolerated because his very
presence serves as proof of the far more powerful
Divinity which is gracious enough to permit the
Devil's existence. The proper way to look at the
Devil, then, is as the "Widersacher," the attorney
for the other side.[5]

Maximilian Rudwin maintains that in modern literature "the Devil's chief function is that of a satirist."[6] Having made the point that the Devil provided the inspiration for a number of masterpieces—by Dante, Calderon, Milton, Goethe, Marlowe, Byron—Rudwin concludes that "the modern Devil is a great improvement on his prototype of medieval days" because modern writers have used the Devil as a clever critic who "directs the shafts of his sarcasm against all the foibles and faults of men."

Since satirists work by distortion, it is not surprising that when they choose the Devil as spokesman they load his side of the scale. In his review of Byron's *Cain* Jeffrey complained that the whole argument of the poem was directed against the goodness of God and the rationale of religion, while "the Devil and his pupil have the field entirely to themselves." Similarly, the title character in Melville's *Confidence-Man* is the Devil having a pleasant time in a corrupt world. And there is a revealing passage in Mark Twain's unpublished "The Great Dark": "I need not point out that the Superintendent of Dreams exactly corresponds to God in *What Is Man?* Watch him become Satan."

In 1957 Dr. George Gallup polled Americans and Englishmen concerning their belief in the actual existence of the Devil. Among Americans 61 per cent said they believed; among Englishmen, 34 per cent. Forty-two per cent of the English were sure that there is no Devil; only 26 per cent of the Americans were willing to go that far.

THE FACT THAT references to sex have always been a prime source of entertainment has long been known, and many satirists utilize sex as an aid to sustaining narrative interest. Edgar Johnson's *Treasury of Satire* is full of sexual allusions; apparently Johnson felt that the political and social allusions in older satires would interest modern readers less than references to sex. He was quite right.

It is a significant point, and one frequently made, that Greek comic drama originated in those religious rituals which celebrated sexual activity. Maxwell Anderson suggests that tragic drama is an expression of the divine in man, and comedy of the animal in man, and that the animal's sexual interests have been vividly represented. Professor F. M. Cornford, the eminent classical scholar, a long time ago made a similar distinction between the functions of sex in comedy and tragedy. Having discussed the emphasis on phallic symbols and fertility, Cornford concluded that comedy "has been marked all through its history by an erotic tone, and in its lower manifestations relied openly on the stimulus of sex attraction."[7]

Freud devoted a whole book, *Wit and Its Relation to the Unconscious*, to analysis of humor and satire. The relevant point here is Freud's application of the censor-evasion technique to the wit-making process. Society represses the basic desires, Freud says—and the strongest desires it represses are sex and aggression. Man gets around this censorship by talking instead of doing—and by talking indirectly enough and wittily enough so that he can be safe and entertaining at the same time. Since sex is man's basic need, Freud concludes, dirty jokes are the most popular form of humor. Havelock Ellis, in complete agreement, thought the need of adults for obscene literature is as great as that of children for fairy tales, in both cases providing relief from "the oppressive forces of convention."

Whatever the reason, satirists from Aristophanes to Aldous Huxley knew that allusions to sex were an easy method of sustaining the reader's interest and the audience's pleasure. No recondite explanation is necessary. In every society references to sex arouse pleasure of one kind or another. People enjoy sex and allusions to sex, and satirists have always catered to this desire. A few years ago the Dried Fig Advisory Board in the United States had to order an additional 15,000 copies of its promotional pamphlet; the public had snapped up the first 20,000 copies of *The Love Life of a Fig*.

Consequently, sex is a strong component in the satire of Rabelais, Petronius, Huxley, Lucian, Waugh, Aristophanes, Juvenal, Voltaire, Cabell, and Apuleius. The influence of Rabelais on the later work of Anatole France is seen in the coarser humor of that work. Lewis Carroll wrote indignant letters to the press when he spotted indecency in art or literature, so it is refreshing to learn from

Dr. Phyllis Greenacre, a psychoanalyst, that "there is less substitution in *Gulliver* of other body parts for the phallus than is to be seen in *Alice in Wonderland*."[8] There is also reason to think that the popularity of Nabokov's *Lolita* is not entirely due to satire.

The times temper the expression. What Aristophanes' characters were permitted to say is not likely to be repeated on American television. Certain scenes in Molière's plays tend to be underplayed by contemporary actors. But, paradoxically, the modern novel has used sex more freely than any literary form since the Restoration drama; and satirists have not ignored the opportunity. In the novels of Günter Grass, Joseph Heller, Huxley, Orwell, and Beckett sex provides relief, humor, and sheer interest. And in the movie, *Dr. Strangelove*, the Russian prime minister has to be traced to the house of his mistress, while the American general is continually interrupted during a Pentagon emergency by telephone calls from his oversexed girl friend. Scholars, of course, are immune to temptations of this kind.

Sentiment

SATIRE, it is usually assumed, appeals primarily to the intellect. But in spite of Bergson many satirists have blended sentiment with critical humor to retain the reader's interest and achieve a stronger emotional reaction than would otherwise be possible.

Arthur Koestler's analysis of crying, in relation to laughter, may be relevant here. Having divided human emotions into two categories, self-transcending and self-asserting, Koestler suggests that crying is "a discharge reflex for redundant or frustrated" emotions of the former kind, laughter for the latter. In crying the process is simple and direct, and the discharge preserves the continuity of mood; but in laughter, which is based on a "bisociative pattern" (perceiving an unexpected relationship in two diverse objects or ideas), a separation of thought from emotion occurs.

Among satirists who use a good deal of sentiment in their novels are Fielding, Sterne, Dickens, Lewis, Gogol, Thackeray, Cervantes, and Orwell. It appears in the poetry of Heine, Byron, Hood, and Burns. There is a mixture of sentiment and satire in the work of Washington Irving, Karel Capek, Oscar Wilde, Baudelaire, Sholom Aleichem, and Mark Twain. One of the most popular comedians of the twentieth century, Charlie Chaplin, made sentiment a prime ingredient of his comic material.

From ancient China we get an example of this device: When Po-Yu's mother punished him with a stick, he cried.

She said, "You never used to cry when I thrashed you. Why do you cry today?"

"It used to hurt. But this time Mother's strength is such that it does not hurt. That is why I cry."

Mixture

IN HIS SATIRIC NOVELS Sinclair Lewis used realism, sentimentalism, didacticism, and satire. The mixture of these incongruous elements proved more successful than his attempts, in the following novels, to use only a single method: *The Man Who Knew Coolidge* is pure satire—and a failure; *The Innocents* is sheer sentiment—and a failure; *Mantrap* is melodrama—and a failure; *Bethel Merriday* is realistic narrative—and a failure. In all of his successful novels satire is an important element, but never the only element. Satire invigorates the minute realism of *Main Street*, the sociology of *Babbitt*, the romanticism of *Arrowsmith*. It is true that these ingredients in Lewis' novels seem incompatible; it is also true that his best novels are successful because of and in spite of these ingredients. One critic has suggested that Lewis' literary success varies directly with the amount of satire Lewis uses: The more satire a novel has, the better it is. The theory is plausible but not correct; if it were, *The Man Who Knew Coolidge, Elmer Gantry,* and *Gideon Planish* would be his best novels.

Will Cuppy mixes satire with sound knowledge of history in *Decline and Fall of Practically Everybody* and with sound knowledge of zoology in *How To Tell Your Friends From the Apes.* Molière mixes comedy and moralizing. The writings of Heine provide a miscellany of heterogeneous elements. *Gulliver's Travels* is more widely read for the fantasy than the satire, as is *Alice in Wonderland. Jurgen* was read more for its sexual symbolism than its satiric commentary, and Bierce is better known for his macabre short stories than his bitter criticism. Twain is treasured for his "humor," and Sinclair Lewis for his "realism." Cervantes and Chaplin mix satire with pathos; Shaw and Johnson with philosophy; Fielding, Dickens, and Thackeray with sentiment.

In his history of satire Hugh Walker praises Burns and Byron for demonstrating that the blend of pure poetry with satire results in "something not, perhaps, satirically more effective, but certainly more charming than satire undiluted and unmixed." In Peacock's satire the story counts for nothing and the characters for very little; that is why he never attained popularity in contrast to Thackeray. Of the Victorian writers, Walker concludes, the satire outweighs all other elements only in Peacock and Butler.

Dryden, speaking of the early Latin form of satire called "Varronian," quotes Varro's analysis of his work: "Many things are there inserted, which are drawn from the very entrails of philosophy . . . which I have mingled with pleasantries on purpose, that they may more easily go down with the common sort of unlearned readers."[9] Anatole France vacillates between realism and romanticism, cynicism and sentiment. In *Penguin Island* and *The Revolt of the Angels* he mixes burlesque, history, fables, and mythology with loose women, faithless wives, and lecherous husbands. Satire was an increasingly important element in Thomas Wolfe's novels, though even in *You Can't Go Home Again* it is subordinated to other ingredients. Addison blends satire and pathos. There is a mixture of sentimentality and humor, pathos and wit, in Thomas Hood's poetry.

The variety of devices in Joseph Heller's *Catch-22* is indicated by the number of writers whom critics have listed as influencing his book, including Rabelais, Joyce, Max Shulman, Dostoevsky, S. J. Perelman, Celine, Nathanael West, the Marx brothers, and Nelson Algren. It has been suggested that Heller selects violent, shocking techniques in order to get attention in an age immune to milder forms of criticism. Whatever his reasons, *Catch-22* makes use of exaggeration, parody, surrealism, subtlety, puns, contrast, disparaging symbol, sex, and grotesquerie in a devastating and hilarious satire.

Oscar Wilde's *Importance of Being Earnest*, a high comedy of manners, illustrates the variety of comic techniques possible in satiric drama. There is, first, an incongruous contrast between the suave, witty dialogue and the farcical situations. In addition Wilde uses mistaken identity; two romances; running gags; incongruous groupings; unexpected truths; play on words; distortion in the form of both understatement and exaggeration; epigrams; appeals to the superiority of the audience; and incidental satiric remarks at the expense of aristocracy, the church, snobbery, education, fashion, art, culture, politics, and marriage.

Nor is formal verse satire restricted in its choice of methods. In her study of the genre, Mary Claire Randolph found all of the following devices being used: "miniature dramas, sententious proverbs and quotable maxims, beast fables (often reduced to animal metaphors), brief sermons, sharp diatribes, series of vignettes, swiftly sketched but painstakingly built-up satiric 'characters' or portraits, figure-processions, little fictions and apologues, visions, and apostrophes to abstractions."[10]

With the exception of a few "pure" satires most of the world's satiric literature is a mixture of satiric material with nonsatiric content and of satiric devices with nonsatiric techniques. Whatever rules theorists may propound or scholars seek, the satirist goes blithely on his way, violating the classicist's instructions, laughing at the romantic's illusions, distorting the naturalist's ingredients, blending techniques and mixing materials, concocting what in the Latin word *satura* meant "medley" and for all practical purposes still does. Those satirists who circumvent the limitations of satire most successfully are writers who combine satire with other literary appeals. Writers who dare rely solely on satire find either that they are limited to writing short pieces, or that they have a very small audience or no audience at all.

PART THREE

The Techniques of Satire

CHAPTER FIVE

Theory of Satiric Technique

THE FIRST PROBLEM of the satirist is to hold the reader's interest, while doing something other than what he is pretending to do. Most readers begin with the expectation that they will be either entertained by a narrative or educated by informative exposition. Satire rarely satisfies either of these expectations. Although satirists often use narrative as the basic device, satire does not usually provide suspenseful reading, nor is the reader likely to identify himself with the characters strongly enough to be genuinely concerned over what happens to them.

Because the satirist appeals primarily to the mind, he must divert the mind—and the method he chooses is predominantly playful distortion. He uses all the standard comic devices, plus a number of variations of wit which are more suitable for satire than for uncritical humor. Because he wants to please the mind, he tries to avoid fatiguing the mind—the intellect tires more rapidly than the heart—by splitting up the satiric material into short units and interpolating other appeals between these units. Or he makes the satire subordinate to some form of dramatic narrative.

The satirist has the additional problem of being nasty to his victim without antagonizing the reader, a task simplified considerably by Swift's observation that men recognize the fact that their neighbors are being satirized, but seldom themselves. Still, criticism irritates and overt anger distresses most readers. The satirist has to camouflage the criticism or sugarcoat it somehow to make it palatable. One of the methods traditionally used to achieve this effect is showing the victim as ridiculous rather than wicked. Another is implying that the satirist's own position is just and proper. "The world do not dislike originality, liberality, and independence," warned Sydney Smith, "so much as the insulting arrogance with which they are almost always accompanied."

The satirist must give the impression of infallibility while constantly pointing out the fallibility of others. He cannot afford technical mistakes, for he needs the sustained credulity of his readers. Even a slight doubt can spoil the effect of satire. To avoid the suspicion of sanctimoniousness, he often assumes the pose of detachment; but then he opens himself to the charge of callous indifference. Yet, if he does not restrain his anger, the bitterness of his attack may create sympathy for his victim.

I have defined satire as a playfully critical distortion of the familiar. The word "critical" is intended to distinguish satiric humor from nonsatiric humor, although some scholars think that all humor involves disparagement. And all litera-

ture "distorts" reality, varying only in the degree
of distortion, whether the literary form is labeled
naturalism or expressionism, surrealism or classicism.

The satirist gets much less help from the emotional appeal of his content than do other writers.
He does benefit somewhat from the fact that conflict is interesting, and criticism implies or directly
expresses conflict. But beyond that limited appeal
satire must rely, to a greater degree than most
other forms of writing, on technical excellence.
The satirist must get off his witticism perfectly—
it may be expressed in ten ways, but nine of them
are likely to be ineffective. When exaggeration is
used, it must be brought in very naturally and very
seriously. The reader will tolerate few mistakes
in the work of one whose business it is to be intol-
erant of the mistakes of others.

The easiest sources of humor are sex and
aggression, as a glance at most college humor magazines immediately reveals. But the satirist has to
go beyond these easy sources and convince the
reader that he is using sex and aggression as means
to an end, not as the end itself. For the satirist,
criticism and exposé provide far more appealing
material than praise and agreement. Since he cannot take advantage of some appurtenances of popular literature, he caters instead to the reader's
pleasure in superiority, evasion of the censor, and
release of aggressions.

Satire achieves its effect less by what it says
than by how it says it. *Gulliver's Travels* enter-

tains the reader wholly apart from its satire. *A Modest Proposal* gains its startling effect from the unique manner in which it is written. John P. Marquand claimed that *The Late George Apley* was the first book to combine the correspondence method with a parody of the compiler's commentary. Satire usually shows us familiar things in a new way; it rarely tells us anything new. It is not the originality of ideas that makes the great satires successful; it is the manner of expression, the satiric manner, which makes them entertaining and interesting, stimulating and refreshing.

Dryden credits Persius with discovering "this important secret, in the designing of a perfect satire; that it ought only to treat of one subject; to be confined to one particular theme; or at least to one principally."[1] Juvenal and Boileau followed this rule. But Dryden admits that even Horace violated it, and the word satire itself originally meant a hodgepodge. The fact is that in its long history all kinds of satire have been written, some concentrating on one subject and some covering many. Juvenal solved the problem by devoting a separate "Satire" to each major subject he attacked; but Anatole France's books are, as Chevalier says, "singularly deficient in practically all the conventional requirements and virtues: unity, structure, coherence, independence, etc."

Even the most sophisticated satirists do not consider themselves above using the most elementary comic devices. Shaw (in *Androcles and the Lion*), O'Casey (in *Juno and the Paycock*), and

Wilde (in *The Importance of Being Earnest*) use stock characters and obvious insults for satiric effect. The metaphysical tragicomedy, Samuel Beckett's *Waiting for Godot,* employs a kick in the shins, unbuttoned trousers, dropped pants, and obscene language to inject humor into a prolonged dialogue about the purposelessness of human existence.

Because the satirist cannot rely on the emotional involvement of the reader in the form of empathy or suspense, he uses all the technical devices which help maintain interest in a story. One of these devices is variation—of scene, of incident, of character. Bernard Shaw, for instance, changes scenes in his plays often to provide relief from long discussions. Molière keeps subplots alternating with the main story line. Capek, in *The Insect Play,* offers a different setting in each act, new characters, and a shift in focus so that the spontaneity of each idea is not lost.

Variety of technique is not, of course, limited to satire. A classic example of versatility in finding new ways of showing the ordinary activities of monotonous life is Flaubert's *Madame Bovary.* But satirists even more than realists have to find ways to trick the reader into being interested. And successful satirists have proved remarkably ingenious by providing variety in shifting scenes, unexpected remarks, incongruous behavior, fast pacing, elimination of irrelevant details, and a freshness of approach which gives an impression of more spontaneity than is actually present.

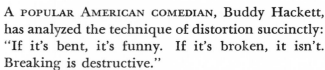

Distortion

A POPULAR AMERICAN COMEDIAN, Buddy Hackett, has analyzed the technique of distortion succinctly: "If it's bent, it's funny. If it's broken, it isn't. Breaking is destructive."

The satirist distorts in many ways. He minimizes the good qualities of the person or institution that he is attacking and magnifies the bad ones. He begrudges praise, unless to use it for contrast. Thus Dryden lists Buckingham's virtues, and Pope Addison's, only to make more startling the subsequent disclosure of their victims' vices. The satirist tries to make isolated instances seem typical. He quotes the one authority who happens to agree with him, or the one statement by a hostile authority which happens to fit the satirist's immediate purpose. In comparing two people whom he dislikes, the satirist is not likely to say "one is better than the other," but "one is not as bad as the other." He exaggerates. He understates. He pulls things out of context. He attributes obviously false motives. He stacks the cards in every way he can.

The satirist has to exaggerate, to overstate, in order to attract attention, for he is usually expressing an unpopular point of view—unpopular not because it is original but because it reaffirms inconvenient principles which society pays lip service to but does not practice. The satirist, like Socrates' gadfly, keeps nagging society and arousing the same resentment that Socrates and

gadflies arouse. Most people are complacently indifferent to the ludicrous inconsistencies of society,
except when they are personally affected by them.
Because men prefer to believe what is comforting
rather than what is true and because men's institutions support them in their illusions, the satirist
feels justified in using unfair devices to achieve
what he regards as a desirable purpose, exposure
of the fake and foolish and evil. Great satirists
tend to deal in black and white, as Aristophanes,
Juvenal, Swift, Voltaire, and Gogol do.

The charge that satire exaggerates is scarcely
a devastating one. All literature exaggerates. Life
is dull and even realists have not been foolish
enough to transcribe it literally. There is an unavoidable concentration for literary purposes, a
manipulation of incidents, an intensification of
character. Poetry exaggerates, realistic literature
exaggerates, romantic literature exaggerates. It is
in degree rather than in kind that satire exceeds
other types of art. Exaggeration is a form of
attack and an indispensable procedure for a satirist.

      Indirection

SATIRE VARIES in degree of indirection from the
blunt invective of Rabelais and Juvenal to the
delicate irony of Max Beerbohm and C. S. Lewis;
from the crudity of *Mad* magazine to the erudi-
tion of James Joyce; from the author comment of
Dickens, Fielding, and Sinclair Lewis to the subtle

use of situation, character, and dialogue by Marquand, Nabokov, Salinger, Mary McCarthy, Gide, and Aubrey Menon.

Although it is possible to describe the style of some satirists as "rough" and others as "smooth," it is impossible to draw a firm line between the two groups. Nor is it safe to assume that a smooth technique is always superior to a rough one. Some of the world's greatest satirists might be described as rough: Juvenal, Twain, Rabelais, Aristophanes. Among smooth satirists we might list Horace, E. B. White, Thurber, Christopher Fry, Norman Douglas, and Anatole France. But where Swift, Petronius, Voltaire, Fielding, Huxley, Gogol, and Orwell belong is debatable.

The alternation of direct and indirect satire is a favorite technique of Sinclair Lewis: He makes an obnoxious character express approval of a foolish or vicious idea, praising it for reasons which the reader is likely to reject. Lewis then addresses the reader directly, attacking the idea. Later the original speaker, or one like him, again defends the same proposition, again giving stupid or vicious arguments on its behalf.

It is generally agreed that the method of amateur correspondents who insert, in parentheses, "Ha-ha" or "Joke" after their attempts at humor, is too obvious. But it is not so easy to determine the optimum degree of indirection. The satirist has the problem of finding the golden mean between excessive obviousness, which makes satire too crude to be satisfying, and excessive subtlety, which keeps some people from getting

the point at all and leads others to reach precisely
the opposite conclusion from that which the
satirist intended. The oversophisticated satirist is
susceptible to literary anemia.

In his "Essay on Satire" Dryden comments on
the difficulty of indirection: "How easy it is to
call rogue and villain, and that wittily! But how
hard to make a man appear a fool, a blockhead, or
a knave, without using any of those opprobrious
terms." The devices of indirection which satirists
use include verbal irony, the mask-persona, burlesque, parody, allegory, and symbol. Satire is, as
David Worcester put it, "the engine of anger,
rather than the direct expression of anger."

The penalty for indirection is a decrease in
the satirist's audience, a decrease proportional to
the amount of subtlety. The reward is greater
appreciation, for subtle humor suffers less from
rereading than does obvious humor; Thurber and
Thoreau and White give repeated, and sometimes
greater, pleasure the second time around. Over-
direct satire of hypocrisy, as in Molière's *Misan-*
thrope, is sometimes more irritating—and consequently less satisfying—than a more subtle attack.
The bitter pill needs sugarcoating, but no pre-
scription exists for the precise amount.

✳   *Externality*

IT HAS BEEN long assumed that satire is concerned
with society rather than individuals, the typical
rather than the unique. Before the twentieth

century (and the appearance of Joyce, Kafka, Pirandello, Proust, and Beckett) scholars assumed that satire deals with the external rather than the subconscious, behavior rather than introspection, the superficial (or at least the obvious) rather than the profound.

Satirists have often been criticized for the "externality" of their work, for their concentration on the act itself rather than on the psychology of individuals who commit the act. But the satirist's objective is different from that of the psychological novelist. Bergson insists that not only satire but all comedy deals with the external. Poetry, he says, is concerned with "inner" observation; but comedy springs from a totally different kind of scrutiny. "It is directed outward. . . . It is on others that observation must be practiced. . . . It will not be more than skin-deep. . . . It will go no farther. Even if it could, it would not desire to do so, for *it would have nothing to gain in the process*." (Italics mine.)

From the satirist's point of view, then, the fact that he deals with externals is not a shortcoming but a virtue; that is exactly what he is trying to do. And it is no criticism of the satirist to speak of Dryden's "external pictures," or "Washington Irving's power to assimilate . . . the surfaces of those materials," or Sinclair Lewis' "stereotypes," or Smollett's concern with "the superficial features of temperament, mannerisms in which men differ, not with the deeper human qualities that unite them."

The satirist needs detachment, but the styles of many satirists have not been detached styles. There is a good deal of subjectivity in the writing of Rabelais, Cervantes, Juvenal, Dickens, Melville, Thackeray, and Sinclair Lewis. Satire usually profits from detachment, and the lack of aloofness makes Shelley's attempts at satire painful reading. Detachment results in more sophisticated satire, but detachment is not a *sine qua non*. Theoretically, perhaps it ought to be, but literary history proves that it is not.

The forms of detachment vary: the pseudo-naiveté of Fielding in *Jonathan Wild* and Mark Twain on the lecture platform; the "deadpan" realism of Hemingway and O'Hara; the impersonality of Camus in *The Stranger;* the ironic tone of Anatole France and E. B. White. There are disadvantages to the method. As we have seen, when one fails to use emotional appeals he cannot expect the benefits of emotional appeals. Also, detachment can be carried to extremes, resulting in romantic irony—the detached satirist observing himself observing the situation.

Brevity

"BREVITY is the soul of wit," said Hamlet. Somewhat earlier Horace listed brevity as an indispensable quality of good satire. Sir Walter Scott thought that "the perpetual scintillation of Butler's wit is too dazzling to be delightful; and we can seldom read far in *Hudibras* without feeling more fatigue than pleasure." Samuel Johnson, writing of Dryden's *Absalom and Achitophel,* warned that "a long poem of mere sentiments easily becomes tedious; though all the parts are forcible, and every new line kindles new rapture, the reader, if not relieved by the interposition of something that soothes the fancy, grows weary of admiration, and defers the rest."

Brevity may be achieved by concentrating the satiric material into a one-sentence review, as Shaw did with his "People who like this sort of thing will find this the sort of thing they like," or by dividing a long satire into self-contained units, as Swift did in *Gulliver's Travels.* But the satirist knows that by one means or another he must control his expression of criticism, for the reader's span of attention is short.

Why is the reader of satire so impatient? A number of possible explanations are offered in Chapter Twelve. Here it will suffice to mention the theory of psychoanalyst Edmund Bergler; in "The Dislike for Satire at Length" he maintains that reading satire is the expression of unconscious rebellion by the frightened child who persists to some extent in every adult. This "slave-rebellion" permits a furtive glance at forbidden material— in this case satire—but a long look is dangerous. People who take more than minute doses of satire, says Dr. Bergler, find it "a dish causing mental indigestion (fear!)."

Satirists have used many different methods to

solve this problem. Sometimes, like Huxley and Waugh and Günter Grass and Joseph Heller, they make novels out of a series of short vignettes about numerous characters, using the perspective of the omniscient observer and scrambling the vignettes into some sort of continuity. Sometimes, like Butler in *Erewhon*, they devote separate sections to different institutions. Sometimes, like Voltaire in *Candide*, they divide a book into a number of "journeys."

Matthew Arnold commented on Byron's "wonderful power of vividly conceiving a single incident, a single situation," and Shenstone noted that "Pope's talent lay remarkably in the condensation of thoughts." It is a talent shared by most verse-satirists, and many writers of satiric prose. Rochester, Donne, Dryden, Heine, La Rochefoucauld, Pope, Swift, Churchill, Martial, Byron, T. S. Eliot, and Auden also have a remarkable talent for condensing witty thought.

But the problem is more complex than a need for brevity. Surprisingly few examples of short satires in narrative or drama have survived. A great many satiric sketches, in narrative and dramatic forms, were written, enjoyed momentary success, and have been long forgotten. But the great satiric short story is rare, and few short plays have achieved satiric distinction. Satire seems to flourish best either in the epigram at one extreme or an extended series of satiric scenes and characterizations at the other, but not in the brief episode itself. Such popular sketches as *Beyond*

*the Fringe, That Was the Week That Was, Second
City,* and revues at *avant garde* nightclubs are often effective at the time they are presented—but are
inconceivable as entertainment a decade later.

 Varieties

THERE ARE TECHNICAL differences between romantic and realistic satire. The former is more likely
to require a creative imagination, to permit
greater leeway in exaggeration, and to use such
devices as nonhuman characters and remote times
and places. But realistic satire also is difficult to
write because there is an almost irreconcilable difference between realism and satire. Realism is,
ostensibly, an attempt to record accurately; satire
is an attempt to distort. In creating characters
there is a sharp conflict between the requirements
of authentic reproduction and the demands of
satiric exaggeration. Realism requires objective
analysis; satire uses biased criticism. Realism needs
characters with both virtues and vices; satire prefers the use of types. Realistic dialogue is often
dull; dialogue in satires tries to be entertaining.

From a corner seat in the front row of a
theater one gets a peculiarly distorted view of a
movie. The characters seem tall and narrow,
movements are jerky, objects are two-dimensional.
The details of ordinary life are present, the scenes
are familiar, but they do not seem real somehow
because we are not accustomed to seeing them

from that particular perspective. Everything seems to be genuine but not quite credible. This is the effect of realistic satire such as that of Sinclair Lewis. We see a mass of minute details, we hear words and phrases exactly as we have often heard them, and we accept momentarily the accuracy of the representation. It is only later that we discern the one-sidedness of selection, the exaggeration, the compression. It is only on careful second glance that we recognize a set on a stage, rather than a scene in life. It is not naturalism but caricature. Yet it is caricature so richly detailed, so accurate in recording the minutiae of ordinary existence, that because we accept these details we are tempted to accept the whole—and to overlook the fact that it is *concentrated* hypocrisy or stupidity or dullness that we are shown. The essence of realistic satire is exaggeration of material whose components are authentic.

The satirist has the right to concentrate absurdities in the dialogue of his characters (as Molière and Jonson and Lewis and Ionesco and Beckett do), but the pretense that such concentration is a realistic representation of life is unwarranted. Satire distorts not only dialogue but also character and situation. The distortion may be aesthetically successful but it is distortion nevertheless. There is a justification for this method, which satirists have frequently offered: Satire is a "quintessence of realism," an art which reproduces the substance of life without necessarily reproducing the precise form of life.

Writers in general and satirists in particular pay little attention to such terms as "realism," "romanticism," "classicism," and the other paraphernalia of the scholar's cubicle. "Impressionistic" satire has been written by James Joyce in *Ulysses* and *Finnegans Wake,* "naturalistic" satire by Chekhov and Ibsen, and "expressionistic" satire by Capek, O'Neill, Toller, Kaiser, and Kafka. Satirists refuse to fit into neat categories. Ibsen was a realist at one stage, a symbolist at another. Lagerkvist has experimented with a number of techniques, and has managed to be ironic in all of them. So has Anatole France. Satire is not limited to a particular genre or milieu, and there is no point in trying to prove that one method is best.

CHAPTER SIX

The Technique of Incongruity

UNCRITICAL humor is not satire, nor is all satire humorous. But since satirists use all the comic devices for the purpose of criticism, to see how satire works it is necessary to examine four basic techniques of humor: incongruity, surprise, pretense, and catering to the superiority of the audience.

The incongruity theory is the most popular of all explanations of humor. The incongruity device makes use of the fact that certain kinds of inappropriateness result in amusement.

Schopenhauer suggests that "the cause of laughter in every case is simply the sudden perception of the incongruity between a concept and the real objects" which that concept is supposed to represent. For Schopenhauer a generalization about things is never an accurate substitute for the thing itself: Every concept in effect squeezes individual objects out of shape to make them fit the concept; humor arises when one suddenly perceives an incongruity between the concept and the object, as in Shakespeare's remark, "There was never yet philosopher that could endure the toothache patiently."

An obvious weakness of the incongruity theory is its failure to account for numerous instances of disharmony which do not cause laughter. It is only certain kinds of incongruity that result in humor; other kinds cause fear, horror, shock, or disgust. No theory of humor has been able to identify categorically those incongruous situations which always provoke laughter.

Arthur Koestler maintains, in two brilliant books *(Insight and Outlook* and *The Act of Creation),* that all humorous situations are variants of "the bisociation of form and function, the whole and the part." Every humorous device, he contends, involves "distortion of function." For example, Koestler says that we find eccentric clothes comic because we have gotten into the habit of regarding conventional clothes as "functional parts of their wearer," so that an unusual article of apparel focuses our attention on "its unfunctional aspects," thus becoming absurd and incongruous.

Not all scholars accept incongruity as the explanation of humor. One of the more ingenious attempts to disprove the theory is that of Dr. Edmund Bergler. He insists that we laugh not at incongruity itself but at the proof it offers that our teachers were wrong. In our youth, Bergler says, we were taught that there is logic in the world, that all things are "congruous" to the educated person. But subconsciously we suspect that this is not true, and incongruity delights us by furnishing evidence to the "child in the adult" that the logic which once was forced upon us is faulty. We triumph in this exhibition of the educator's inadequacy, and we laugh at the fallibility of our former superiors.[1]

There is no lack of incongruities in the theater of the absurd. In Beckett's plays truncated old parents live in ash cans in the son's room, a woman half-buried in the earth conducts a rambling two-hour monologue, and an old man strokes and consumes a large number of bananas. Ionesco turns people into rhinoceroses, permits a gigantic corpse to drive a young couple from their apartment, shows an old man talking to chairs, and entitles a play *The Bald Soprano*. Brecht presents a prostitute who masquerades as a business tycoon, Adamov centers a play around a pinball machine, and Ghelderode shows angels swinging on trapezes. In a stage set for one of Duerrenmatt's plays the room has one window opening on a Nordic city with a Gothic cathedral and apple trees, another on a Mediterranean view with classical ruins and cypress trees. And Genêt has Negroes wearing the masks of whites as they impersonate deities dancing around a bier to music by Mozart.

Somewhat incongruous is the line in Wilde's *Importance of Being Earnest*: "And, speaking of the science of Life, have you got the cucumber sandwiches cut for Lady Bracken?" Robert Benchley remarks solemnly, "Personally, if you ask me I feel that we as a nation eat too much buttered toast." And in Evelyn Waugh's satiric novels incongruity is continually demonstrated. The cloying sentimentality of the human cemetery is parodied by the pets' Happy Hunting Grounds; cards are sent to owners on the anniversaries of their dogs' deaths; chimpanzees and birds are given elaborately ritualistic funerals; and Aimee writes letters to the lovelorn columnist, an alcoholic journalist who calls himself the Guru Brahmin. In *Handful of Dust* a vicar who had served in India most of his life delivers his old sermons to a rural English congregation; he speaks of "the harsh glare of the alien sun" in a freezing church and adds, "we have for companions the ravening tiger and the exotic camel, the furtive jackal and the ponderous elephant." In *Decline and Fall,* Waugh concocts a party at which Mrs. Melrose Ape and her angels, Chastity, Humility, and Divine Discontent sing songs like "There Ain't No Flies on the Lamb of God." And Pennyfeather, on his first day as a teacher, offers his students "a prize of half a crown for the longest essay, irrespective of any possible merit."

The court scene in Carroll's Wonderland provides incongruities in the form of absurdity, unexpected logic, puns, grotesqueries, and several other varieties of nonsense, including the use of live flamingos for mallets in the Queen's croquet game. The strutting Lilliputians are incongruous, and the optimistic philosophizing of poor Pangloss is incongruous. So are France's baptized penguins.

ALL SATIRE is exaggeration. It always intensifies,
or contrasts dramatically, or emphasizes one thing
at the expense of something else. But it does so
more obviously than other literary forms and
achieves humor because, in James Feibleman's
happy phrase, by "confusing the categories of
actuality," exaggeration implies that these categories are ultimately unimportant. By distorting
accepted values, exaggeration makes them seem
ludicrous.

Slapstick is a variety of exaggeration which
even subtle satirists do not hesitate to use when it
suits their purpose, and Bernard Shaw often used
crude devices to communicate sly ideas. "Vulgarity," Shaw said, perhaps in defense of his own
practice, "is the necessary part of a complete
author's equipment."

Perhaps the best-known exaggerator was
Baron Munchausen, with his tales of hunters who
kill several birds with a single shot; stewed icicles;
fried pyramids; talking monkeys; and a cherry tree
growing out of a deer's head. From Franklin to
Twain exaggeration has been a dominant characteristic of American humor, especially on the part
of frontier humorists. Other Americans have contributed to this technique. "That guy would steal
a hot stove and come back later for the smoke,"
said Wilson Mizner. To a conceited movie producer he remarked, "A demitasse cup would fit

over your head like a sun-bonnet." Describing his flight from an armed madman, he said, "I got up enough lather to shave Kansas City."

H. L. Mencken tended to overstatement. "No man," he wrote, "is genuinely happy, married, who has to drink worse gin than he used to drink when he was single."

Henny Youngman tells this one: "I saw a man lying in the street and asked him if he was sick. 'No,' he says, 'I found a parking place and I'm holding it while my wife buys a car.'" Will Rogers sent his niece a picture postal card of Venus de Milo from Italy; he wrote on it: "See what'll happen to you if you don't stop biting your nails."

It is surprising how widespread is the notion that all British humor is quiet and understated. One has only to cite Dickens, Shakespeare, Fielding, Sterne, and W. S. Gilbert as examples of wild exaggeration. Describing what it was like to preach at St. Paul's in London, Sydney Smith said, "The temperature is several degrees below zero. My sentences are frozen as they come out of my mouth, and are thawed in the course of the summer, making strange noises and unexpected assertions in various part of the church." And: "Heat! It was so dreadful that there was nothing for me to do but take off my flesh and sit in my bones." Carroll's Alice swims in a pool of her own tears. Some readers detect a slight element of exaggeration in *Gulliver's Travels*. And Evelyn Waugh described the Welsh band in *Decline and Fall* in these words:

Ten men of revolting appearance . . . low of brow, crafty of eye, and crooked of limb. They advanced huddled together with the loping tread of wolves. . . . They slavered at their mouths, which hung loosely over their receding chins, while each clutched under his ape-like arm a burden of curious and unaccountable shape.

All satirists exaggerate, some pretending to be realists like Sinclair Lewis, others openly admitting their buffoonery like Rabelais. Aristophanes exaggerates and Cervantes and Voltaire and Gogol and Molière and Kafka. Eugene Field overstated things somewhat when he wrote, "He is so mean, he won't let his little baby have more than one measle at a time." So did Philip Wylie, in his attacks on Moms, teachers, and everyone else.

One might expect conditions in an absurd world to be absurd, and Ionesco does his best to demonstrate. In his plays banality is exaggerated, clichés are exaggerated, conformity is exaggerated, stupidity is exaggerated, and coincidences are exaggerated. Nor is slapstick out of place, and in *The Killer* people urinate on stage, bang each other on the head with police clubs, and indulge in all sorts of rough-and-tumble activities. The satiric world of Nathanael West offers a distorted picture, and in *A Cool Million* the Horatio-Alger-like protagonist is swindled, robbed, jailed, maimed, scalped, shot, cheated, whipped, beaten, and finally killed. And Heller's *Catch-22* is loaded with such incidents as Halfoats striking oil, Scheisskopf planning to rivet soldiers together to insure a perfect parade, Major Major Major signing Washington

Irving's name to all documents, and Nately's whore chasing Yossarian all over Italy in her preposterous attempts to kill him.

The exaggeration of satirists is not as purposeless as it tries to appear. What the satirist exaggerates is the bad, the foolish, the hypocritical; what he minimizes or omits is the good, the sensible, the honest. The resulting scene is not only exaggerated but heavily biased—against the victims of the satirist's attack.

Invective. Mencken's attack on the low-caste man illustrates the method of sheer invective:

> The world gets nothing from him save his brute labor, and even that he tries to evade. In two thousand years he has moved an inch: from the sports of the arena to the lynching party—and another inch: from the obscenities of the Saturnalia to the obscenities of the Methodist revival. So he lives out his life in the image of Jahveh. What is worth knowing he doesn't know and doesn't want to know. What he knows is not true. The cardinal articles of his credo are the inventions of mountebanks; his heroes are mainly scoundrels.[2]

The fact that invective is one of the earliest forms of satire does not necessarily prove that it is the easiest. There is a tenuous line between abuse and invective; no mathematical formula differentiates between them. A reader's attitude, intelligence, and knowledge help him decide whether the satirist has uttered a devastating criticism or an ill-natured grumble. For satiric purposes invective needs originality of expression. Indignation is not enough—it may make the reader uncomfortable. Sincerity is not enough—a fool can be sincere. The reader must admire the form of the attack and share, at least momentarily, the intensity of the anger.

In his anthology of insults, Max Herzberg lists among terms of abuse the dog (especially the female of the species), the pig, the snake, the fox and vixen, the wolf, the jackal, the jackass, the hyena, the vulture, the buzzard, the rat, the skunk, the toad, the goose, the sheep, and the louse. He notes also size—shrimp, runt, pinhead, hippopotamus; social inferiority—vulgarian, scum, rabble, riffraff, plebeian, *hoi polloi*, "the great unwashed"; poverty—beggar, hobo, ragamuffin; recently acquired wealth—upstart, parvenu, *nouveau riche;* rusticity—hick, rube, hayseed, clodhopper, yokel; youth—baby, kid, adolescent; age—crone, dotard, hag, gaffer; and color—red in politics, black-hearted, white-livered, green in experience, yellow in reference to courage.

Some satirists have been especially proficient in the use of invective: Juvenal, Swift, Dryden, Pope, Byron, the first Samuel Butler, Charles Churchill, St. Jerome, Junius, Mencken, Twain, and Ambrose Bierce—the last perhaps the most devastating in American literature with his pugnacious, blunt name calling.

That invective is not limited to western culture is suggested by the following letter, sent by Hetman Ivan Sirke to Sultan Mohammed IV.

You Turkish Satan. You damned brother of the Devil. What manner of beast are you? The evil one vomits what you swallow. We fear not your army, you Babylonian cook, Macedonian Stavebinder, brewer of Jerusalem, Alexandrian goat-thief, Egyptian swine-herd, Tartar ram, seed of the very Devil, clown of Hades, swinesnout, horse's tail, red-haired she-dog, unbaptized skull. May the Evil One catch you!

This abuse was addressed directly to the victim. Another form of invective talks about the victims instead of to them. In the "Vision of Judgment" Byron described George III in these terms:

"God save the King!" "It is a large economy
In God to save the like."

And the Earl of Shaftesbury seemed, to Dryden:

In friendship false, implacable in hate,
Resolv'd to ruin or to rule the state.

A fair example of invective is provided by Swift in Chapter 10 of the Voyage to the Houyhnhnms:

I enjoyed perfect health of body, and tranquillity of mind; I did not feel the treachery or inconstancy of a friend, nor the injuries of a secret or open enemy. I had no occasion of bribing, flattering, or pimping to procure the favour of any great man or of his minion. I wanted no fence against fraud or oppression: here was neither physician to destroy my body, nor lawyer to ruin my fortune; no informer to watch my words or actions, or forge accusations against me for hire; here were no gibers, censurers, backbiters, pickpockets, highwaymen, housebreakers, attorneys, bawds, buffoons, gamesters, politicians, wits, splenetics, tedious talkers, controvertists, ravishers, murderers, robbers, virtuosos; no leaders or followers of party and faction; no encouragers to vice, by seducement or examples; no dungeon, axes, gibbets, whipping posts, or pillories; no cheating shopkeepers or mechanics; no pride, vanity, or affectation; no fops, bullies, drunkards, strolling whores, or poxes; no ranting, lewd, expensive wives; no stupid, proud pedants; no importunate, overbearing, quarrelsome, noisy, roaring, empty, conceited, swearing companions; no scoundrels raised from the dust upon the merit of their vices; or nobility thrown into it on account of their virtues; no lords, fiddlers, judges, or dancing-masters.

Not everyone accepts invective as a form of satire. Gilbert Highet calls it "a near-neighbor" of satire, but not properly satire. There is something to be said for Highet's position. Unlike other satiric devices invective does not pretend to be something other than what it is; on the contrary, it passionately insists on being taken literally, and its effectiveness depends on the assumption that it means just what it says. There is usually no humor in invective. It depends on emotion rather than logic, fervor rather than innuendo. Perhaps pure invective—distinguished from the subtle insult and the indirect attack—should not really be categorized as a satiric device. But Morris Bishop maintains that the humor of the Elizabethans relied largely on abuse "elevated to a kind of lyrical drama." And Northrop Frye, discussing invective as a form of satire, admits that we enjoy hearing people cursed: "Almost any denunciation, if vigorous enough, is followed by a reader with the kind of pleasure that soon breaks into a smile."[3]

In general most readers feel that the broad spectrum of satiric attack encompasses both subtle insult and inspired vituperation.

Reductio ad absurdum. As a satiric device the *reductio ad absurdum* is an extreme form of exaggeration. It may magnify one fault of a character to the exclusion of all other qualities, giving us stereotypes in Plautus, Molière, Jonson, Restoration comedy, and expressionistic theater. It may carry to a logical, and ridiculous, conclusion a popularly accepted concept, as in *Erewhon, Squaring the Circle, Gulliver's Travels, Brave New World, 1984, A Clockwork Orange,* Sinclair Lewis' novels, Per Lagerkvist's stories, and Evelyn Waugh's satires. Or it may pretend to accept an opponent's argument and carry it on to an unacceptable conclusion, as Mencken does when he says, "If the average man is made in God's image, then such a man as Beethoven or Aristotle is plainly superior to God."

All satiric utopias make use of the *reductio ad absurdum.* The satirist pretends that his opponent's idea is excellent; he applies it to an actual situation; he not only applies it but exaggerates its inappropriateness to the ultimate degree, until it is preposterously clear that the idea is ridiculous.

Huxley pretends to accept the assumption

that science can solve all of men's problems and then reduces the assumption to absurdity by pushing it to its logical extremes: decanted babies, five conditioned classes of human beings from Alphas to Epsilons, sex orgies instead of religion, and so on. Orwell pretends to accept the assumption that totalitarianism can solve all of men's problems and then reduces the assumption to absurdity by pushing it to its logical extremes: Big Brother, two-way television spying, Anti-Sex League, Thought Police, preposterous slogans, "two-minute hate" rituals, Newspeak, permanent war among the three powers with alliances constantly shifting, and the continuous rewriting of history to make events of the past seem to match the immediate present. Both Huxley and Orwell found before they died that nature was imitating their art far more rapidly than they had expected.

In Aristophanes' *Frogs* a scale is brought on stage to weigh the poetry of Aeschylus and Euripides, in an effort to decide who is the greater poet. Waugh's *Loved One* makes the commercializing of death hilariously funny. Kafka's *Trial* and *Castle* reduce all life to absurdity. Swift's *Modest Proposal* eliminates hungry children by providing recipes for cooking them. And Harry Golden offers his Vertical Segregation Plan as a solution to the integration problem in southern schools: Since Negroes have always been permitted to associate with whites in department stores, shops, and supermarkets where people carry on their activities standing up, all that is necessary to achieve instant integration in schools is to remove all seats from classrooms.

At the end of an essay defending capital punishment and severe penalties for crime, Ambrose Bierce prophesied that if present policies were continued, by the year 2015 all the good people would be in enclosures and all criminals would roam free. In *War With the Newts* Capek ridicules the research methods of historians by having a doorman save the longest newspaper clippings about newts, regardless of their accuracy or profundity. Hasek's good soldier Schweik creates chaos in the army by literally following the instructions his officers give him. Saki tells a story about the problems a woman ran into when she was compelled to speak only the truth.

Anatole France's intention in *Penguin Island* is not really reverent when he makes a nearsighted bishop mistake penguins for men and baptize them, creating problems in heaven and on earth. An efficiency-minded store owner in Ionesco's *Killer,* irritated by the frequent stops his delivery boys make to urinate, figures out a system for a once-a-month four-and-a-half-hour urinating time. The fantasies of nonentities come to reality when three men in Genêt's *Balcony* patronize a brothel where they are dressed and treated like a bishop, a general, and a judge. In the satiric sketches called *Beyond the Fringe,* a speaker on nuclear warfare recommends to his British audience that the best-known defense against radiation is hiding oneself in a brown paper bag. Nathanael West describes Miss McGreeney, "the woman who wrote the biography of the man who wrote the biography of the man who wrote the biography of Boswell."

In *Catch-22* the exponent of free enterprise, U.S. Lieutenant Milo Minderbinder, buys advertising time on the radio programs of Axis Sally and Lord Haw Haw, as well as on Allied stations; Yossarian substitutes for a dead soldier in a hospital so that the soldier's parents can have the comfort of watching their son die; the soldier in white has been so completely covered by bandages that the nurses do not find out he is dead until a long time after his demise. And in *The Tin Drum* two former members of the Home Guard personally carry out the execution of an anti-Nazi postal clerk. There is nothing vindictive in this murder years after the war ended; they are simply carrying out an order they had been unable to carry out during the war.

After the Caucus Race in Wonderland, when all have run around aimlessly for some time, they ask, "But who has won?" The Dodo replies, "Everybody has won and all must have prizes." Then the prizes turn out to be worthless. The contemporary Polish satirist, Mrozek, uses the *reductio* device effectively in several short stories. In a small town, for example, a matron keeps a live rebel caged in her living room; it is presumably more chic than keeping a bird. In another story a lion refuses to eat Christians in the arena; he anticipates a trend toward Christian dominance. Stolen telegraphs are replaced, in a third story, by men stationed every hundred yards to yell out the messages. And, finally, a housewife confesses to the priest that her husband is made entirely out of plasticene. The priest suggests annulment. "Annulment?" she says. "But we have three children."

As usual, the absurdities in life are indistinguishable from those in fiction. A Louisiana prison warden forbade the exchange of letters between a Negro in death row and a woman in Sweden; the warden wanted no race mixing. When Bobby Kennedy was first mentioned as a candidate for the Senate from New York, Gore Vidal suggested that Prince Philip be nominated instead: "He has done as much for New York and is genuine royalty." The proliferation of "queens" chosen for publicity purposes has led to a Miss Storm Sewer of 1965. When the real estate men in a college town opposed the school's plan to build apartments for married veterans, a faculty member wrote a letter to the local paper, suggesting that the housing problems of the veterans could be solved more economically by divorces and infanticides. And it is pleasant to learn that the whole idea for *The Inspector-General* may have come from Pushkin's casual remark to Gogol that he was once mistaken for a government official.

Caricature. Caricature in literature operates by choosing an objectionable quality, attributing it to an individual or a group, then describing the victim only in terms of that disagreeable characteristic. In carrying out this process, oversimplification is the basic requirement. To the degree that oversimplifying is unfair, caricature is certainly unfair. It distorts, by exaggerating and twisting out of shape both objects (individuals, groups, institutions) and ideas. By exaggerating the hypocrisy or selfishness or inconsistency, the satirist exposes it to public view and degrades the victim.

Arthur Koestler's analysis is, as usual, stimulating:[4]

The main techniques of caricature are based on bisociations of the perceptual and the conceptual fields, of form and function, and of the part and the whole. . . . The distorting mirror operates by exaggerating one dimension (e.g., the vertical) at the expense of another. The caricaturist distorts not simply in a spatial direction, but by "exaggerating" spatial form in a direction which is already indicated by nature. . . . But this exaggeration and fixation is not . . . in itself sufficient to produce a comic effect. The exaggeration must produce an effect which is at the same time *visually plausible* and *biologically impossible,* that is, absurd.

The defense of the caricaturist which satirists offer is one which most victims of caricature are likely to deny: The caricature is a more accurate representation of the victim than his actual appearance. The caricature, in Ernst Kris's words, "is truer than reality itself," for it shows more of the essential quality and provides "a likeness more true than mere imitation could be." By finding "the perfect deformity" instead of seeking perfect form, the caricaturist penetrates beneath mere outward appearance to expose the essential ugliness or pettiness of the subject.

In art, caricature has a long history. Certainly one of the earliest examples of the genre is a caricature on stone of the Pharaoh Akhnaton, carved by a royal artist more than 3,300 years ago and hidden until archaeologists uncovered it in the 1930's. The artist had an easy time; Akhnaton had big ears, a thin neck, big mouth, sharp chin, and a head that bulged at the back. In China a few centuries later artists began to distort maliciously the features of unpopular models. And we can still see in European cathedrals the caricatures of medieval sculptors.

The caricature of art is usually limited to individuals, although Diego Rivera, Orozco, and Siqueiros have satirized such institutions as the church, the military, landowners, and government. In essence all social satire is a form of caricature, exaggerating the weaknesses of groups and institutions and ideas and minimizing their virtues. Much of what has been said about the social sources of satire is illustrative of the caricaturizing technique, and the work of a writer like Kafka can be viewed as a caricature of life.

The caricature of individuals will be discussed in Chapter Ten. But the device is used so often that it is worth giving a few examples here. Molière's Tartuffe and Harpagon, Jonson's Volpone, Dickens' Pecksniff are classic types. Aristophanes reduced Socrates to a shallow Sophist, Euripides to a sophomoric skeptic, Dionysus to a coward, Cleon to a scoundrel, and Hercules to a glutton. Mrs. Dudgeon, in Shaw's *Devil's Disciple,* is a caricature of excessive religiosity. The characters in *The Inspector-General* and *Dead Souls* are almost all caricatures. The wicked women of Juvenal and the silly women of Jane Austen and the preposterous women of Evelyn Waugh are caricatures. So are the creations of Rabelais and Lucian and Al Capp.

It is not surprising that in the theater of the absurd, caricature should prove a useful method of accentuating absurdity. Ionesco, Adamov, Genêt, Beckett, and Ghelderode use caricature to emphasize the irrationality, disorder, and purposelessness which, they feel, authentically reflect the real world. But Oscar Wilde in *The Importance of Being Earnest,* and Elmer Rice in *The Adding Machine,* and Capek in *R. U. R.,* and Brant in *Ship of Fools,* and Ring Lardner in his gallery of defectives also relied on caricature to express their criticism. As did Daumier and Hogarth and Dürer and Gillray and Cruikshank and Goya and Rowlandson and George Grosz and Herblock and Bill Mauldin.

 ## *Understatement*

UNDERSTATEMENT may be defined as exaggeration in reverse: By magnifying nonchalance, understatement refuses to accept the "categories of actuality," just as exaggeration refuses to accept them.

Literary historians have noted a tendency among individuals and cultures to progress from an early use of exaggeration to greater use of understatement as the individual or the culture matures. There is some truth in this observation, and there are many exceptions. Children sometimes use understatement, as well as college students. Primitive societies, especially if they value stoicism highly, use understatement freely. (When the use of understatement has become habitual it is no longer humorous, for it then expresses acceptance rather than distortion of current values.) Anglo-Saxon poetry is full of litotes. Esther Warner found that the African natives among whom she lived considered understatement as amusing as exaggeration.

Thurber's cartoon is a classic example of understatement: The detached head of a dueler is calmly saying, "Touché." When young Victoria Lincoln asked why Lizzie Borden was shunned by her neighbors, Mrs. Lincoln explained, "You see, that lady was very unkind to her mother and father." A famous football coach showed considerable restraint when, after a defeat, he told his fumbling fullback, "It's better to have the ball with you when you cross the goal-line." When a French soccer player who had been booed by the fans pulled down his trousers and bowed to the crowd in four directions, the executive committee suspended him for what they called a "thoughtless gesture." And Harry Graham, whose Little Willie jokes delighted Victorian Englishmen, contributed the following verses:

> Willie poisoned his father's tea;
> Father died in agony.
> Mother came, and looked quite vexed:
> "Really, Will," she said, "what next?"

and

> In the drinking well
>   Which the plumber built her,
> Aunt Eliza fell.
>   We must buy a filter.

In stories by Saki characters say:

I know if I were served up at a cannibal feast I should be dreadfully annoyed if anyone found fault with me for not being tender enough, or having been kept too long.

and

Her husband gardens in all weathers. When a man goes out in the pouring rain to brush caterpillars off rose trees, I generally imagine his life indoors leaves something to be desired.

Having seen Russian soldiers raping and murdering in Danzig, Günter Grass's Oskar remarks, "You didn't joke with the Russians." And Ambrose Bierce wrote, in "Owl Creek Bridge," "The liberal military code makes provisions for hanging many kinds of persons, and gentlemen are not excluded."

Sydney Smith's versatility resulted in humor which ranged from biting social satire to playful nonsense, including understatement:

> The Scythians always ate their grandfathers; they behaved very respectfully to them for a long time, but as soon as their grandfathers became old and troublesome and began to tell long stories, they immediately ate them. Nothing could be more improper, and even disrespectful, than dining off such near and venerable relations.

In Shaw's *Androcles and the Lion* a number of casual statements are made about the persecution of Christians and the callousness of Roman soldiers. Then, after Spintho has been devoured, the Keeper says:

> Now [the lion's] appetite's taken off, he won't as much as look at another Christian for a week. . . . What call had he to walk down the throat of one of my lions before he was asked?

James Thurber is particularly adept at describing eccentric or outrageous behavior with a calm detachment which pretends to regard the activity as perfectly normal. Capek, in *Adam, the Creator,* has Adam simplify the act of creation in his comment to Alter Ego: "You just make a figure out of clay, and then you breathe the breath of life into it." And Don Marquis often used understatement: "Cleopatra idly flicked a slave from the garden roof to the crocodiles below as she talked with the journalist." Archy says of Mehitabel, "She may have mislaid her morals somewhere, but I admire her spirit." To the press floor above his office, Marquis sent this message:

> Floor, do not yield! A falling press
> Would be a nuisance, more or less.

Evelyn Waugh's Lady Circumference says, in *Decline and Fall,* "Sorry if we're late. Circumference ran over a fool of a boy." Mark Twain observed that "a soiled baby, with a neglected nose, cannot be conscientiously regarded as a thing of beauty." Gilbert and Sullivan's Lord Chancellor in *Iolanthe* explains that he had pointed out "to myself that I was no stranger to myself—in point of fact, I had been personally acquainted with myself for some years. This had its effect." And in Hardy's poem, "In the Cemetery," mothers are arguing over flowers on the graves of their children, not knowing that because of a new drain all of the bodies had been dumped together. A cemetery worker who is listening remarks:

> As well cry over a new-laid drain
> As anything else, to ease your pain.

Benchley's humor relied to a considerable extent on understatement: "Whereas, for example, a puppy might be able to eat only the toe of a slipper, a child might well succeed in eating the whole shoe . . . which, considering the nails and everything, would not be wise." And Will Cuppy delighted in the device: "This was the year in which Cesare [Borgia] murdered his older brother Giovanni, a stabbing case. Always up to something, that one." And: "Lucrezia was rather fond of her young husband, and the marriage might have grown into something fine and permanent if Cesare hadn't strangled him after a couple of years."

Two understatements in particular have caught the fancy of twentieth-century readers. In a *New Yorker* cartoon the designer watches the crash of his new plane and says casually, "Well, back to the old drawing board." And a great many people who never read *Animal Farm* are familiar with Orwell's slogan: "Some animals are more equal than others."

 ## Contrast

IN A BROAD SENSE contrast is present in all comedy, all irony, all satire. To get a laugh, the contrast should be sudden. To elicit a smile or crinkling of lips, the contrast may be revealed gradually, sneaking up on the reader or spectator until he realizes that there is an odd discrepancy between what he expected to be told and what he actually is being told, or between the way in which such material is usually communicated and the way it actually is being communicated. Among the many ways of using contrast for satiric effect are disparity between manner and matter (as in Jonathan

Swift), inserting irrelevant matter in presumably serious statement (as Richard Armour specializes in doing), interpolating comic interludes in tragedy (as in Shakespeare), casually mixing formal language and slang (as in *The New Yorker*), and incongruous grouping (Twain: "Only kings, editors, and people with tapeworms have the right to use the editorial 'we' ").

The most striking effect of the detached style is the resulting contrast between manner and matter. The ironist writes calmly, gently, in restrained terms, never growing melodramatic or excited or indignant, about the horrors of war and hypocrisy of man and ingratitude of friends and faithlessness of women, as casually as if there were nothing unusual about his subject matter at all, as if it were familiar and expected behavior. This method is used successfully in Voltaire's *Candide* and Swift's *Modest Proposal,* Waugh's *Loved One* and Duff's *New Handbook of Hanging.* At a lighter level the contrast between manner and matter makes successful parody and travesty in verse and in prose, as in Pope's *Rape of the Lock,* Stephen Potter's *Gamesmanship,* and the monologues of Bob Newhart and Robert Benchley.

Hemingway's exploitation of the contrast implicit in the pose of "humanitarianism" is examined by Kenneth Burke: Hemingway "has introduced the most skillfully incongruous terms, gentle words, approbational words, highly Christian words, for events to which we habitually applied words of a wholly resentful order." The contrast between his restrained, casual tone and the intensity of his bitterness has made Swift the greatest English ironist. Auden uses the ingenuous form of the popular song to communicate complex and somber ideas. Evelyn Waugh presents— casually, impersonally, in understated terms—absurd, exaggerated, shocking events. The powerful effect of Camus' *Stranger* comes from a similar detachment. And one of the most effective devices in Wilde's *Importance of Being Earnest* is the contrast between the sophisticated dialogue and the absurd plot.

Heine illustrates the method in the following reminiscence:

> We were schoolmates . . . and I said, "Wilhelm, get the kitten, she just fell in," and he gaily climbed down on the board across the brook, pulled the cat out of the water but fell in himself, and when they pulled him out he was wet and dead. The kitten lived for a long time.

The Devil's Disciple illustrates Shaw's mastery of contrasting manner and matter:

RICHARD: I think you might have the decency to treat me as a prisoner of war, and shoot me like a man instead of hanging me like a dog.
BURGOYNE: Now there, Mr. Anderson, you talk like a civilian, if you will excuse my saying so. Have you any idea of the average marksmanship of the army of His Majesty King George the Third? If we make you up a firing party, what will happen? Half of them will miss you; the rest will make a mess of the business and leave you to the provo-marshall's pistol. Whereas we can hang you in a

most workmanlike and agreeable way. *(Kindly)*
Let me persuade you to be hanged, Mr. Anderson?

RICHARD: Thank you, General. That view of the case
did not occur to me before. . . . To oblige you,
I withdraw my objection to the rope. Hang me,
by all means.

BURGOYNE: Will twelve o'clock suit you, Mr. Anderson?

RICHARD: I shall be at your disposal then, General.

Sinclair Lewis often uses contrast for satiric
purpose. In *Main Street* sophisticated Carol Kennicott arrives in Gopher Prairie the same day as
naive Bea Sorenson; Carol is shocked by the
provincialism and dinginess of the town, Bea
is thrilled by its cosmopolitanism and color. In
Elmer Gantry idealistic Christian minister Frank
Shallard is crippled by a gang of fundamentalist
hoodlums while fraudulent Elmer Gantry achieves
high preferment in the church. The unsuccessful
attempt of the Babbitts to curry favor with the
wealthy McKelveys by giving a dinner for them is
paralleled by the ineffectual attempt of the poor
Overbrooks to curry favor with the Babbitts. And
in *Work of Art* the career of an honest hotel keeper
is contrasted with that of his wealthy brother, a
writer of popular trash.

In *A House-boat on the Styx* Bangs mixes human beings like Shakespeare and Queen Elizabeth
with such literary characters as Hamlet, Yorick,
and Charon. There is obvious contrast between
Don Quixote and Sancho Panza, and between
Chaucer's prioress and the wife of Bath. The

athlete in Housman's poem who died young was twice carried into town shoulder-high: after winning the race and, a little later, in a coffin to the grave. Chevalier observes of Anatole France's characters that they "are almost, as it were, separable from their destinies: their potentialities and their fate rarely coincide." The contrast between the Houyhnhnms and the Yahoos is strong enough to have made Victorian scholars question Swift's sanity. And some of Bill Mauldin's most effective cartoons contrast civilian clichés with soldiers' attitudes, as when Willie says to his broken-down rifle, "I've given you the best years of my life."

The disparity between her petty egotism and the magnitude of war makes the woman in Betjeman's "Westminster Abbey" an object of satire. The alternation of brief episodes in *Brave New World* serves to contrast natural impulses and conditioned responses. Lardner's "Love Nest" reveals an ironic contrast between the insensitive husband's notion of his home life and the tragic emptiness of that life from the wife's point of view. Jane Austen shows discrepancies between form and fact in the middle-class world she dissects. And Kafka measures the ape against human standards in "A Report to an Academy," and Gregor against an insect's needs in "The Metamorphosis."

Voltaire places the idyllic Eldorado episode between a dangerous adventure among cannibals and an unpleasant experience in the following section. Samuel Beckett scrambles formal language and slang, gloomy experiences in a comic framework and comic experiences in a gloomy framework, and the ludicrous incongruities of tramps using pedantic language. And in all of Pirandello's plays contrast is an integral element— contrast between illusion and reality in *Right You Are If You Think You Are*, between art and life in *Six Characters in Search of an Author*, between the medieval world and the modern in *Henry IV*, between an individual's actual personality and the public image in *To Clothe the Naked*.

One of the most effective ways of using contrast is the rhetorical trick of "grouping." This consists of mixing with a number of undesirable items one item which is generally regarded with approval. To make the incongruity clear, the satirist uses parallelism, setting up a balanced pattern of adjectives or phrases so that the reader prepares his mind to expect a group of similar impressions. The sudden realization that one of the impressions is not similar at all results in a pleasant shock—and satire, as in Mencken's remark: "These savages were so low that they had not even invented bows and arrows, usury, the gallows, or the notion of baptism by complete immersion."

The grouping technique is used by many satirists. Mencken in particular relies on it, his measured style finding parallelism an especially appropriate device: "He believed in spiritualism, or democracy, or the Baconian theory, or some other such nonsense." Sydney Smith, a clergyman himself, said, "What a pity it is that we have no amusements in England but vice and religion." A century later Julius Lewis, a professor in Johannesburg, consoled the Englishmen in South Africa for being a minority: "I think they will endure their fate with the aid of two major consolations. One is golf and the other is wealth." Voltaire criticized the English for having sixty religions but only one gravy.

William R. Inge, the "gloomy Dean," announced late in life, "I believe neither in heaven, hell, nor the British Socialists." Will Cuppy tells us that "the orangutan likes stewed apples, toast, cocoa, and soap." Heine wrote, "The inhabitants of Goettingen are generally divided into students, professors, philistines, and cattle."

❋ *Disparaging Comparison*

LIKE THE POET the satirist makes copious use of similes, analogies, and metaphors. But the satirist's comparisons are characterized by special qualities. They are usually exaggerated and often impertinent. The satirist sees an incongruous relationship between objects which to most people seem totally unrelated. As the microscope and Geiger counter reveal the unseen in the physical world, the satirist's peculiar perspective discloses unobserved similarities in the world of men.

Poets, humorists, and madmen all use unexpected analogies. During one phase in certain mental illnesses, the patient sees relationships among objects that more normal people fail to see. But it would take a courageous sage to separate the three groups definitively on the basis of analogies they make. All that one can safely say is that in comic comparison, as Sydney Smith remarked, "There is an apparent incongruity and a real relation." Humor is always a distortion of the familiar, and the humorous comparison is simply one form of this distortion.

The range of satiric analogy is enormous. Some satirists (Nabokov, Auden, Cuppy, Joyce, Mary McCarthy, Kingsley Amis) use erudite similes for comic effect. Some use unexpected comparison for sheer delight (Sydney Smith: Macaulay is "a book in breeches." Heine: "The Napoleon days, when coffee was made out of acorns, and princes out of nothing at all.") Some use analogy for pointed social criticism (Thoreau: "It would be easier for [a man] to hobble to town with a broken leg than with a torn pantaloon.") And some use elaborately contrived metaphors for tragicomic effect, as Melville does with the whaleman comparison and Günter Grass does with the midget drummer in *The Tin Drum*.

Here are a few satiric metaphors and analogies:

SYDNEY SMITH: [Life in the country is] a kind of healthy grave.
SHAW: A man is like a phonograph with half a dozen records. You soon get tired of them all; and yet

you have to sit at table whilst he reels them off to every new visitor.

(When Ellen Terry asked permission to publish some of their correspondence): I will not play the horse to your Lady Godiva.

[In the preface to *Man and Superman,* Shaw says it is commonly] assumed that the woman must wait, motionless, until she is wooed. Nay, she often does wait motionless. That is how the spider waits for the fly. But the spider spins her web.

HEINE: It is indeed a pity that our great public knows so little about poetry; almost as little, in fact, as our poets.

MENCKEN: . . . as easily as the Yahveh of John Calvin slips into the prayers at a hanging.

Howells' discoveries are not disclosed in terms of passion, but in terms of giggles.

An actor, encountering a worthy girl, leaps from the couch to the altar almost as fast as a Baptist leaps from the altar to the couch.

[The popular song] at its loftiest . . . is never far from the poetry of a rooster in a barnyard.

A professor must have a theory, as a dog must have fleas.

The last movement of Beethoven's *Eroica* is voluptuous. Try to play it with your eyes on a portrait of Dr. Coolidge. You will find it as impossible as eating ice-cream on roast beef.

SWIFT: She wears her clothes as if they were thrown on with a pitchfork.

Religion is a cloak . . . conscience a pair of breeches; which, though a cover for lewdness as well as hastiness, is easily slipped down for the service of both.

FRANCE: Thérèse is heavy as a sack of coal and slow as justice.

MARQUIS: Writing a book of poetry is like dropping a rose petal into the Grand Canyon and waiting for the echo.

GOGOL: [A woman's face] as narrow and long as a cucumber, [and a man's face] round and broad, like Moldavian pumpkins.

(At the governor's party Chichikov sees the tailcoated men as flies settling on lumps of sugar.)

FRED ALLEN: Over the radio, Portland's voice sounded like two slate pencils mating.

Pull up a platitude, Portland, and sit down.

EPICTETUS: [Man is a] soul dragging a corpse around.

WOOLLCOTT: I must get out of these wet clothes and into a dry martini.

EUGENE FIELD: Last night Hampden played King Lear. He played the king as though he expected someone else to play the ace.

 Epigram

EPIGRAMS can be concocted more mechanically than other satiric devices. One method consists of changing a cliché slightly, so that an incongruous effect is produced. (Huxley: "And while there is death, there is hope." Twain: "All the modern inconveniences.") Another way is the coining of a cynical definition. (Mencken: "Conscience: the inner voice which warns us that someone is looking." Bierce: "Diaphragm: a muscular partition separating the disorders of the chest from disorders of the bowels.") A third method is stating pungently a belief widely held but rarely expressed. (Proverb: "Poverty is not a sin, but it's a great deal worse.") A variation of this method is a new way of stating an old idea. (Mencken: "Man weeps to think that he will die so soon; woman, that she was born so long ago.") And a fourth, the most difficult, is a polished statement of an original idea, as in Montaigne, Confucius, Nietzsche, Shaw, La Rochefoucauld, Shakespeare, Emerson, Schopenhauer, and Bacon. (Thoreau: "The mass of men lead lives of quiet desperation.") All of these methods rely on balanced construction and economy of words.

Scholars who categorize aphorisms by structure have found two types, the "open" maxims of Bacon and the epigrammatic turns of La Rouchefoucauld. Two different mental processes lead to these aphorisms: A "flash of insight" produces the La Rochefoucauld variety, whereas the Baconian kind is "the result of gradual clarification." But the motivation is not always psychological: China has given the world a great many epigrammatists who had to be terse simply because they did their writing on narrow bamboo sticks.

The epigram must interest; it should stimulate, as the observations of Thoreau and Pascal force men to reexamine their assumptions. It may simplify—usually oversimplify. But epigrams do not necessarily edify, for each reader judges subjectively; and individual differences determine whether a statement is a brilliant epigram or a shallow platitude, whether La Rochefoucauld is a cynic or a realist.

The epigrammatist faces two temptations and usually succumbs to both: being witty rather than being fair and being witty by being cruel. Logan Pearsall Smith, a lifelong epigrammatist, asked, "And what pursuit is more elegant than that of collecting the ignominies of our nature and transfixing them for show, each on the bright pin of a polished phrase?" But Voltaire, who also had some acquaintance with satiric literature, concluded, "A witty saying proves nothing."

Cliché Twisting. Cliché twisting is a form of parody; the writer tricks the reader into expecting a familiar pattern, then suddenly introduces an incongruity which distorts the pattern. Charles Addams' cartoons provide illustrations:

In a circus tent, Mother says testily, "Wait a minute. . . . I've only got three hands."

One cannibal woman says to another: "Do you smell someone burning?"

Another cannibal mother, holding her boy by the hand, says, "I'm worried about him, doctor. He won't eat anybody."

One bear asks another, as they come out of a cave, "What in the world was the matter? You tossed and turned all winter."

After General MacArthur's farewell speech to the Congress, a number of variations appeared, among them "Old blondes never fade, they just dye away," and "Old soldiers never die, but young ones do."

IRVIN S. COBB (when he heard his mean boss was ill):
My God, I hope it's nothing trivial.
GEORGE ADE: Early to bed, early to rise, and you will
meet very few prominent people.
DISRAELI: Every woman should marry—but no man.
MENCKEN: Temptation is an irresistible force at work
on a movable body.
TWAIN: Familiarity breeds contempt—and children.

Be good—and you'll be lonesome.
WILDE: He hasn't a single redeeming vice.

A man cannot be too careful in the choice of his
enemies.

One of those characteristic British faces that, once
seen, are never remembered.

I am dying beyond my means.

Give me the luxuries, and anyone can have the
necessities.
TALLULAH BANKHEAD (after seeing a play by Maeter-
linck): There is less in this than meets the eye.
JOSEPH HELLER: Some of my best friends are enlisted
men.

Orwell uses political slogans for satiric effect
in *Animal Farm* and *1984,* changing the Ten Commandments and Marxist clichés to make his point.
And Thurber sometimes ends his fables with the
same device:

You can fool too many of the people too much
of the time.

He who hesitates is sometimes saved.

Samuel Beckett makes an admirable effort to
sum up his philosophy in *The Unnamable:* "Here,
at least it seems to me, is food for delirium."

Satiric Definition.

BIERCE:

> Conservative: A Statesman who is enamored of existing evils, as distinguished from the Liberal, who wishes to replace them with others.

> Admiration: Our polite recognition of another's resemblance to ourself.

> Painting: The art of protecting flat surfaces from the weather and exposing them to the critic.

> Revolution: In politics, an abrupt change in the form of misgovernment.

> Hers: His.

> Fiddle: An instrument to tickle human ears by friction of a horse's tail on the entrails of a cat.

MENCKEN:

> Adultery: Democracy applied to love.

> Self-respect: The secure feeling that no one, as yet, is suspicious.

> Historian: An unsuccessful novelist.

LASKI: A liberal is a man with both feet planted squarely in midair.

PERSIAN DEFINITIONS:

> Angel: A hidden tell-tale.

> Lawyer: One ready to tell any lie.

> Faithful Friend: Money.

> Learned Man: One who does not know how to earn his livelihood.

RICHARD ARMOUR: Two-party system: political system composed of two parties, the Ins and the Outs.

ARTEMUS WARD: An optimist is anybody who doesn't give a darn what happens, as long as it happens to somebody else.

WILDE: Conscience and cowardice are really the same thing.

PROVERB: Rich relations are close relations; poor relations are distant relations.

Don Marquis: A pessimist is a person who has had to listen to too many optimists.

An optimist is a guy who has never had much experience.

Aldous Huxley: Chastity: the most unnatural of all the sexual perversions.

Nationalism: the theory that the state you happen to be subject to is the only true god, and that all other states are false gods.

Teaching is the last refuge of feeble minds with classical education.

Shaw: Martyrdom . . . is the only way in which a man can become famous without working.

Cynical Wit.

Anonymous: Those who can, do; those who can't, teach; those who can't teach, teach others how to teach.

Twain: Man is the only animal that blushes. Or needs to. If you pick up a starving dog and make him prosperous, he will not bite you. That is the principal difference between a dog and a man.

Wilde: The only thing to do with good advice is pass it on.

Fashion is what one wears oneself; what is unfashionable is what other people wear.

Hubbard: In order to live off a garden, you practically have to live in it.

La Rochefoucauld: If we never flattered ourselves we should have but scant pleasure.

Usually we praise only to be praised.

The refusal of praise is only the wish to be praised twice.

Shakespeare: Every one can master a grief but he that has it.

It is a wise father that knows his own child.

Men have died from time to time, and worms
have eaten them, but not for love.

Policy sits above conscience.

A man may fish with the worm that hath eat of a
king, and eat of the fish that hath fed of that
worm.

One form of cynical wit balances two elements, neatly set up to stress the incongruity.
William Bolitho writes, "No Englishman dreams
of being King; his history denies the possibility;
his poetry denies the desirability." A Jewish proverb says, "The hat's all right, but the head's too
small." Another proverb says, "Rich people swell
up with pride. Poor people swell up with hunger."
Somerset Maugham wrote, "People ask you for
criticism, but they only want praise." And Hes-
keth Pearson, speaking of traditional choices of
careers among "upper" families in England, re-
fers to "the profession of body-killer being the
most respectable alternative to that of soul-saver."

Paradox. The American College Dictionary de-
fines paradox as "a statement or proposition
seemingly self-contradictory or absurd, and yet
explicable as expressing the truth." A. R. Thompson's comment is also helpful: "An irony says the
expected and means its opposite, whereas a paradox says and means the opposite of the expected."
    In a meticulous analysis of the structure of
paradox, Harold Pagliaro concludes that most

paradoxes can be divided into two parts, related to each other by one of the following means: antithesis, analysis, synthesis, equation, or comparison. He explains why these devices affect the reader more intensely than does mere repetition: "The force of repetition is mechanical; the force of the other devices of polarity is electric; through the use of paradox, they close the circuit between poles and transform the two into a unique one." There is an emotional effect in paradox, Pagliaro suggests, due to the fact that opposites are interdependent; the paradoxist mischievously selects contradictory views about matters that the reader had long assumed were settled, and the shock comes from "the almost simultaneous destruction and reconstruction of received opinion."[5]

WILDE: If one tells the truth, one is sure, sooner or later, to be found out.

Being natural is simply a pose.

Each man kills the thing he loves.

When the gods wish to punish us they answer our prayers.

A cynic knows the price of everything and the value of nothing.

Whenever people agree with me I always feel I must be wrong.

Women, as some witty Frenchman once put it, inspire us with the desire to do masterpieces, and always prevent us from carrying them out.

CHESTERFIELD: At court people embrace without acquaintance, serve one another without friendship, and injure one another without hatred.

Incongruity

A man who tells nothing, or who tells all, will equally have nothing told him.

SWIFT: Ambition often puts men upon doing the meanest offices: so climbing is performed in the same posture with creeping.

Vision is the Art of seeing Things invisible.

Every Man desires to live long: but no Man would be old.

Some People take more care to hide their Wisdom than their Folly.

HALIFAX: Just enough of a good thing is always too little.

MENCKEN: Women, one may say, have to subscribe to absurdities in order to account for themselves at all.

PROVERB: No choice is also a choice.

ROBESPIERRE: I am the slave of liberty.

SHENSTONE: I know not whether encreasing years do not cause one to esteem fewer people and to bear with more.

SHAKESPEARE: Some rise by sin, and some by virtue fall.

THOREAU: Men say that a stitch in time saves nine, and so they take a thousand stitches today to save nine tomorrow.

STENDAHL: God's only excuse is that he does not exist.

MONTAIGNE: There are some defeats more triumphant than victories.

Nothing is so firmly believed as that which we least know.

Man is certainly stark mad. He cannot make a flea, and yet he makes gods by the dozen.

DON MARQUIS:
Prohibition makes you
want to cry
into your beer
and denies you the beer
to cry into

CHESTERTON: A man is angry at a libel because it is false, but at a satire because it is true.

We are never free until some institution frees us, and liberty cannot exist till it is declared by authority.

You can never have a revolution in order to establish a democracy. You must have a democracy in order to have a revolution.

CONFUCIUS: If everyone dislikes it, it must be looked into; if everyone likes it, it must be looked into.

LA ROCHEFOUCAULD: Passion often renders the most clever man a fool, and sometimes even renders the most foolish man clever.

We are often obstinate through weakness and daring through timidity.

The evil that we do does not attract to us so much persecution and hatred as our good qualities.

To establish ourselves in the world we do everything to appear as if we were established.

KIERKEGAARD: What one especially praises in Christ is precisely what one would be most embittered by if one were contemporary with it.

Because writers like Wilde, Shaw, and Chesterton sometimes abuse the paradox, there is a tendency to undervalue it. But in spite of Josephine Tey's charge that the paradox is a "cheap and convenient method" and "the easiest way to sound witty," there is a good deal more to an effective paradox than that. To synthesize neatly the contradictions—or apparent contradictions—of life is not easy, and the number of brilliant paradoxes is limited.

CHAPTER SEVEN

The Technique of Surprise

IMMANUEL KANT defined laughter as "the affection arising from the sudden transformation of a strained expectation into nothing." One has been prepared to think along a certain channel and is trustfully proceeding on that path when he is abruptly switched to a totally unexpected direction. He undergoes a complete transformation of mental set, from seriousness to triviality, and this collapse of an emotional attitude explains how an intellectual process can create an emotional effect. For example, Dorothy Parker says of an author: "He is a writer for the ages—the ages four to eight."

One flaw in Kant's theory is the fact that humor is *not* always the transformation of a strained expectation into nothing. The humor of exaggeration operates by giving the reader more than he expects, not less. The clown who pulls a hundred bananas out of his pockets, the closet which cascades dozens of objects, and the ship cabin full of Marx brothers and plumbers and servants and visitors provide a transformation into more than is ordinarily expected.

Herbert Spencer explained this effect in

terms of physiology: The humorous situation or anecdote creates an expectation—the body tenses, blood comes to the skin, etc.—and the emotion has to be released somewhere. Since the joke culminates in a climax for which tears or screams would be inappropriate, laughter provides the only readily available means of release.

Unexpected Honesty

BECAUSE civilized society requires a great deal of pretense—one is not supposed to make unkind remarks, or use profanity, or discuss sex in public, or divulge his selfish motives—an honest statement can under certain conditions be amusing. It is not truth that is humorous; it is only truth at a socially inappropriate, or inconvenient, or embarrassing moment that is humorous. It is still distortion of the familiar that causes the humor, but in this case the *untruthful* remark is the expected one, so that the truth suddenly strikes us as a surprise. We realize immediately that the surprise is pleasant because we enjoy the violation of an artificial restriction.

Much of the "humor" of children's remarks consists simply of naive honesty at inopportune moments, such as the comments of Dennis the Menace or the Peanuts ménage. The clown, fool, and court jester use this stratagem, being permitted (as "abnormal" members of society) to express inconvenient truths. The device is used often by the personae (see Chapter Ten) whom the satirist employs to express his criticism of society.

Freud identifies one species of comic form as the *naive*. It appears when someone "puts himself completely outside of inhibition, because it does not exist for him"; it is necessary for the audience to be convinced that the person genuinely lacks this inhibition, otherwise we should regard it as impudence rather than naiveté and be indignant rather than amused. The mechanics of laughter at this naiveté, says Freud, are easy to understand: "An expenditure of that inhibition energy which is commonly already formed in us suddenly becomes inapplicable when we hear the naive, and is discharged through laughter." The naive one supposedly has no intention of making us laugh; he is certain (or pretends to be certain) that his remarks and actions are quite proper. But the audience has inhibitions and knows it has them.

As with incongruity, though, one more condition is required for the unexpected to be funny. The reader or spectator must be at ease and feel that the subject is not dangerous to him or particularly relevant to his own status. (The beatnik often expresses unpleasant truths but he is usually not amusing because he is too shrill, too intense, and too successful in communicating to his audience a sense of personal involvement.)

The frank admission of cowardice or greed is often entertaining, whether in the form of wit or genuine naiveté. When Bernard Shaw, campaigning for social reform, was asked what he would do if violence arose, he replied, "If the revolution came, I'd hide under the bed." Mrs. Alice Roosevelt Longworth, having seen Calvin Coolidge at a series of dinners where he had eaten without entering the conversation, said, "You go to so many dinners. You must get terribly bored." "Well," said Coolidge, "a man must eat."

Heine admitted that he understood perfectly his motive in criticizing Goethe: "It was envy." Diogenes the Cynic, asked what wine he liked best, replied, "Another's." And Cicero gives this example of Roman humor:

FIRST MAN: "What do you think of a man who is caught in adultery?"
SECOND MAN: "He is too slow."

On a recent quiz program the master of ceremonies asked the woman who had just won $600, "What's the first thing you're going to do with that money?" "Count it," she said.

Finally, W. C. Fields once said, "When I was young I was the biggest thief at large. Then, when I . . . had plenty of dough, my character changed. From then on there was nothing I hated worse than a thief."

But most of the satiric effect of unexpected truth comes not from confessions of shortcomings but from refreshingly unanticipated statements. John Kendrick Bangs, having run for mayor and been defeated, was asked by a *New York Times* reporter, "To what do you attribute your defeat?" "Too few votes," said Bangs.

When Gandhi visited King George on a ceremonial occasion, reporters asked the Indian whether he was embarrassed by wearing a loincloth. "No," said Gandhi, "the King has enough clothes on for both of us." In Shaw's *Devil's Disciple,* Major Swindon asks indignantly, "What will History say?" General Burgoyne replies, "History will tell lies as usual." John Erskine, in his satiric novels about such people as Galahad and Helen of Troy, is particularly skillful in making mythical characters discuss their motivations with complete candor. And much of the humor of Kingsley Amis' books comes from unexpected frankness, such as Lucky Jim's honest hatred of professors, the academic bureaucracy, and hypocritical maneuvering for social advantage. A Bill Mauldin cartoon shows President De Gaulle saying, "Why do you Americans stay where you aren't wanted?" Behind him is a French cemetery filled with American graves.

Joseph Heller uses the unexpected-truth device frequently in *Catch-22.* Of the protagonist he says, "Yossarian had decided to live forever or die in the attempt, and his only mission each time he went up was to come down alive." Doctor Daneeka responds to a patriotic appeal: "I don't want to make sacrifices. I want to make dough." And the following exchange takes place between Yossarian and his superior officers:

YOSSARIAN: I don't want to fly any more combat missions.
MAJOR: Why not?

YOSSARIAN: I'm afraid.
MAJOR: That's nothing to be ashamed of. We're all afraid.
YOSSARIAN: I'm not ashamed. I'm just afraid.

Lewis Carroll is another writer who found unexpected truth a convenient mechanism. "Oh, I'm not particular as to size," Alice hastily replied; "only one doesn't like changing so often, you know." "I don't know," said the caterpillar. Before that, Alice had said, "I think you ought to tell me who *you* are first." "Why?" asked the caterpillar.

Many readers have found a painfully accurate description of their own predicament in the Red Queen's remark, "Now here, you see, it takes all the running you can do, to keep in the same place."

With characteristic cheerfulness Samuel Beckett says in *Murphy*, "The sun shone, having no alternative, on the nothing new." The General's mood in *The Pirates of Penzance* is more playful:

For my military knowledge, though I'm plucky and adventury,
Has only been brought down to the beginning of the century.

A great many epigrams, we have seen, are built on the succinct admission of inconvenient facts. Upton Sinclair observed, "It is difficult to get a man to understand something when his salary depends on his not understanding it." And Byron asked, reasonably enough:

Think you, if Laura had been Petrarch's wife,
He would have written sonnets all his life?

Not all of Wilde's epigrams were mere plays
on words. "Duty," he said, "is what one expects
from others." And, "Experience is the name

." Shaw's characters
iths, as Undershaft,
nd Alfred Doolittle
the statements of
t *The Misanthrope*
ter play.

e *and Fall*, Penny-
ich the boys at the
uldn't try to *teach*
quiet."

the poetry contest
age read aloud and
In an aside to the
he least idea what
, Socrates says, "Is
es replies, "If I'm
, But if I owe, for-

Who Married a
yer friend Fumée:
en't you deceiving
lawyer in court?"
ollowing dialogue
ering being made

DOCTOR: You are a judge. What disadvantage is there in a judge's being deaf?

FUMÉE: None at all. Believe me, I am a practicing lawyer. There is none at all.

DOCTOR: What harm could come to justice thereby?

FUMÉE: No harm at all. Quite the contrary. Master Botal could then hear neither lawyers nor prosecution, and so would run no risk of being deceived by a lot of lies.

A character in Pirandello's *The Pleasure of Honesty* observes, "It's much easier to be a hero than a gentleman. Anyone can be heroic from time to time, but a gentleman is something you have to be all the time. Which isn't easy."

 Unexpected Logic

BECAUSE SOCIETY has accustomed us to think in certain conventional patterns, we are startled by tricky deviations from those patterns. A child is delighted when he is first told why the chicken crossed the street, or what the bear saw when he went over the mountain. In more ingenious ways unexpected logic was the basic comic method of Gracie Allen. Mahomet was not trying to be humorous when he adapted himself to the mountain's immobility, but the remark seems amusing to us.

Oscar Wilde uses the device so often that it becomes a mannerism, but it is effective nevertheless, as in his remark, "In this world there are only two tragedies: one is not getting what one

wants, and the other is getting it." There is unexpected logic in the reply of an old Indian in
Minnesota who forecast a long cold winter. "How
do you know?" a reporter asked. "I saw white men
putting up many snow-fences," he explained. And
Mencken observed: "All the great villainies of history, from the murder of Abel to the treaty of
Versailles, have been perpetrated by sober men."

There is an anecdote about a wealthy man
who gave very little to charity. The solicitor, trying to shame him, said, "Even your son has given
more money than you have." The father replied,
"How can you compare me to my son? He has a
rich father. I have none."

The English tell about the lunatic, looking
over the wall of the asylum, who says to a fisherman:

"Been there long?"
"All day," says the fisherman.
"Caught anything?"
"No."
"Come inside."

Swift liked to use unexpected logic. In *A
Modest Proposal,* suggesting that unemployment
and famine can be alleviated by eating children,
he says, "I grant this food will be somewhat dear,
and therefore very proper for landlords, who, as
they have already devoured most of the parents,
seem to have the best title to the children."

In Kafka's *Castle* the rank of officials is determined by the work each does not do; the people

scurrying about are servants, while those moving slowly are high-ranking dignitaries. A character in *The Picture of Dorian Gray* says, "I like Wagner's music better than anybody's. It is so loud that one can talk the whole time without other people hearing what one says." Shaw says, "When a man wants to murder a tiger he calls it sport; when a tiger wants to murder him he calls it ferocity." The powerful Ferrovius, in *Androcles and the Lion,* urged to control his anger and refrain from hurting the gladiators, says, "It does not hurt a man to kill him."

Illogic is a conspicuous element of Lewis Carroll's humor. The Dormouse is telling about three little sisters who lived at the bottom of a well.

"What did they live on?" said Alice.
"They lived on treacle," said the Dormouse, after thinking a minute or two.
"They couldn't have done that, you know," Alice gently remarked. "They'd have been ill."
"So they were," said the Dormouse; "very ill."

Wilson Mizner reached a conclusion which many scholars, including authors of books on satire, share: "If you steal from one author, it's plagiarism. If you steal from many, it's research." Tom Lehrer expresses a similar attitude in "Lobachevsky." Elbert Hubbard offered a rare reason for optimism: "Don't lose faith in humanity: think of all the people in the United States who have never played you a single nasty trick." In Capek's *The Power and Glory,* when Dr. Galen is asked, "Would you let the whole world die of the White Scourge?" he replies, "Why not, if those in power would let the human race be exterminated by war?" And in Huxley's *Ape and Essence* the people worship the Devil instead of God because the devastation of World War Three proves his superiority to God.

The following dialogue takes place during the poetry contest in Hades between Aeschylus and Euripides in *The Frogs:*

AESCHYLUS: We fight not here on equal terms.
DIONYSUS: Why not?
AESCHYLUS: My poetry survived me; his died with him. He's got it here, all handy to recite.

Don Marquis on occasion resorts to logic which is unconventional. "Man must have laws," he says, "for the progress of humanity consists of the violation of laws." And the narrator in "Reveries of a Bigamist" defends himself in these terms:

The man who marries just once proves only his ignorance of women. The man who marries many times proves, in spite of his disillusionments, his faith in women.

In *The Physician in Spite of Himself* Molière twists logic a bit.

SGANORELLE: That's enough. . . . You were lucky to find me.
MARTINE: What do you mean, lucky to find you? A man who is bringing me to the poorhouse, a drunkard, a good-for-nothing, who eats up everything I've got—

SGANORELLE: That's a lie. I drink part of it.
MARTINE:—who is selling off, bit by bit, everything in the house—
SGANORELLE: We mustn't let our possessions possess us.
MARTINE:—who has even got rid of my own bed—
SGANORELLE: You won't sleep so late.
MARTINE:—who won't leave a single stick of furniture in the house—
SGANORELLE: That makes moving easier.

An incident in *Decline and Fall* illustrates how Evelyn Waugh's characters use logic to suit their ends. When Clutterbuck is awarded the track prize, Lady Circumference protests:

> "But he only ran five laps."
> "Then clearly he has won the five-furlong race, a very exciting length."
> "But the other boys," said Lady Circumference, almost beside herself with rage, "have run six lengths."
> "Then they," said the Doctor imperturbably, "are first, second, third, fourth, and fifth respectively in the Three Miles."

A similar kind of reasoning leads Mark Twain, in "The Negro Mate," to make the captain agree that the murderer should have a trial—after the captain has executed him. In *The Pirates of Penzance* Frederick decides that since he was born on February 29, he is not really twenty-one years old, but five, and goes back to the pirates. And *Alice in Wonderland* concludes, after the boy baby has turned into a pig: "If it had grown up it would have made a dreadfully ugly child: but it makes a rather handsome pig, I think."

Tristan Bernard used his facile wit not only in

his plays but in life, as Cornelia Otis Skinner's anecdotes in *Elegant Wits* show. When he was bumped by a workman carrying an enormous grandfather clock on his shoulders, Bernard said good-naturedly, "Why don't you wear a wristwatch like everybody else?" After applying for admission to the French Academy, Bernard immediately sent a note withdrawing his application, explaining, "The costume costs too much. I'll wait until someone dies who is my size." When he was an old man, Bernard became quite deaf but refused to get a hearing aid: "What's the use? One hears the same things."

In *Catch-22* Heller uses unexpected logic for bitterly effective satiric purposes. Yossarian decides that "the enemy is anybody who's going to get you killed, no matter which side he's on." A soldier complaining to a nurse is told, "It's not your leg. It belongs to the U.S. government." Dunbar increases his life span by cultivating boredom on the theory that when one is bored, time passes more slowly. And Heller satirizes one kind of proof in the following passage:

Doc: What makes you so sure Major Major is a Communist?
Black: You never heard him deny it until we began accusing him, did you? And you don't see him signing any of our loyalty oaths.
Doc: You aren't letting him sign any.
Black: Of course not. That would defeat the whole purpose of our crusade.

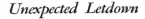

Unexpected Letdown

THE ANTICLIMAX illustrates Kant's theory of "frustrated expectation": a buildup, interest, tension—then such small result that excess energy has to be disposed of somewhere, and goes into a laugh or a smile.

Bernard Shaw's remark is an example: "In moments of crisis . . . I size up the situation in a flash, set my teeth, contract my muscles, take a firm grip on myself and, without a tremor, always do the wrong thing."

Whistler, as a teacher of art, was interviewing students.

WHISTLER: Where have you studied?
FIRST STUDENT: With Chase.
WHISTLER: Couldn't have done better. And you?
SECOND STUDENT: With Bonnet.
WHISTLER: Couldn't have done better. And you?
THIRD STUDENT: I have never studied anywhere.
WHISTLER: Couldn't have done better.

In one of his early comedies, *The Bank*, Charlie Chaplin makes an officious entrance, pompously goes into the vault, then comes out carrying his mop, pail, and janitor's clothes.

George Gobel opened a television program with: "Good evening, ladies and gentlemen and many, many others. I'd like to wish you all a safe and sane holiday tomorrow night when the nation turns out to celebrate the 494th birthday of Vasco da Gama."

A familiar example is this one:

The family gathered around the dying store-keeper.

"Is Mother here?" he asked.

"Yes, John," she said.

"Is my son Charles here?"

"Yes, Dad, I'm here."

"My daughter Mary?"

"Here I am, Dad. We're all here."

"All of you here," cried the dying man, sitting up in the bed. "Then who is watching the store?"

In an essay on Dreiser, Mencken wrote, "Such books as *Jennie Gerhardt* and *The Titan* excel in everything, save workmanship." Tristan Bernard, when the waiter brought the third kind of soup that Bernard had said he couldn't eat, explained, "I'm sure they're all delicious, but I don't have a spoon." The King in Carroll's Wonderland, after the Messenger has shouted in his ear, threatens, "If you do such a thing again I'll have you buttered." In *My Life and Hard Times*, Thurber said he couldn't remember the servants too well "except the one who set the house on fire and I can't remember her name." And Ambrose Bierce was expressing his characteristic optimism when he wrote

My! how my fame rings out in every zone—
A thousand critics shouting—"He's unknown."

✳ *Unexpected Event* (Dramatic Irony)

THE TERM "dramatic" is used here not in reference to the theater but to differentiate ironic events and situations from verbal irony (which is discussed in Chapter Eight). The definition of dramatic irony in *Webster's Second Unabridged Dictionary* is as good as any: "a state of affairs or events which is the reverse of what was expected; a result opposite to and as if in mockery of the appropriate result."

In its most familiar form dramatic irony appears in the irony of life. Our newspaper points out that the young man killed by an auto while crossing the street in his home town had recently completed fifty combat missions as an Air Force pilot. We are told there is an ironic moral in the suicide of a Hollywood star. And we are familiar with certain historical ironies: Clisthenes introduced the punishment of "ostracism," which banished offenders from their native land; shortly afterwards Clisthenes was ostracized. Eutropius persuaded the Emperor to abolish the safety of "sanctuary"; later, having fled to a church to escape punishment, he was returned to the Emperor and executed. The man who invented the guillotine was executed on it. The man who built the Bastille was imprisoned in it. And the bishop who invented the Iron Cage, a torture chamber so small that the victim could neither stand nor lie in it comfortably, was the first man confined in it.

But it is the irony of literature rather than the irony of life that we are concerned with. Although many attempts have been made to classify the categories of nonverbal irony, the classifications always overlap. It is hard to distinguish between tragic and cosmic irony, or between cosmic and dramatic irony, or, sometimes, between dramatic and comic irony. What shocks one person amuses another. And dramatic irony is often harder to recognize than verbal irony; more concentrated effort is required on the part of the reader to rearrange and juxtapose apparently unrelated incidents than to discern a double meaning in a phrase.

Nevertheless, we might look at a few attempts to divide irony into convenient pigeonholes. One scholar lists Socratic, Verbal, Tragic, Romantic, and Practical Irony.[1] ("Romantic" irony is a term used to describe a writer's detached amusement at the behavior of his characters or his own reactions —a form of self-mockery.) David Worcester identifies verbal irony, irony of manner, irony of fact, and cosmic irony. A. R. Thompson recognizes two kinds of nonverbal irony: (1) irony of character, in which the true character of a person is "in painfully comic contrast to his appearance or manner" and (2) irony of events, in which the outcome is "incongruous to the expectation, with painfully comic effect."

In the Victorian novel alone, Frances Russell found four kinds of ironic situations: "Dramatic Irony," where ignorance is not bliss; "Reversed Wheel of Fortune"; "Granted Desire," which turns out tragically; and "Lost Opportunity." Another device, called "Sophoclean Irony," makes a character say something the full significance of which he does not perceive; but the audience perceives it and anticipates his doom. And Gilbert Highet dismisses the whole problem: " 'Dramatic irony' is a particular type of theatrical effect which has no inherent connection with satire."

The list of ironists is endless. In one form or another, almost all comic writers use irony—and almost all tragic writers.

Though irony is traditionally regarded as detached and indifferent, Anatole France does not agree. "The Irony which I invoke is not cruel," he says. "It mocks neither love nor beauty. It is gentle and kindly." At the conclusion of *The Revolt of the Angels* Satan, having dreamt that he had vanquished the Lord but then merely changed places with him in an unchanged world, renounces the revolt. And the "Procurator of Judea" ends with Pontius Pilate saying, "Jesus? Jesus—of Nazareth? I don't remember."

Irony varies in Twain from Tom Sawyer's trick with the whitewashed fence to the Devil's tricks in *The Mysterious Stranger*. Flaubert awards a worn-out old woman a medal for fifty years' labor, in *Madame Bovary*. The boy whom Don Quixote has rescued from a beating gets a bigger thrashing the moment Quixote leaves. In Petronius' *Satyricon* Trimalchio pays a trumpeter to keep reminding him how much of his lifetime has gone. "In his own grece I made him frye," says Chaucer's Wife of Bath.

The poetic justice of *The Egoist* is ironic because the victim falls into a pit of his own digging. In the dramatized version of Eudora Welty's *Ponder Heart*, the simple-minded defendant congratulates both his attorney and the prosecutor when they make what seem to him interesting points. Helen of Troy, in John Erskine's novel, contemptuously deflates her sanctimonious daughter's attempts to justify Helen's behavior.

The most familiar example of tragic irony in Western literature is Oedipus' obstinate search for the killer of his father. It is ironic that he causes his own downfall, and there is no humor or playfulness in the situation. *Oedipus,* the critics insist, belongs under tragedy, not under satire.

But other instances of what is sometimes called cosmic irony are not so clearly identifiable as pure tragedy. The two tramps in Beckett's play are waiting for Godot—who does not come. This could be a tragic concept, but the play is loaded with comic business, witty lines, and satiric devices. Beckett's protagonists, in *Waiting for Godot* and other works, are not tragic characters in the traditional sense but mock heroes in an unconcerned universe. Kafka's people are tried for unspecified transgressions against unidentified regulations in strange courts. Why some people die while others survive Camus' plague remains puzzling to some readers, but the contrast between man's pretensions and the universe's indifference is obvious. And Sartre's fiction and drama emphasize the ironic dilemma of men who pretend there is a God.

Again, the range of subtlety is considerable. Thomas Gray says bluntly:

The paths of glory lead but to the grave.

and

Some mute inglorious Milton, here may rest,
Some Cromwell guiltless of his country's blood.

But in West's *Day of the Locust* the ironies are
less obvious; people's lives are pushed in one direction or another by mere chance; opportunities
are blindly ignored; wishes bring the opposite effects from the ones desired; and men unknowingly
destroy what they want to save.

At still another level of indirection, Pirandello demonstrates that truth can be one thing to one
person and something entirely different to another.
Is the wife Signora Frola's daughter, whom Ponza
remarried under a delusion, or is she another woman whom he married after the death of his first
wife? The wife herself in *Right You Are, If You
Think You Are* refuses to explain: "I am she
whom you believe me to be." And the six characters in search of an author are dropped, a critic
suggests, "in much the same way that God left
man ignorant of his destiny."

In a short story, "E Va Bene," Pirandello describes a baby who had been nearly suffocated during a protracted delivery and made no sound until
the midwife slapped him. Pirandello comments,
"For on entering into this world one must cry."
And Death, in Ionesco's *Killer*, is represented by
a giggling dwarf with a black patch over one eye.

Shelley's poem is popular with young readers
because the irony is obvious, yet seems to be somehow significant:

"My name is Ozymandias, king of kings:
Look on my works, ye Mighty, and despair!"

Nothing beside remains. Round the decay
Of that colossal wreck, boundless and bare
The lone and level sands stretch far away.

In the Bible it is ironic that Haman is hanged
on the same gallows he ordered built to hang
Mordecai. Having installed a secret "doomsday
machine," triggered to go off automatically when
their country is attacked, the rulers of Russia are
unable to prevent the catastrophe, even when
they want to, at the end of *Dr. Strangelove.* And
in *Hamlet* poisoned swords are accidentally exchanged; Rosencranz delivers a letter ordering his
own death; and the wrong person drinks the
poisoned cup.

The irony of fate affects the lives of Hardy's
characters; when a letter slips under a rug instead
of a door, and remains unseen, the lives of both
Tess and Angel are tragically affected. Jude the
Obscure makes the wrong choice, or has it made
for him, at every crossroad of his life. And in
the "Satires of Circumstance" Hardy presents a
series of tableaux: In one a dog admits to his
dead mistress that he was digging on her grave not
out of loyalty but simply to bury a bone; he had
forgotten she was buried there. At tea a young
wife happily entertains a female guest, not knowing that the visitor was her husband's first, and
present, choice. And a tubercular husband unexpectedly walks into a draper's shop, to find his
wife ordering material "soon required for a widow,
of latest fashion."

Maupassant's most famous story is about two
people who slave for fifteen years to replace a

necklace—which proves to have been worthless.
Another Maupassant character picks up a piece of
string on a day when a purse has been lost—and
cannot convince anyone that he is innocent of
theft. The death of the brilliant young Bazarov,
in Turgenev's *Fathers and Sons*, seems shockingly
purposeless. Several soldiers in Ambrose Bierce's
Civil War stories find that they have shot at
friends and relatives. Hemingway's Macomber is
killed a day after he has found his courage; after
escaping from the war to Switzerland, Catherine
Barkley dies in childbirth. And Oscar Wilde's
Dorian Gray, in spite of his crimes and vices, remains young and angelic; his portrait ages and
deteriorates.

Housman's people remain strangers and afraid
in a world they never made. Camus' Mersault is
executed not because of his crime but because
society resents his rejection of its hypocrisy. In
Sartre's "Wall" the condemned man pretends to
confess that his loyalist friend is hiding in the
cemetery; by pure chance the friend quarrels with
his host and leaves home to hide in the cemetery;
after he has been shot there, the prisoner is freed.

The dwarf Oskar, in Günter Grass's *Tin
Drum*, not sure which of two men is his real father,
is largely responsible for the deaths of both. To
intensify the irony, both die because they happened
to be in the wrong place at the wrong time. And the
columnist in West's *Miss Lonelyhearts* originally
took the job out of cynical hope for professional
advancement. But the pathetic letters he receives

so affect him that he decides he is Christ and becomes obsessively involved in the lives of his correspondents. At the end, trying to perform a miracle, he rushes towards the cripple whose wife he had seduced and is accidentally shot to death.

Mark Twain was kind enough, in *The Mysterious Stranger*, to offer men two paths to happiness—insanity or death. But other satirists have extended man's troubles even beyond death. Sartre's *No Exit* presents a group of recently deceased characters who learn to their horror that hell consists simply of existing for eternity as the same contemptible creatures they had been while they were alive. Lagerkvist develops a similar theme in "The Lift That Went Down Into Hell." And Huxley, having shown in *After Many a Summer Dies the Swan* that the prolongation of human life results merely in bestiality, makes a character in *Time Must Have a Stop* discover after dying that existence in the next world is just as boring as it had been on earth.

Waugh crowds a series of ironies into *Handful of Dust*. Early in the book a man enviously calls Tony Last one of the happiest men he knows: Tony has money, a beloved son, a devoted wife, an attractive home. But by the time the book ends, the money has proved inadequate, the son is killed, the wife has betrayed him, and Tony loses his chance to escape from his jungle prison because he had been given a sleeping potion at the time explorers came to look for him.

All sorts of ironies take place in Kafka's

Castle, including the fact that K is not expected and everything turns out to be different from what he had imagined. He had been hired as a land surveyor but ends up working as a janitor, although there had never been any need for either a janitor or a surveyor. K thinks that Barabbas is very important and eagerly awaits his arrival, but Barabbas turns out to be only an assistant to the village cobbler. And the letter that Barabbas brings proves to have been intended for an earlier surveyor, long gone. On their wedding night, K and Frieda awake to find that two assistants had been sitting in the room all night staring at them.

Several incidents in *Moby-Dick* may be called cosmic irony. After finally locating Moby-Dick, the "Pequod" passes him in the night so that the whale ends up chasing the ship. Ishmael, the most inexperienced whaler, is the only one saved. A coffin becomes Ishmael's life preserver. Ahab causes his own destruction by concentrating on the destruction of Moby-Dick. The captain of the "Rachel," who is searching for his drowned son, rescues the orphan Ishmael. The prophecy of an insane man, Elijah, comes true. Queequeg, convinced that his god wants Ishmael to choose their ship, insists that Ishmael do so and the "Pequod" takes Queequeg to his death. Queequeg recovers from a critical illness in time to drown when the "Pequod" goes down.

Fedallah's prophecy, of the manner of Ahab's death and his own, seems as unlikely to come true as the witches' warning to Macbeth, but in quite realistic terms it is fulfilled. Ahab finally locates Moby-Dick by ignoring the compass and following his intuition. Starbuck, the moral antagonist who is momentarily put in charge of Ahab's life by holding the supporting rope, finds that his morality keeps him from destroying Ahab. Queequeg terrifies a man who has teased him, then leaps into the sea to rescue him. The Pequods are an extinct tribe of Indians—and the ship "Pequod" is traveling to extinction. The color white conventionally represents goodness—but the white whale is a symbol for evil. Another captain who has lost a limb to Moby-Dick has learned his lesson—he avoids the white whale and remains alive.

Stephen Crane was intrigued by cosmic irony. In "The Open Boat" the lighthouse, symbol of help, is deserted; the oiler, strongest and hardest working man in the boat, is the only one who drowns; the man on shore waves at the boat but cannot communicate with it; the men on the beach are unable to help the boat land; the closer to shore, the stronger the waves.

The Red Badge of Courage too is full of ironies. Henry Fleming's wound is inflicted by a soldier in his own army, not by the enemy, when Henry is fleeing, not charging, but it is interpreted as a sign of heroism instead of cowardice. The loud soldier becomes humble; the coward becomes brave. Trying to escape from the horror of war, Henry stumbles over a corpse in the forest. Having fought bravely, the soldiers overhear their general describe them as incompetent mule drivers. The loud soldier who expects to get killed writes a farewell letter, which proves to be unnecessary. Henry's heroic feats stem from hysteria. And there is the added irony that this war book, written before Crane had ever seen a battle, proved to be his most successful work; later writings, based on actual observation of war, turned out to be less convincing.

Perhaps the most famous example of this kind of irony is the Samara anecdote. A servant in Bagdad rushes home and tells his master, "I just met Death in the market place and she threatened me. Let me borrow your horse and escape to Samara." The master gives him the horse, then goes to the market and says to Death, "Why did you threaten my servant?" Death replies, "I did not threaten him. I made a gesture of surprise when I saw him in Bagdad, for I have an appointment with him tonight in Samara."

In many instances, dramatic irony stems not from a cosmic source (whim or indifference in heaven) but from social causes, the absurdities and contradictions of man-made customs. For example, to test mankind's definition of humanity Vercors wrote a novel in which a man mates with an ape for the sole purpose of forcing society to determine the legal status of the offspring. And in Shirley Jackson's "lottery" a pleasantly bucolic ritual ends in socially approved murder.

In a depression-era short story by Albert

Maltz, a worker loses a finger in a factory accident and is paid insurance money as compensation; later, in need of money, he cuts off another finger at home and ingenuously brings it to the insurance office. Gogol's Chichikov travels around Czarist Russia buying up the names of "dead souls" for tax purposes. "A Charmed Life," in Mary McCarthy's novel, turns out not to be charmed after all. At the end of *Point Counterpoint* the secretary whom Burlap has just discharged (because she knew the truth about his character) goes home to commit suicide, while Burlap spends the evening with his new mistress pretending that they are two little children having a bath together. And Huck Finn is disturbed because his humane and generous acts violate the moral law society has taught him.

The lighter plays of Sartre, such as *The Respectful Prostitute*, are full of subtle social irony. And in Maupassant's "Boule de Suif" a prostitute is persuaded by her respectable companions to sleep with a Prussian so that the companions can escape—and is later shunned by them for her immoral act.

Social irony pervades the lives of Ring Lardner's lower- and middle-class characters, who do not understand their motivation, their social position, or their real relationship to other people, and proceed to disillusioning climaxes. Sometimes the irony is more pointed, as in the long monologue by the barber in "Haircut" who does not realize that a murder was committed in the incident he has

described. And in "A Day With Conrad Green"
a cynical Broadway producer who tries to steal
another man's idea for a story is furious when he
learns that his intended victim had stolen it
himself.

Genêt pushes irony far enough to insist that,
to maintain its images, society needs the outcasts
of the world. In Camus' "Artist at Work" Jonas
is a dedicated, unrecognized artist, until at the age
of thirty-five he becomes famous. After that time
he is forced to talk about art instead of creating
it. Finally, in desperation, he produces his "mas-
terpiece," a blank canvas with the word "solitary"
or "solidary." And a Frenchman in another Camus
short story, having helped an Arab escape, knows
that the Arab's friends will cynically assume that
he betrayed the man, and waits to be murdered
by them.

The ironic situation which is amusing belongs
under satire because, in most such cases, implied
criticism is present. In a large number of instances
the humor derives from references to sex. Viewers
still enjoy Aristophanes' *Lysistrata*, in which the
women of Athens deny their husbands sexual
privileges until they stop the war. In Maupassant's "Madame Tellier's Excursion" the town
brothel is temporarily closed while the prostitutes
travel, in holiday clothes, to attend confirmation
services for the madam's niece. The young widow
mourning by her husband's tomb vows eternal
loyalty to the dead man—and quickly succumbs to
the handsome soldier guarding the body, in Chris-

topher Fry's *A Phoenix Too Frequent.* Günter
Grass's *Tin Drum* begins when a man fleeing the
police hides under the wide skirts of a peasant
woman who is working in a potato field; he uses
the interlude, while the police are questioning her,
to impregnate the woman. The sexual proclivities
of a twelve-year-old girl add interest to *Lolita.*
And Square's dignity is somewhat ruffled when
Tom Jones finds him hiding in Molly Seagram's
bedroom.

But sex is not the only source of comic irony.
Strepsiades, in Aristophanes' *Clouds,* sends his son
to the philosopher's school to learn sophistry, by
use of which Strepsiades hopes to avoid paying his
debts. The son learns sophistry—and uses it to
justify beating up his father. In *Dr. Strangelove,*
an infantry battle rages in front of a "Keep Off the
Grass" sign; nuclear bombs bear such labels as
"Dear John" and "Hi there"; and the loyal officer,
who has finally secured the secret code for recall-
ing the ill-fated bomber, is unable to telephone
Washington because he does not have enough
coins and cannot persuade the telephone operator
that this is an emergency.

The range in subtlety is very wide. By swal-
lowing pills in Wonderland, Alice grows either
too small to accomplish her objective, or too large.
The psychoanalyst in E. B. White's "Second Tree
From the Corner" spends the hour talking to the
patient about his own problems. In Ionesco's
Chairs an old man hires an orator to give his message to the world; the orator turns out to be a

mute, makes a few unintelligible sounds, then writes meaningless scribbles on the blackboard. John Tanner, the sophisticated antifeminist in Shaw's *Man and Superman*, is easily led into marriage by Ann Whitfield.

The husband who pays a doctor to give his mute wife speech lives to regret it, in Anatole France's *Man Who Married a Dumb Wife;* his spouse becomes such a chatterbox that he hires the same doctor to make him deaf. Topaze, in Marcel Pagnol's play, is a despised dolt as long as he remains honest; when he becomes a crooked financier, wealth and women pour in. Thurber's meek little man tricks the bullying efficiency expert who is about to reorganize his department; he visits her home, pretends to be a dope addict, and makes wild threats against the boss. When the woman reports this behavior no one believes her, she has a nervous breakdown, and the mild man is left sitting in the "Catbird Seat." The immoral characters in Norman Douglas' *South Wind* are so much more attractive than the conformists that normal values seem inverted.

There is comic irony in *Pinafore* when Ralph and Captain Corcoran learn that they had been accidentally exchanged in childhood, and in *Iolanthe* when Iolanthe reveals herself as the Lord Chancellor's supposedly dead wife. The Major in Saki's "Bag" is planning to hunt the fox, not knowing that Vladimir has accidentally killed it. In Molière's plays people are likely to hear unpleasant truths about themselves while eavesdropping, as

Orgon does under the table while Tartuffe tries to seduce his wife. The miser Harpagon is unpleasantly surprised to find that the stranger who wants to borrow money at exorbitant rates is his own son. And Scapin persuades his greedy father to hide in a sack, then beats him while pretending to protect him. The clerk in Gogol's play, who is mistaken for the Inspector-General, readily assumes the role, while the townspeople hypocritically adapt their behavior to the misconception under which they labor.

Melville gets a good deal of comic irony into *Moby-Dick*. The Quaker captain, Peleg, sanctimoniously spouting religious maxims, cheats everyone he can. His sister, Charity, gives the crew gifts which they do not want. While cutting up the whales they have captured, the sailors eat whale steaks and burn whale oil in the lamps. The ships they meet have ironic names: smelly "Rosebud," decrepit "Jungfrau," unhappy "Delight." There are ironic parallels between the religious rituals of the pagan Queequeg and the pious Christians. Ahab has replaced with whalebone the leg he lost to a whale. A harpooner slips and falls into the dead whale, almost drowning. The ambergris from a stinking diseased whale is the most precious component of fragrant perfumes. And the protocol of eating order in the officers' mess keeps the third mate continually hungry.

The ironies of war are usually not comic, but satirists have managed to ridicule even mass murder. In Orwell's *1984* the three powerful super-

states which control the earth keep shifting alliances among themselves to wage permanent war, a
condition which might seem absurd to a Martian
visitor but quite accurate to a modern historian.
The American entrepreneur in *Catch-22*, Lt. Milo
Minderbinder, who rents out his planes to the
highest bidder, signs a contract with the Germans
to bomb his own squadron, and does. Later he
arranges with both Germany and the United States
to bomb the bridge at Orvietto; but since both
sides are already at work on that operation, he does
nothing and collects from both. Because Colonel
Cathcart wants to be a general, he keeps raising the
number of missions his men have to fly—but man-
ages to fly only four himself. Dr. Daneeka's wife,
learning that as far as government aid is concerned,
Daneeka is worth much more to her dead than
alive, pretends that he is dead and collects the
money. The military police ignore Aarfy's murder
of an Italian girl but arrest Yossarian for coming
to Rome without the proper pass. Lt. Orr keeps
crashing his plane—actually, he is practicing to
fake a plane crash and desert. The most important
man in the Air Force is Private First Class Winter-
green; as mail clerk, he misdirects important messages. To relieve the boredom of censoring mail,
Yossarian sometimes deletes all modifiers, or all
articles, or signatures. He signs some letters as
Washington Irving, and three Criminal Investiga-
tion Department men, unknown to each other, are
sent to the island to look for a spy named Washington Irving; they spy on each other, and the one

hiding in the hospital catches pneumonia. For his cowardice in not bombing the objective, Yossarian is given a medal and promoted; otherwise, Colonel Cathcart would have to turn in a report unfavorable to his squadron's record. And a private whose name is Major Major so confuses the computing machine that he is promoted, becoming Major Major Major.

Irony appears in various manifestations: the power of Swift, the ingenuity of Huxley, the urbanity of France, the geniality of Fielding, the persistence of Voltaire. While the sun continues to rise in Hemingway's sex-centered novel, impotent Jake keeps accompanying Brett on a series of assignations. Ironic events occur in Hardy's "satires of circumstance" and Edgar Lee Masters' *Spoon River Anthology.* And the ironic spirit is characteristically demonstrated by H. L. Mencken's prank of collecting as many of the vituperative epithets used against him as he could find and publishing the compilation as *Menckeniana—A Schimpflexicon.*

CHAPTER EIGHT

The Technique of Pretense

THE TERM "censor-evasion" is Freud's, and it was he who expressed most forcefully this theory as an explanation of what he called "tendency-wit," a form of humor that most people would call satiric. As Freud saw it, "Wit makes possible the gratification of a craving (lewd or hostile) despite a hindrance which stands in the way." By eluding the hindrance, wit provides pleasure. Inasmuch as civilization, in the form of the social "censor," forbids or disapproves of many primary pleasures, man resents the censor and dislikes renouncing his pleasures. Wit provides the means by which we can evade the censor and at least talk about forbidden subjects.

Freud uses the phrase "tendency-wit" because he believes that the pleasure this kind of wit offers comes from gratifying a tendency. Both external and internal forces oppose the gratification of such "tendencies" as sex, aggression, cynicism, and skepticism, the first two being the most frequent sources. Wit helps remove the inner inhibitions, says Freud, and combats such forces as reason, critical judgment, and suppression.

Freud assumes that from infancy man feels repressed. Somebody is always telling him what to do and what not to do; mother, nursery supervisor, teachers, father, police, sergeants. Evasion of this restriction, this censorship, gives pleasure. It relieves, in this case, the aggressive rather than the sexual drive, and it functions by eluding the censor instead of assaulting him.

All censor-evasion devices are based on pretense—the pretense that the satirist is talking about something other than what he is really talking about, or the pretense that the satirist is naive and does not understand the implications of what he is saying.

In an earlier period, the court jester served this function of expressing forbidden desires. Today the hostile joke attests to the prevalence of resentment against authority and the pleasure of expressing that resentment in an indirect way. Bibler provided a series of cartoons for college newspapers, in which the faculty was consistently ridiculed. The popularity of Bernard Shaw and Mencken came in part from their expressing ideas ordinarily forbidden. Even popular entertainers like Bob Hope and Red Skelton provide pleasure by violating some social restrictions; their rebellion is always insignificant, and the objects of their criticism are usually superficial. But the audience likes it.

Percy Hammond, the music critic, intentionally misspelled the names of people he wanted to annoy. When American soldiers on occupation duty in Germany were ordered to begin wearing neckties, they obeyed—putting on the most gaudy, luminous, and objectionable ties they could obtain. Satirist Henry Morgan followed the radio commercial for a razor with a skit about a man who saved a minute shaving, got to the street earlier than he had to, and was run over by a car. Morgan did not keep his sponsor long.

On his seventieth birthday the French playwright, Henri Bernstein, remarked sadly, "Mirrors aren't what they used to be in my youth." And W. C. Fields, watching one of the flats shake in the middle of his act, turned to the audience and said, "They just don't build houses the way they used to."

When Twain visited Whistler, he ran a finger over one of his paintings. "Be careful," Whistler cried, "it isn't dry." "That's all right," Twain said. "I have gloves on."

Among the devices for avoiding the censor are verbal irony, parody, disguise and deception, the persona-mask, the symbol, and allegory.

Verbal Irony

To the ancient Greeks, irony meant dissimulation in speech, often in the Socratic sense of pretending to seek enlightenment. Verbal irony uses such mechanisms as sham praise (Shaw: "Bulgarians of really good standing wash their hands nearly every day"; Cuppy: "In fairness it must be said that Cesare did not always commit his own murders. He had most of them done by one Micheletto, a natural son of Old Man Micheletto"); implying the opposite of what one is saying (Mencken: "the gifted Professor Dr. Stuart P. Sherman"), or something quite different from what one is saying ("But Brutus is an honorable man"); and varieties of pseudo naiveté, including absurd suggestions made with apparent sincerity *(A Modest Proposal);* praise of harmful things under the pretense that they are good *(The Screwtape Letters),* or of obviously false, hypocritical, or ludicrous motivations for behavior *(Jonathan Wild);* recognition of a person or date for the wrong and irrelevant reason (Cuppy, *Decline and Fall of Practically Everybody);* referring vaguely to important people as nonentities or subordinates (France, *Procurator of Judea);* treating a small point in detail and minimizing the obviously important elements (Thurber); and assuming that the minutiae which interest the writer fascinate everybody (Benchley).

When challenged about the accuracy of a statement he has made, the user of verbal irony may agree to modify it, and does, by changing the least important part of his original statement, or by restating the criticism in even stronger terms. Or, he reduces to absurdity an analogy which his opponent has used by pretending to accept the analogy literally and carrying it through to a ludicrous conclusion. Another favorite device of ironic writers is to state repeatedly that the actions they are describing are those of a far-distant or long-gone people, and that the issues under discussion have long ceased to be timely. Still another form of irony is describing a desirable condition by pretending to describe the actual condition.

Verbal irony varies in subtlety and when it is overobvious we are tempted to call it sarcasm. Sinclair Lewis' irony is direct: "Main Street is the climax of civilization. That this Ford car might stand in front of the Bon Ton Store, Hannibal invaded Rome and Erasmus wrote in Oxford cloisters. What Ole Jensen the grocer says to Ezra Stowbody the banker is the new law for London, Prague, and the unprofitable isles of the sea; whatever Ezra does not sanction, that thing is heresy, worthless for knowing and wicked to consider." The ironist in the following anecdote was more subtle. Invited by two dishonest millionaires to the unveiling of their portraits, he looked at the adjacent pictures and asked, "But where is the Saviour?"

The irony of the prophet Elijah was direct. Watching the priests of Baal invoking their idols, he taunted: "Cry louder! Baal is a god, but perhaps he is talking, or walking, or traveling, or perhaps he is sleeping and must be awakened." William Shirer was more subtle when, in his censored radio broadcasts out of Berlin during the war, he managed by innuendo to convey information to American audiences which the German officials did not detect.

There was irony in the report of an Indian native on the hunting prowess of a visiting Englishman: "Our guest shot beautifully, but heaven was very merciful to the birds." George Gobel announced on a television program: "The National Safety Council predicted there would be 407 accidents due to careless driving over the weekend . . . and so far only 209 have been reported. . . . Now, some of you folks just aren't trying."

Naval trainees in World War Two called the exercise period "Happy Hour." Alva Johnston said, "Nobody seems to have worked out a satisfactory method of training writers to write. Colleges are good on punctuation marks, but not on what to put between them." Wilde remarked that "America was really discovered by a dozen people before Columbus, but it always was successfully hushed up." And H. L. Mencken felt that "The United States, in spite of its gallant resistance, has been swept along in the general direction of human progress."

Perhaps the most sustained piece of verbal irony in English is *Jonathan Wild*. Among Victorian writers, Frances Russell notes that ironic language appears in flashes in Lytton and Disraeli, increases in Trollope, and is most pervasive in Peacock, George Eliot, Thackeray, Meredith, and Butler. Jane Austen is habitually ironic in speech but does not stress the irony of fate, whereas Hardy consistently utilizes the irony of fate but seldom uses ironic language.

When Romeo says that the wound is probably slight, the fatally stabbed Mercutio replies, "No, 'tis not so deep as a well, nor so wide as a church-door; but 'tis enough, 'twill serve." Some of Hamlet's best lines are ironic, within the context of the play. Bernard Shaw's plays are saturated with verbal irony. Mencken, a militant atheist, explained that he finally got married because "The Holy Spirit informed and inspired me." In "My Favorite Murder" Ambrose Bierce wrote, "Altogether, I cannot help thinking that in point of artistic atrocity my murder of Uncle William has seldom been excelled." The title Stephen Crane chose for his poem on the horrors of war is "War Is Kind." Saki described one of his characters in these words: "He believed in company prospectuses, and in purity of elections, and in women marrying for love, and even in a system for winning at roulette."

The irony of Fielding in *Jonathan Wild* is sustained but not really subtle:

Jonathan Wild had every qualification necessary to form a great man. As his most powerful and predominant passion was ambition, so nature had . . . adapted all his faculties to the attaining those glorious ends to which this passion directed him. . . . He was entirely free from those low vices of modesty and good nature. . . . His lust was inferior only to his ambition.

Orwell satirizes totalitarian slogans by coining for *1984* such terms as "War Is Peace," "Big Brother," "facecrime," "Ministry of Love" (for the police), "Ministry of Truth" (for the propaganda office), "Newspeak," and "Doublethink." In "An

Argument Against Abolishing Christianity" Swift offers a number of ridiculous reasons for attending church. And Twain says, in *The Connecticut Yankee:* "I will say this much for the nobility: that tyrannical, murderous, rapacious, and morally rotten as they were, they were deeply and enthusiastically religious." And Lewis names the city of conformity "Zenith."

In *The Genius and the Goddess,* Huxley has a character say: "Pneumonia, the old man's friend. Now they resuscitate you so that you can live to enjoy your arteriosclerosis or your cancer of the prostate." And Pirandello indulges in romantic irony when he makes the manager say in *Six Characters in Search of an Author,* "Is it my fault if France won't send us any more good comedies, and we are reduced to putting on Pirandello's works, where nobody understands anything, and where the author plays the fool with us all?"

Finally, the verbal irony of Anatole France is demonstrated by the following two passages from *Penguin Island.* "For many years Orberosia bestowed her favors upon neatherds and shepherds, whom she thought equal to the gods. But when she was no longer beautiful she consecrated herself to the Lord." "Although children died in marvellous abundance and plagues and famines came with perfect regularity to devastate entire villages, new Penguins, in continually greater numbers, contributed by their private misery to the public prosperity."

THE SPIRIT of parody was succinctly expressed by Elbert Hubbard when, registering at a hotel, he noticed that the last entry read: "Richard Harding Davis and Man." Hubbard wrote: "Elbert Hubbard and Satchel."

The imitation of even an innocuous statement can be amusing, if the imitation is in a different tone of voice, or out of context, or in some other way implies that the statement is being repeated for the purpose of arousing derision or amusement. There is a standard comedy routine in which a man thinks that he is looking into a mirror; it is actually transparent glass, and a "double" on the other side imitates every gesture and facial expression.

Precisely why such imitation is funny has never been fully explained, although many writers have tried to do so. "By an obscure psychological law," says Aldous Huxley, "words and actions in themselves quite serious become funny as soon as they are copied; and the more accurately . . . the funnier."[1] Blaise Pascal agrees: "Two faces that are alike, neither comic in itself, excite laughter when together through their likeness." Bergson thinks that similarity provokes laughter because it suggests the mechanical, automatism, whereas each human being is different and unique. But Bergson's theory does not account for those "mechanical" objects which do not provoke our laughter, such as a military parade or a line of chorus girls or precision swimmers or ballet dancers.

As a rule, only objects which are familiar can be parodied successfully. The parodist should be expert in the medium he is using: pianist Victor Borge parodies Liberace, dancer Imogene Coca burlesques the ballet, musician Beatrice Kay parodies songs. It may be, as E. B. White says, that "good parody should be funny in itself, whether or not one has read the book or author parodied," but very few parodies are genuinely entertaining to an audience unfamiliar with the object being imitated.

To be the subject of parody one must have sufficient individuality of style or content to be distinguished. That individuality may consist of significant originality or mere eccentricity. Parody serves as criticism by emphasizing the affectations and excesses of style, and the superficiality and absurdity of content. And parody provides strong evidence that satire need not have anything to do with morality—unless one accepts the argument that bad writing is immoral.

Low burlesque, as Worcester sees it, is the process of diminishing and degrading the object; it creates a standard below its victim and makes the reader measure him against that standard. High burlesque compares by placing our standard above the victim, thus making his shortcomings stand out sharply. Low burlesque, Worcester explains, compares its subject with what is base and sordid. "High burlesque, on the other hand, depends not on noticing similarities but on noting differences. Contrast rather than comparison is its method." Furthermore, "Conventionally, high burlesque treats a trivial subject in an elevated manner, and low burlesque treats an elevated subject in a trivial manner." R. P. Bond, in his study of English burlesque poetry, makes further distinctions, putting parody and mock-heroic under high burlesque, and travesty and Hudibrastic verse under low. Parody and travesty imitate particular models, Bond suggests, whereas the mock-heroic and Hudibrastic poems mock the manner of a whole class of writing.

But scholars do not agree in defining terms. Edgar Johnson, for example, considers both parody and travesty forms of burlesque: "Both are a kind of literary parody. But parody . . . burlesques the style of its original; travesty retains the original subject-matter and throws the style overboard." And Dwight Macdonald distinguishes among travesty, burlesque, and parody in his excellent anthology, *Parodies.*

Parody includes pseudo biography and pseudo natural history, as Will Cuppy writes it; pseudo history as Sellers and Yeats in *1066 and All That,* Richard Armour in *It All Started With Columbus,* Myers in *Beowulf to Virginia Woolf,* and Donald Ogden Stewart in *Parody Outline of History* have written it; pseudoadvice books, such as Thurber and White's *Is Sex Necessary* and Tressler's *How To Lose Friends and Alienate People.* Rewriting folk tales, fairy tales, and fables in cynically modern terms (Thurber, George Ade) is another device. John Erskine was an expert in this field.

"Give us this day our daily stone," says a

Nathanael West character. The narrator in Camus' *Fall* addresses God in these terms: "Our Father, who art provisionally here. . . ." Hemingway's waiter mutters, "Our nada who art in nada, nada be thy name. . . . Give us this nada our daily nada. . . ." In Samuel Beckett's *Molloy* these lines appear: "Our Father who art no more in heaven than on earth or in hell, I neither want nor desire that thy name be hallowed, thou knowest best what suits thee. . . ." Joyce parodies the Lord's Prayer in *Finnegans Wake* and the Apostles' Creed in *Ulysses*. And in his parody of American funeral services, Evelyn Waugh offers this prayer for dogs at the Happier Hunting Grounds mortuary, paraphasing Job: "Dog that is born of bitch hath but a short time to live, and is full of misery."

The inhabitants of Huxley's *Brave New World* date their calendar After Ford, make the sign of the T instead of the cross, and call their ruler His Fordship Mustapha Mond. They parody fervid religion by participating in sexual orgies. In *Ape and Essence*, the sign of horns replaces the sign of the cross, and in elaborate ceremonies and hymns the survivors of atomic war parody Christian ritual. The beasts in Orwell's *Animal Farm* pretend to obey The Seven Commandments and follow the human example of modifying all of them before the book ends. Robert Burns' Holy Willie makes his prayer a perversion of genuine worship. And Orwell, in *Keep the Aspidistra Flying*, parodies I Corinthians when he writes: "Though I speak with the tongues of men and angels, and have not money, I am become as a sounding brass, or a tinkling cymbal."

But religious parody is not limited to Christianity. Aristophanes makes the women in *Lysistrata* imitate for satiric purposes the sacred procedures of Greek worship: parodying the oath-taking ritual, the women use a wine jug to represent their sacrifice and wine to symbolize blood. And Harrer, a German who lived in pre-Communist Tibet, tells us that during the annual drama week, performances were given in the Dalai Lama's summer palace. One of the acting groups satirized all aspects of Tibetan life, including the religious institutions. They parodied the holy ritual of the Oracle, burlesquing the dance and the mystic trance itself. Men dressed as Buddhist nuns, mimicked their alms-begging techniques, and pretended to flirt with the monks. Apparently the audience, from the highest abbots down, found the performance immensely entertaining.

No aspect of society has been safe from the parodist's mocking attention. Englishman Henry Labouchere parodied the English national anthem, and American Ambrose Bierce parodied the American national anthem. But the great bulk of parody, for obvious reasons, consists of literary satire, imitating either individual writers or literary genres. *Candide* is, in part, a parody of the adventure fiction popular in Voltaire's day, and *True History* is a parody of travel tales enjoyed by Lucian's contemporaries. Nathanael West's *Cool Million* burlesques the Horatio Alger type of story. Fielding ridiculed heroic drama in *Tom Thumb the Great* and Richardson's sentimental novel, *Pamela,* in *Shamela.* The Gothic novel is made to appear absurd in Jane Austen's *Northanger Abbey.* Gilbert and Sullivan created delightful parodies of grand opera, Mark Twain burlesqued graveyard poetry in *Huckleberry Finn,* and Stephen Leacock wrote funny parodies of the ghost story and the detective story. And Murray Schisgall's *Luv* parodies the techniques of the theater of the absurd and the mannered pessimism of existentialist philosophers.

Joseph Heller's *Catch-22* is full of parodies, such as the Glorious Loyalty Oath Crusade organized by Captain Black to get revenge on Major Major Major and the repeated parody of Charles Wilson's remark, "What is good for the country is good for General Motors and what's good for General Motors is good for the country." The profiteering Milo Minderbinder sells the gas, which is supposed to inflate life jackets, and the morphine, which is supposed to be available for wounded men, and leaves in their place notes stating, "What's good for M and M is good for the country."

But most parodies are of individual writers or of particular pieces. After listening to the President once too often, Oliver Jensen wrote "The Gettysburg Address in Eisenhowerese," beginning with this sentence: "I haven't checked these figures but 87 years ago, I think it was, a number of individuals organized a governmental set-up here in this country, I believe it covered certain Eastern areas, with this idea they were following up based on a sort of national independence arrangement and the program that every individual is just as good as every other individual."

When Mencken and George Jean Nathan dominated American criticism with their iconoclastic pronouncements, Don Marquis wrote this parody of Eugene Fields's "Wynken, Blynken, and Nod":

MENCKEN, NATHAN, AND GOD

> When God protested, they rocked the boat
> And dumped him into the sea
> For you have no critical facultee
> Said Mencken and Nathan to God.

Lewis Carroll parodied Isaac Watts's "How does the little bee" with

> How doth the little crocodile
> Improve his shining tail,
> And pour the waters of the Nile
> On every golden scale!
> How cheerfully he seems to grin,
>   How neatly spreads his claws,
> And welcomes little fishes in
>   With gently smiling jaws.

Robert Southey's "The Old Man's Comforts" begins with "You are old, Father William." Carroll's parody proceeds from there:

> "You are old, Father William," the young man said,
> "And your hair has become very white;
> And yet you incessantly stand on your head—
> Do you think, at your age, it is right?"

Carroll also parodied Sir Walter Scott's "Bonnie Dundie," Wordsworth's "Resolution and Independence," Isaac Watts's "The Sluggard," Mary Howitt's "The Spider and the Fly," G. W. Langford's "Speak Gently," and Jane Taylor's "Twinkle, Twinkle, Little Star." Perhaps his best known parody, though, is of James M. Sayles' "Star of the Evening," the chorus of which reads:

> Beau-ti-ful star,—
> Beau-ti-ful star,—
> Star of the eve-ning,
> Beau-ti-ful, beau-ti-ful star. . . .

Carroll's version:

> Beautiful soup, so rich and green,
> Waiting in a hot tureen!
> Who for such dainties would not stoop?
> Soup of the evening, beautiful Soup!
> Soup of the evening, beautiful Soup!
> Beau-ootiful soo-oop!
> Beau-ootiful soo-oop!
> Soo-oop of the e-e-evening,
> Beautiful, beautiful soup!

Of the making of parodies there is no end. In ancient Greece the traveling minstrels who recited Homer's poems were followed by less reverent entertainers who burlesqued the same stories. "The Battle of the Frogs and Mice," probably composed in Greece in the fifth century B.C., parodied the Homeric epic. During the Fools' Carnivals of the Middle Ages, many holy rituals were mocked, particularly in the Drunkards' Mass.

In *The Dunciad* Pope has lines parodying the Aeneid; Aristophanes parodied scenes from Euripides and Aeschylus, and lines from Socrates; Byron burlesqued Southey's "Vision of Judgment" in his own poem with that title. More recently, Hemingway parodied Sherwood Anderson in *The Torrents of Spring,* and E. B. White parodied Hemingway in "Across the Street and Into the Grill." Edith Wharton parodied Henry James in "A Backward Glance," Faulkner parodied Sherwood Anderson in an early work, and Corey Ford parodied a number of modern writers in *The John Riddell Murder Case.* Allen Ginsberg's "Howl" is ridiculed by Louis Simpson's "Squeal." In recent years *The New Yorker* magazine has been the best source of literary parody; and Peter DeVries, Wolcott Gibbs, Clifton Fadiman, and other wits have imitated derisively the styles of such writers as Thomas Wolfe, Faulkner, and other contemporary novelists.

 Disguise and Deception

ONE OF THE FAMILIAR comic devices is disguise in dress, especially when a man dresses as a woman or a servant as a master. A woman dressed as a man is not nearly so funny, and some critics have suggested that it is the tradition of male superiority which makes the Charley's Aunt routine especially satisfying. But in the servant-dressed-as-master device the opposite kind of reversal takes place, so the explanation cannot be that simple. Koestler accounts for the humor of disguise on the grounds that attention is called to the clothing in a "disjunctive" way—out of context, so that the incongruous elements are more apparent.

Bergson's explanation is that disguise, like surprise, dissolves our prepossessions. A person wearing odd clothes is in effect disguising himself. The disguises of individuals are comic, and every social stereotype is comic, because they are all expressions of rigidity, inelasticity. All ceremonies possess comic elements, being in a sense "clothing," and are acceptable only when they are in the appropriate context. When a ceremonial object or gesture loses this familiar relationship with its purpose, the manner becomes incongruous and comic.

Quite a different explanation of the humor of disguise is offered by Dr. J. Y. T. Greig, a psychologist who applies his theory of ambivalence: disguise is a variation of the childish game of peek-a-boo, retaining the ambivalence of mock fright and making disguise a popular device of stage comedy.

Examples are: the impostor *(The Importance of Being Earnest, Gargantua,* Aristophanes' *The Frogs, Charley's Aunt,* Duke and Dauphin in *Huckleberry Finn,* Genêt's *Balcony)*; mistaken identity (Plautus, Cervantes, Shakespeare, Molière, *The Inspector-General)*; and other misrepresentations and mix-ups (Barth's *Sot-Weed Factor,* Jonson's *Alchemist,* Machiavelli's *Mandragola,* and Wycherley's *Country Wife).*

THE MASK or "persona," the pretense of being another person, is a favorite device of the satirist. In a sense, of course, all fiction uses the device. But the satirist is especially successful in making the mask serve his satiric purposes. The mask is particularly useful to the satirist, providing him with greater freedom, an alter ego, and protection from possible attack.

The relationship of the satirist to his persona is not likely to be as close as that of the ventriloquist to his dummy; nor is it likely to have results as drastic as the nervous breakdown of the unfortunate ventriloquist who claimed that his dummy kept saying nasty things to him. But Walter Blair notes that of the twelve American literary comedians he discusses, ten "intermittently or consistently wrote in the guise of comic characters."[2]

Satirists have shown an inclination for the persona device both in their personal lives and in their writing. Thackeray, for example, was preoccupied with masks; in his fascination with comic disguise Lewis resembled Dickens, whom he greatly admired. Lewis often tested monologues at parties and on streets before putting them into books and on occasion masqueraded in public as a traveling salesman, a foreigner, and his own father. Among Swift's personae are Dean, Drapier, Bickerstaff, and Gulliver; also, Author of *A Tale of a Tub,* Member of Irish Parliament, Three Writers on Church and State, Two Advisers on Style, Simon Wagstaff, The Examiner, du Baudrier, and others.

Genêt has found the mask a particularly useful device. In *The Blacks,* for example, the blacks impersonate whites, then impersonate the appearance they present to the whites, then impersonate the image whites present to them, and so on. In *The Balcony* the masses turn to Madame Irma's brothel for new images to replace the images they had overthrown. Consequently, Madame Irma dresses as the queen, and the customers recreate their illusions as judge, general, and bishop, assuming images to satisfy the mob's need for ritual images. The nation, then, is ruled not by authorities but by masks. And in *The Maids* Genêt has the two maids play the roles of mistress and maid, while the mistress herself is continually choosing fantasy roles to play—and all these female parts are played by boys.

Among the methods of presenting the persona, ostensibly the simplest form is that of the satirist speaking in the first person under his own name. But since what he says may not literally be what he believes, this technique may well be, as several critics have observed, the subtlest use of the device. Anatole France writing ironically under the name of Anatole France, Twain pretending to speak as Twain, Voltaire posing as the spokesman for Voltaire have provided examples of this method. An acceptable variation has the satirist speaking under his own name in the third person, as when a character identified as Horace speaks in some of Horace's *Satires,* or Pope puts statements in the mouth of a speaker he calls Pope.

Another method approved by scholars is the

use of a first-person narrator who pretends to be someone other than the satirist himself. Thus the speaker in *A Modest Proposal* poses as a man who is not Swift; the narrator of *We* pretends to be a Russian engineer, not Zamiatin; Addison makes comments through the person of Mr. Bickerstaff.

The technique presumably furthest removed from direct author comment is making the persona a fictional character, as Waugh uses Paul Pennyfeather and Byron uses Childe Harold and Twain uses Satan and Ionesco uses Beranger and Orwell uses Winston Smith. But even this device is no guarantee of objectivity, as Sinclair Lewis implied when he parroted Flaubert's remark: Asked who the model for Carol Kennicott was, Lewis replied, "C'est moi."

Nor is the nature of the persona any more clearly defined than the technique. Maynard Mack, for example, correctly identifies the voices of Pope's personae as: (1) "the voice of the man (ethos) of plain living, high thinking . . . who hates lies, slanders, lampoons," (2) "the voice of the *naif*, the ingenu, the simple heart," (3) "the voice of the public defender . . . the satirist as hero."[3] But these are not the only spokesmen for the satirist. A large gallery of rogues, some much less amiable than others, have expressed the satirist's point of view in Petronius' *Satyricon*, Le Sage's *Gil Blas*, Grimmelshausen's *Simplicissimus*, Jippensha's *Hizakurige*, Morier's *Hajji Baba*, and many other picaresque tales. Still another persona is the cynical commentator, such as Oscar Wilde's

Lord Henry, Norman Douglas' Count Caloveglia, and the Devil in his frequent appearances as satiric spokesman. And the satirist's persona is not always moral, naive, or heroic in the work of Huxley, Nabokov, Schnitzler, Genêt, and Bernard Shaw.

Scholars disagree about the relationship of the satirist to his personae. One extreme position is the assumption that the persona is the author himself speaking. The other extreme is the hypothesis that the persona is definitely not the satirist himself. There are objections to both assumptions. In spite of some scholars' insistence on the detached nature of the persona, the result of the persona's actions and statements is always an attack on what the satirist himself wants attacked and a defense of what the satirist himself wants defended. After all, the personae of Swift and Horace and Juvenal and Voltaire and Thackeray do express, in various ways, the same criticism of society which each of these satirists wants to express. The content of satire is historically identifiable material—specific individuals, institutions, issues—and it is remarkable how often the effect of the persona's behavior supports the satirist's own position.

Similarly, there are weaknesses in the persona-is-the-satirist-himself hypothesis. Often the personality presented in the satire is quite different from the satirist's own temperament. Writers whose honesty, morality, and integrity were suspect have created personae who are models of proper behavior. Nor can we assume that satirists who use rogues as protagonists are necessarily rogues themselves. Furthermore, a single persona never reveals the complete personality of the writer; Lewis, Swift, and Twain use many diverse characters to express disparate aspects of their vision of the world.

The personae of satirists range from the ingenu to the sophisticate, the plain good man to the confirmed cynic. They include the court jester, the *naif* like Candide, the moralist, the amiable humorist, the rogue of the picaresque tale, the outsider like Oskar in *The Tin Drum,* the detached realist like Yossarian in *Catch-22* and Blunschli in *Arms and the Man,* the skeptical realist like Mr. Dooley, the sophisticated cynic in *The Picture of Dorian Gray,* and the Devil in his manifestations as a satiric commentator. But no generalization about the personae of one writer—Swift or Pope or anyone else—or one technique can cover all the variations used by Giradoux, Wilde, Huxley, Waugh, Pirandello, Beckett, Nathanael West, Ionesco, Andreyev, Bernard Shaw—or even Bob Newhart.[4]

 Symbol

LIKE THE POET, the satirist uses symbols frequently, but his reason for using them is not quite the same as that of the poet. The poet uses symbols to represent things; the satirist sometimes uses symbols to misrepresent things. He often makes use of symbols as a means of indirection and distortion.

For example, by pretending that it is animals or puppets he is describing, instead of men, the satirist makes his criticism indirectly; by ascribing to animals human characteristics, he is, presumably, distorting human beings.

Freud observed some similarities between wit and dream—distortion, indirection, the puzzle-element. There is some value in the comparison, although dreams are rarely comic. The symbolic content of satires like *Gulliver's Travels* and *Alice in Wonderland* is similar to the material of dreams.

Symbols that satirists use are remarkably varied. Certain objects, such as clothing, have proved particularly suitable, and Swift's *Tale of a Tub* and Carlyle's *Sartor Resartus* make effective use of them. But practically everything has been utilized by satirists for symbolic representation, or misrepresentation. Man as puppet has already been discussed. The mirror is a popular device for satirists. Don Quixote's windmills and Capek's robots suffered the fate of oversuccessful symbols and have become clichés.

A well-mined source for satiric symbols, *Gulliver's Travels* offers Lilliput as England; the King as George I; High Heels and Low Heels for Tories and Whigs; Big Endians and Little Endians for Catholics and Protestants; Flimnap as Walpole; and red, blue, and green garters as Orders of Garter, Bath, and Thistle. Political dexterity is symbolized by balancing on a tightrope, and the cushion which saves a falling minister from injury turns out to be a mistress who shares the King's favors. Other works of Swift also use symbols to a considerable degree, especially *A Tale of a Tub*. And the Houyhnhnms have been interpreted by some readers to stand for reason in man, the Yahoos for bestial emotions.

Kafka's fiction uses symbols for metaphysical and allegorical purposes and suffers from the fact that most readers are uncertain of what the symbols are intended to represent. Almost every object that appears in Kafka, from the apple thrown at Gregor by his father in "The Metamorphosis" to trials, castles, and cages for artists, has been interpreted as a symbol for something or other by various critics. The study of Kafka can become a lifetime occupation, and whoever indulges in it soon finds a great many images which distort, critically, the familiar world.

Another popular source for symbols, James Joyce, also offers a great many satiric images. The milk-woman in *Ulysses*, bearing the promise of life, may be a symbol for the church; but her breasts are old and shrunken. Leopold Bloom, who represents modern man, is a Chaplinesque little figure in a baggy suit, timid, persecuted, and cuckolded. As eminent critics have shown, everything in *Ulysses* and *Finnegans Wake* is a symbol, and many of the symbols are pejorative.

Günter Grass has loaded *The Tin Drum* with enough satiric symbols to keep a generation of graduate students busy: Freudian symbols; the color white; triangles; a midget; hospitals; womb symbols (hospital bed, hiding under grandmother's

skirt, mother, stepmother Marian, midget Ros-
witha); drums; statues of Christ and Niobe; a
keeper named Bruno; a song about a witch black
as pitch; a magic drum; "The Onion Cellar"; a
dialogue between a moth and a bulb; the scars on
Herbert's back; a rug; a chopped-off ring finger—
there is no end to the deluge, and every symbol is
derisive, sometimes gently melancholic but more
often bitter, brutal, and devastating.

Often the very titles of satiric works identify
the basic image. Thackeray's *Vanity Fair,* Gold-
ing's *Lord of the Flies,* West's *Day of the Locust,*
Capek's *R. U. R.,* Ionesco's *Rhinoceros,* Genêt's
Balcony (of a brothel, which represents the world),
Lagerkvist's "The Lift That Went Down Into
Hell," Sartre's "No Exit," Camus' *Plague* and
Stranger and *Fall,* Beckett's *Endgame,* and Grass's
Cat and Mouse state the sardonic symbol in the
title, and go on from there. Fortunately, not all of
them emulate Ionesco's *Amedée,* which symbolizes
the death of married love by having a corpse grow
fifteen years in the couple's bedroom while toad-
stools sprout in the living room.

 ## *Satiric Allegory*

THE EXACT MEANING of the word "allegory" is hard
to determine, for its connotations are not limited
to a dictionary definition. The original implica-
tion of ethical instruction is still accepted by some
scholars, ignored by others. The Greek word *al-*

legoria meant "description of one thing under the image of another," and *Webster's Second Unabridged Dictionary* gives this definition: "the veiled presentation, especially in a figurative story or narrative, of a meaning metaphorically implied, but not expressly stated. An allegory is a prolonged metaphor in which, typically, a series of actions are symbolic of other actions, while the characters often are types or personifications."

In *Satiric Allegory: Mirror of Man,* Ellen Leyburn brings the definition up to date: "We can, then, call allegory the particular method of saying one thing in terms of another, in which the two levels of meaning are sustained, and in which the two levels correspond in pattern of relationship among details." The definitive qualities of the genre, she thinks, are judgment and indirection.

After citing a number of satirists, from Lucian to Orwell, who have used allegory for satiric ends, Professor Leyburn lists the following characteristics that allegory and satire have in common: indirection; economy, as a result of intensification; detachment; conveyance of the general by the particular. The form is appealing because it engages both the imagination and the intellect; it offers a riddle, and lets us solve it. Among examples of the genre, she lists *Absalom and Achitophel, A Tale of a Tub,* and *Battle of the Books* as "Allegories Controlled by Plot"; *MacFlecknoe* and *Hudibras* as "Allegories of Mock Heroes"; Aesop's *Fables,* Swift's *Beasts' Confessions,* selections from Johnson's *Idler,* Joel C. Harris' *Uncle Remus,*

Chaucer's *Nun's Priest's Tale,* Orwell's *Animal Farm,* Munro Leaf's *Story of Ferdinand, Reynard the Fox,* and Spenser's *Mother Hubberds Tale,* as "Animal Stories"; *Gulliver's Travels* and *Erewhon* as "Satiric Journeys"; and Morris' *News From Nowhere,* Bellamy's *Looking Backward,* Huxley's *Brave New World,* and Orwell's *1984* as "Future Worlds."

Capek's plays *(R. U. R., The Insect Play, The Makropolous Affair, Adam the Creator)* offer a series of allegories about false roads to salvation. Each play proposes a popular formula for the redemption of the world; each new world fails. In *R. U. R.* the mechanized world fails because it has no soul. *The Insect Play* derides the "return to nature" theory; the lower levels of life exhibit the same deficiencies—greed and brutality and hypocrisy—as human beings. In *The Makropoulos Affair* the concept that longevity brings happiness is disproved; those who choose a three-century life are as miserable as Swift's Struldbrugs. And *Adam the Creator* decides that innovation can be dangerous; it is more sensible to make the best of the world we have than to remake it completely.

Swift's *Tale of a Tub* is an allegorical account of Christian history. Martin, Jack, and Peter represent the split in the church—Anglicanism, Dissent, Catholicism. Their clothes are Christian life, and as reforms are made, the garments are changed.

It is possible to read Grass's *Tin Drum* as an allegory and to see Oskar the midget as a symbol for the undeveloped German conscience and his later growth to five feet as a sign of inadequate improvement. The book rejects both Naziism and orthodox religion and expresses the satirist's disgust with the modern world.

Some allegories contain a good deal of incidental satire, although their primary intention is not satiric—*Pilgrim's Progress, The Divine Comedy, Piers the Ploughman*. And contemporary literature is rich in allegorical implications. The short stories of Lagerkvist and his *Dwarf* and *Barabbas* are allegoric. So is Kos's report of Yugoslavia's reaction to *Big Mac, the White Whale*. John Barth's *Giles Goat-Boy* is an allegorical satire of modern education, religion, politics, and practically everything else. Mrozek, the Polish satirist, in his first collection of short stories includes an account of several Communist clerks who read a description of themselves in bureaucratic propaganda as eagles, took the jargon literally, and began to fly. Most of the other stories, including the title narrative, *The Elephant*, are allegorical satires about totalitarian society.

In Genêt's plays we can never believe what we see; there is allegorical comment in *The Maids, The Deathwatch, The Balcony*, and *The Blacks*— and the mocked rituals are mirrors of the world. Kafka's allegories—in *The Trial, The Chinese Wall, The Castle*, "The Doctor," "The Hunger Artist," and most of his other works—have been discussed and debated but not conclusively interpreted. Ionesco's *Killer* and *Rhinoceros*, Beckett's

Waiting for Godot, and Joyce's *Ulysses,* as well as plays of Duerrenmatt, Tennessee Williams, Albee, Max Frisch, Thornton Wilder, Brecht, Giradoux, O'Neill, Pinter, Cocteau, Kaiser, Wedekind, and Ibsen contain varying amounts of allegorical material.

The writer of allegory no longer uses personifications as characters; modern readers and spectators would be bored. His problem is finding concrete and specific representations—characters, incidents, milieu—for the abstractions and generalizations he wants to discuss and the metaphysical point he wants to make. It is sometimes a tightrope to walk; if he follows the abstraction too closely, the allegory may turn out to be rigid or artificial. But if he is too free in his treatment, the idea he wants to communicate may be lost. Some satirists—and many modern playwrights—have proved particularly adept at creating a new kind of satiric allegory particularly suited for the twentieth-century audience.

CHAPTER NINE

The Technique of Superiority

NEXT TO THE THEORY of incongruity, the most popular explanation of humor is that we laugh because we feel superior. Obviously this bald statement is insufficient: superiority alone is not enough to cause laughter, and *incongruity must be present* in some form before comic pleasure is experienced. But so many writers have accepted the superiority theory that their view is worth examining.

The authority most often quoted is Thomas Hobbes: "Laughter is nothing else but a sudden glory arising from a sudden conception of some eminency in ourselves, by comparison with the infirmity of others, or with our own formerly." A man who is laughed at, says Hobbes, is "triumphed over"; that is why we do not laugh when our friends or we ourselves are the subject of jest.

In different ways this concept has been elaborated upon by other writers. Bergson thinks that laughter is society's way of pushing the nonconformist back in line by humiliating him. In all laughter Bergson sees "an unavowed intention to humiliate and nature has implanted even in the best of men a spark of spitefulness which makes this activity universal and socially useful." Stephen Leacock insists that laughter originated as a primitive shout of triumph, and more recently Albert Rapp traced all humor to the single prototype he calls "thrashing laughter," the laughter of triumph after a physical duel. Laughter at sexual or other forbidden topics Rapp considers a temporary victory over social taboos. A. M. Ludovici identifies the smile as the vestigial remnant of an animal's fang baring when he triumphed. Humorist Irvin S. Cobb was convinced that "nearly all humor is founded on the idea of embarrassment or ridicule or suffering for somebody else."

Derision is not limited to our own culture. A popular German clown of the medieval period, Conrad Pacher, began his successful career as a court jester by hanging a boy on a tree because he was scabrous. The western Indians among whom Whittaker lived practiced a humor which was sometimes very cruel and involved "the most cutting and effective ridicule." Anthropologist Beck found that the humor of personal humiliation was rarer among the Woodland Indians than it was among whites, but his friends were not perfect and chose names describing physical deformities to identify their less fortunate colleagues.[1]

That superiority is a basic element of Chinese satire is admitted by George Kao: "The teller of these tales can feel definitely superior to his fellow beings— . . . physical defects and mental deformities . . . poor scholar . . . teacher's incompetence and downfall . . . every doctor a quack . . .

every cook a thief . . . greedy guests and miserly hosts . . . impatient maidens marrying backward 'son-in-laws' . . . the henpecked husband . . . moron jokes."

Eskimos appeal to the pleasure of superiority in direct fashion. Dr. Ralph Piddington describes Eskimos using public degradation as a means of maintaining social status. "If a man has been wronged, he has the right to make a public speech, trying to make the wrong-doer appear as ridiculous as possible. The latter then gives a similar speech. The one who is made to appear more ridiculous is, *ipso facto*, in the wrong."

Enid Welsford, listing the common traits of the buffoon in the Middle Ages, includes his appeal to the superiority of the simple, coarse people; heartlessness, the callous, brutal form; grossness; obscenity; "the normal functions of the human body have always provided the human race with inexhaustible sources of merriment."

Dr. Bergler believes that all laughter, not just that of satirists, is an expression of aggressive desire. According to Dr. Bergler, everyone is disturbed by the difference between the ideal man he had hoped to become and the imperfect man he actually is. Laughter is a pseudoaggressive expression of our pleasure at finding that other people are also imperfect, and there is nothing kindly about the process.

The sources of superiority vary. It has been suggested that our pleasure in puns stems from superiority to the language itself. Laughter at other races, other religions, other nationalities, is laughter at socially "inferior" groups, giving pleasure by identification with the superior group. Most racial jokes are superior and insulting, usually at the expense of a stereotype representing the nation or race. This has been demonstrated by telling the same joke to different groups, changing in each case the name of the butt of the joke. When the butt's name was that of a nonmember of the group which was hearing the joke, the group laughed heartily. Otherwise, it did not.

Certainly superiority plays a part in the pleasure one gets from Ambrose Bierce's one-line review, "The covers of this book are too far apart," and Mark Twain's remark, "A very good library could be made by leaving Jane Austen out." Superiority is at work when one enjoys Sibelius' comment about a popular American conductor: "He is a fine man, interested in many things—but not, I think, in music." And in H. L. Mencken's definition: "Democracy is that system of government under which the people, having 37,000,000 native-born adult whites to choose from, including thousands who are handsome and many who are wise, pick out a Coolidge to be head of state."

 ## Small Misfortunes

A GREAT DEAL of humor is based on the discomfiture of other people, in the form of *faux pas*, practical jokes, and revelation of ignorance or social inadequacy. Writers like Thurber, Leacock, Benchley, and Jerome K. Jerome made exaggerated accounts of their own small misfortunes an important source of their humor.

As long as no one is seriously hurt, we enjoy the mishaps of others. It is no longer considered proper to laugh at the crippled and the insane, as it was in Shakespeare's day, nor is the sight of a man being boiled in a huge pot as hilariously funny to us as it reportedly is to cannibals. But the humor of movie cartoons consists to a startling extent of pain inflicted on victims who seem impervious to injury.

One of Charles Addams' most popular cartoons shows a man who has painted the floor and suddenly realizes that he is stuck in the only dry corner.

Untermeyer tells of a guest at a large party who said to the host, "Who is that ugly woman sitting by herself?" "That," said the host, "happens to be my sister." "Of course," said the embarrassed guest, "I didn't notice the resemblance."

In a cosmic sense perhaps Bergson is right and all misfortunes are due to the victim's inability to adjust himself to circumstances; these misfortunes demonstrate the kind of mechanical rigidity which Bergson finds at the source of all humor. But, although few of us are willing to apply this dogma to ourselves, it is sometimes hard to draw the line between pleasure at small misfortunes and sadistic gratification at the degradation of others. Readers seem to have enjoyed the scenes of punishment in

Candide, Ben Jonson's plays, *Gulliver's Travels,* Saki's stories, and the whipping of servants, wives, and dignified gentlemen in Molière's plays and of miscellaneous unfortunates in *Don Quixote.*

Slapstick devices provide a great deal of satiric humor, from Aristophanes to Joseph Heller. Incongruity is a source of humor in slapstick, but superiority is also present, for there is always a loss of dignity suffered by the victim, and the audience revels in it. There is a surprising amount of slapstick in avant garde theater, particularly Ionesco and Beckett, the metaphysical concepts of the latter having been conveyed by pantomime, falling trousers, pinching shoes, hat trading, pratfalls, and slipping on banana peels. And that classic satire, Gogol's *Inspector-General,* has an eavesdropper fall into a room when the door breaks off its hinges; the mayor dons a hatbox; a love note the impostor writes on the back of an old bill is read aloud as "trust in God's mercy two salted cucumbers."

The practical joke, most people think, appeals to our sense of superiority. Whether the practical joker's motivation is sadism or insecurity or exhibitionism, or all three, is not certain. Bergson explains the practical joke as an illustration of his theory that "the mechanical encrusted on the living" results in humor. The victim of a practical joke, Bergson thinks, is similar to a runner who falls, and both are comic for the same reason—they have demonstrated "mechanical inelasticity."

One of Jonathan Swift's most successful prac-

tical jokes was at the expense of a popular fortune-
teller. Swift circulated among Londoners a prophecy of Partridge's death at a particular moment,
then distributed an account of the death. The dis-
traught Partridge, running around London in-
sisting that he was alive, became a laughingstock
and had to leave town. Later Ben Franklin, with
an eye on the dollar, used the same device when
he began publishing *Poor Richard's Almanack*.
Franklin predicted the death of a rival publisher
and in subsequent issues pretended that the death
had taken place.

Although some scholars deny that the practical joke is a satiric device, Gilbert Highet defends it. In his *Anatomy of Satire* he considers
the hoax a form of "parody in action."

 ## Unmasking

SATIRE FREQUENTLY "unmasks" somebody or something. That people get pleasure out of such exposés is unquestionable. The popularity of "peep-
hole" columnists, of "confidential" magazines and
books, and of gossip is evidence of the universal
human desire to have individuals and institutions
proved not nearly so good as they pretend to be.
Much of the pleasure presumably comes from our
consciousness of our own imperfections; it is gratifying to learn that others are also guilty of inadequacy or hypocrisy.

The devices which result in unmasking degrade the dignity of a person by calling attention to what Freud calls one of his "common human frailties," usually the fact that his mental functions depend upon his physical needs. Obviously, the greater the profession of virtue the more keen the pleasure of spectators when the pretense is exposed.

One form of unmasking is unintentional self-exposure, the revelation of a defect by a person trying to conceal it. Don Marquis' Mehitabel says, "To hell with anything unrefined." Pooh-Bah proudly announces, "I am . . . a particularly haughty person." And an old Chinese joke book tells of a scholar who received a letter from a friend asking him to buy a bird-cage for him. He forgot to make the purchase and, when the friend arrived, the scholar told him, "I'm sorry I didn't get your letter about the bird-cage."

A particularly charming example is the answer a student wrote on a history examination: "I don't know who the Albigensians are, but whoever they are and wherever they are I wish them a Merry Christmas."

We enjoy the pleasure of unmasking in the last words of Nero: "Jupiter! What an artist is lost to the world! What an artist!" We see it in Robert Owen's remark: "All the world is queer save thee and me—and even thee art a little queer." In the complaining letter of the old lady whose son had sent her to the Catskills for a vacation: "The food here is plain poison. And such small portions." In the advice of a psychiatrist to a patient who had confessed a childish fear of thunder: "That's ridiculous. Thunder is a natural phenomenon. There's nothing to be afraid of. Whenever you hear thunder, do what I do. Put your head under the pillow and it will go away."

Two religious anecdotes further illustrate unmasking. The priest put into the dying moneylender's hand a silver crucifix. "Very light, very light," murmured the dying man. "I can give no more than ten francs." In the other story a very pious old Jewess is taken to the hospital. The daughter undresses her mother and is shocked to find a crucifix. "Mother," she gasps, "how could you? Why are you wearing it?" The old lady mutters, "Just in case."

Finally, there is Ausubel's story about the old man on a hot train, moaning to himself, "Oh, am I thirsty." After hearing the complaint repeated a number of times, another passenger gets off at the next stop and brings the man a glass of water. "Thank you," says the old man and drinks. A little later he sighs, "Oh, was I thirsty."

Unmasking in satire is not limited, of course, to relatively innocuous pretenses such as these. Satirists unmask more serious hypocrisies—political, religious, and social—on the parts of human beings and their institutions. But they achieve humor by the same methods of indirect exposure, combining wit with criticism, that these anecdotes use. Ring Lardner presents a series of characters who reveal in letters, monologues, and diaries weaknesses that they are not conscious of revealing. Huck Finn's father exposes his ignorance and prejudice in sanctimonious orations intended to conceal those characteristics.

Lewis' Babbitts repeatedly reveal their inadequacies without being conscious of the revelation. But other characters unmask the hypocrites in the satires of Molière, Jonson, Aristophanes, Voltaire, France, Thackeray, and Gogol.

 ## *Ignorance*

IGNORANCE—in the form of social naiveté, mispronunciation, misspelling—has long been a favorite subject of humorists and satirists. Although some scholars think that incongruity is the source of amusement in these cases—because there is a startling difference between conventional behavior and the victim's—most critics feel that it is a sense of superiority that provides the pleasure. Usually it is the "inferior" deviation, or what the group assumes is an inferior deviation, that is laughed at, not a superior form of divergence. It is the weakest, the slowest, the most stupid who is laughed at, not the strongest, fastest, or most brilliant. A feeling of superiority is the reason we laugh at an individual who does not practice the social usages which we accept, such as wearing correct clothes at appropriate affairs, eating in the manner and with the implements we approve, pronouncing words as our locality pronounces them. It may be cultural superiority, such as that of *The New Yorker;* or intellectual superiority, assumed by professors toward students; or the superiority of experienced laborers to the apprentice. It consists primarily of the pleasure of knowing something that the victim does not know.

Snobbery is the reason for laughter by an older, or "higher," or sophisticated social group at the childish, the crude, the naive. This includes laughter by urbanites at farmers and laughter by farmers at the expense of city folk. It is the laughter at the superstitions of others and acceptance of the foibles of one's own group. It perpetuates such remarks by a fight manager as "We wuz robbed" and "He should of stood in bed." And it accounts for readers' pleasure in meeting the ignoramuses of Sinclair Lewis, Ring Lardner, and Mark Twain, and the ingenus of Voltaire, Johnson, Grimmelshausen, and Waugh.

Mispronunciation must have been a familiar source of humor by the time Aristophanes used it to ridicule a barbarous god in *The Birds*. Koestler is correct in observing that mispronunciation suddenly calls our attention to a detail, disrupting the usual pattern. But the disruptive detail is funny only when it is considered a sign of inferiority.

Similarly with dialect. The laughter at dialects varies with the social rating of the nationality represented (a French accent is considered by American audiences charming, but Russian, Yiddish, and southern Negro are ludicrous). Familiar variations are the stutter, a cheap but easy humorous device, and the lisp, which James Barrie as well as Gilbert and Sullivan used for comic effect.

Misspelling also pleases us by making us feel superior to the unfortunate speller—unless Koestler is right and a misspelled word, by providing a sudden "bisociation," becomes "a minor functional monstrosity." Instead of permitting us to see the word as we usually do—"a functional whole or a Gestalt configuration"—misspelling disrupts the pattern and calls our attention to an incongruous detail.

Although Josh Billings wrote, "There ain't no more wit and humor in bad grammar and spelling than there is in being crosseyed," Billings' "Farmers' Allminax" earned him $30,000 a year.

Some interesting misspellings by students have been immortalized in collections of *Boners*.

Christianity became popular because it promised immorality to the lower classes.

The couple was united in holy deadlock.

Gypsy Rose Lee is having her navel dramatized. As she is going to get married soon, she is busy getting her torso ready.

It was raining cats and dogs, and there were poodles in the road.

Absentmindedness has been analyzed as "the application of one habitual or professional pattern of thought or behavior to a situation which requires a different one." "Garbles" and "Slips That Pass in the Night" are forms of absentmindedness.

Ridiculing a German professor, a writer attributed to the pedant the following examples of absentmindedness:

I see a great many pupils who are absent.

Gotha is not much further from Erfurt than Erfurt is from Gotha.

Julian first killed himself, then his father.

Tacitus says the ancient Germans were as tall as our Honor Guards.

A bitter war ensued on page 94.

He drew his sword and shot him.

In an American collection of student boners, these gems appear:

Abraham Lincoln was born in a little log cabin, which he helped his father build.

Magna Charta provided that no free man should be hanged twice for the same offense.

You should always say hippopotami when there are more than one hippopotamuses.

In Aristophanes' *Birds* we find a pleasant example of absentmindedness when Poseidon exclaims, "Now, by Poseidon, there. . . ." And the Red Queen in Wonderland keeps shouting, at inappropriate moments, "Off with his head."

 ## *The Banal*

AN UNEXPECTED RELATIONSHIP between the madman and the conformist is observed by W. H. Auden. Auden's point is this: a human being should be unique, identical with no one else. But banality creates the illusion of identity; people who express their ideas in clichés make it impossible to differentiate the experience of one person from the experience of another. The cliché user, then, is "the megalomaniac in reverse." While the madman thinks of himself as being someone else—such as Napoleon, or God—"the banal man thinks of himself as being everybody else, that is to say, nobody in particular."

The banal character is a familiar figure in satiric literature—Molière, Dickens, and Ben Jonson have used him. Sinclair Lewis' Babbitt has become a word in the dictionary. Ring Lardner's characters converse in clichés, such as "don't do nothing I wouldn't do." The superficiality of Nathanael West's characters makes banality a dominant quality of their existence. The use of jargon by educated stereotypes makes them absurd, in novels of Kingsley Amis and somber reports of sociologists. Lenina Crown, Polly Trotzky, and their conformist colleagues speak in clichés in *Brave New World,* as do the citizens of *1984.* And *Dr. Strangelove* is enriched by the banal remarks of General Buck Turgidson during the tension of an unauthorized nuclear bombing.

Ionesco delights in satirizing the banality of the bourgeoisie. Line after line of dialogue in *The Bald Soprano* consists of nothing but trivialities and clichés. People lose their identity, resulting in a number of characters, male and female, named Bobby Watson. And in *The Shepherd's Chameleon,* a critic named Bartholomeus comes in, later followed by Bartholomeus II and Bartholomeus III.

Nor is the language of the Red Queen entirely spontaneous in her conversations with Alice.

" 'Garden,' " she says—"I've seen gardens. . . ."
On another occasion, "When you say 'hill,' " the
Queen interrupted, "I could show you hills. . . ."
Or, "You may call it 'nonsense,' if you like, but
I've heard nonsense. . . ."

In *Waiting for Godot* the following dialogue
takes place between the two tramps:

ESTRAGON: And what did he reply?
VLADIMIR: That he'd see.
E: That he couldn't promise anything.
V: That he'd have to think it over.
E: In the quiet of his home.
V: Consult his family.
E: His friends.
V: His agents.
E: His correspondents.
V: His books.
E: His bank account.
V: Before making a decision.
E: It's the normal thing.
V: Is it not?
E: I think it is.
V: I think so too.

Insult

IF THE AGGRESSIVE drive is as important to man as
most psychiatrists assume, the poison tongue must
have preceded the poison pen. The insult, the
jibe, the retort vary in subtlety, originality, and
vehemence. They appeal sometimes to superiority,
sometimes to censor-evasion, usually to both simultaneously. And they differ from invective in

that there is always an element of indirection, obliqueness, deviousness.

Freud maintains that, because our hostile impulses towards others have been repressed by society since our childhood, verbal hostility replaces physical attack; we obtain the pleasure of our enemy's degradation by scorning and ridiculing him in the presence of a third person, an inactive spectator who laughs. Wit permits us to evade the restrictions of society and to express our aggressions safely.

The insult is the basic appeal of Clare Boothe Luce's *The Women,* George S. Kaufman's *The Man Who Came to Dinner,* and much of W. C. Fields's comedy. It varies in directness from Wilson Mizner's "You're a mouse studying to be a rat" to Groucho Marx's letter to the Friars Club, explaining why he had resigned: "I just don't want to belong to any club that would have me as a member."

Insults adapt themselves to the times. Bismarck, asked what he would do if England landed troops at Hamburg, said, "Oh, we'd notify the Hamburg police." Half a century later, when an Italian officer threatened, "And if Il Duce ordered us to invade France, who could stop us?" a Frenchman replied, "Monsieur has forgotten the French Customs Service."

Seeing Descartes enjoying a rich meal, the Duke of Duras said sarcastically, "What! Do philosophers partake of such sweet things?" Descartes replied, "Do you suppose that nature has produced all its good things only for fools?"

When bitter enemies Randolph and Clay met on a narrow street, Randolph said, "I never give way to scoundrels." Clay stepped into the gutter. "I always do."

Professor Kittredge of Harvard, having lost his balance and fallen off the edge of the platform, rose calmly and resumed his lecture with the remark, "This is the first time I have fallen to the level of my audience."

When Boileau was asked by Louis XIV his opinion of the King's verses, he replied, "Sire, your majesty wished to write poor lines and did it so well that you proved nothing is impossible for you."

Dorothy Parker said, when she heard that Coolidge was dead, "How can they tell?" When her pompous escort brought her home after a dull evening, he remarked, "I can't bear fools." Miss Parker replied, "That's strange. Your mother could."

A wealthy woman invited Fritz Kreisler to dinner and told him to bring his violin. "If I play," he said, "the fee will be $1,500." "Oh. In that case, don't mingle with the guests." "In that case," Kreisler said, "the fee will be $1,000."

Diogenes the Cynic, walking into a dirty bath, asked, "Where are those washed who wash here?"

At Heifetz's debut at Carnegie Hall, Mischa Elman mopped his brow and said, "It's stifling in here." His companion, Moritz Hofman, replied, "Not for pianists, Mischa."

Heine wrote, "Curious how Napoleon's detractors have all come to horrible ends. Castlereagh cut his throat. Louis the XVIII rotted to death on his throne. And Professor Saalfeld still teaches at Goettingen." Max Baer, having just been beaten for the heavyweight title, was asked how long Braddock would be champion. "Till he fights again," Baer said.

The literary review offers many possibilities for insult, direct and indirect. Heywood Broun, having won a court suit against an actor whom he had called "the world's worst actor," limited his comment on the actor's next performance to the single sentence: "Mr. X was not up to his usual standard." Heine wrote, "Uhland's poetry reminds me of Bayard's horse; it has every conceivable virtue but it is dead."

A friend accused Douglas Jerrold, "I heard you said it was the worst book I ever wrote." "No, I didn't," Jerrold replied, "I said it was the worst book anybody ever wrote."

The pun as an aid to insult is used in the review of a musical performance: "The Smith Quartet played Brahms last night. Brahms lost"; in Eugene Fields's "Mr. H played Hamlet. He played it until eleven o'clock"; and in Percy Hammond's "I have knocked everything except the knees of the chorus girls, and nature anticipated me there."

Nor is the witty insult a modern innovation. A Roman emperor, seeing a Greek who resembled him, asked the young man if his mother had been in Rome. "No, sire," the Greek said, "but my father has."

Brooks Atkinson once wrote, "X-play opened last night. Why?" Dorothy Parker felt that in the performance she had seen, Katherine Hepburn "ran the gamut of emotions from A to B." Mrs. Thomas Carlyle said, after reading Browning's "Sordello," that she still didn't know whether Sordello was a man, a book, or a city. In Huxley's *The Genius and the Goddess* a character evaluates the work of H. G. Wells as "acres and acres of shiny water, but never more than two inches deep," and also asks, "Those ladies and gentlemen in Henry James's novels—could they ever bring themselves to go to the bathroom?" And David Lardner finished his review of a play with the remark, "The plot was designed in a light vein that somehow became varicose."

W. P. Trent wrote, "In *Precaution* Cooper carved the first of his long line of wooden women." Oscar Wilde felt that "Mr. Henry James writes fiction as if it were a painful duty." Heine said, of a handsome minor poet, "All women love Hartmann—all except the Muses." And Dorothy Parker wrote:

> I would rather flunk my Wasserman test
> Than read the poems of Edgar A. Guest.

George Meredith thought that increased sensitivity to laughter and shrinking from being the object of it are important steps on the road to civilization. But if that were the only test of civilization we would still be at a very low level, judging by the amount of ridicule directed at those who are inferior in some way. And it is undeniable that spectators feel, and enjoy, superiority to the misers, hypocrites, poseurs, malingerers, and fops in the plays of Molière and Jonson and most other satiric playwrights. Readers seem to have found pleasure, through the years, in the misfortunes of Pope's victims and those of Dryden, Juvenal, Aristophanes, Voltaire, Swift, St. Jerome, Dante, Hugo, Orwell, Huxley, and Waugh—and the mishaps of characters in the works of all other important satirists.

CHAPTER TEN

Beams and Studs

W HEN a satirist chooses to use narrative as the vehicle for his commentary, he has available the traditional devices of storytelling: plotting, characterization, dialogue. But the satirist uses these devices in a special way, adapting them freely to his specific purposes in each satire.

Plot

PLOT IS rarely the most important component of a satire. The satirist's real purpose is to comment rather than narrate, criticize rather than recite. We get no feeling of inevitability from a satiric plot as we do from tragedy, no conviction that events must progress inexorably in the order that they do. Actually, in most satires it does not particularly matter in what order the events take place. The world does not change much, the satirist seems to tell us, and human beings do not progress appreciably, and the same difficulties remain. We have been given a glimpse of some problems, and have seen some pretensions exposed, but we really have not gotten anywhere. The satirist's vision of the world is communicated by a number of incidents and characterizations and settings and dialogues, rather than continuously developed by a single dramatic plot line. Like Housman the satirist usually concludes that the world is the old world yet, and nothing now remains to do but begin the game anew.

Most satiric works simply do not meet the classical requirements for proper plot. They violate Aristotle's rules of causal progression, Francis Fergusson's tragic rhythm of "purpose, passion, and perception," and Suzanne Langer's comic rhythm of "vital continuity." The disorder of satiric structure is sometimes justified by sympathetic critics on the ground that it is intended to be an accurate reproduction of a disorderly world. But the satirist is rarely interested in accurate reproduction—his basic technique is distortion—and a more likely explanation is that the satirist is temperamentally unsuited for prescribed, rigid methods of organization. *Dead Souls, Hudibras,* and Juvenal's *Satires* are unfinished, and the last chapter of *Rasselas* is entitled "The Conclusion, in Which Nothing Is Concluded."

The difficulties satirists often have with endings illustrate their ineptness with extended plotting. Satires usually end in disaster or submission —at best the resignation implied in Candide's "let us cultivate our garden," or the ambiguity with which *Huckleberry Finn* and *The Mysterious Stranger* conclude. "I've never done a single thing

I've wanted to in my whole life," Babbitt finally confesses. Sometimes, as in the theater of the absurd, there is no ending at all, just an arbitrary termination. Satire has the unique distinction, Philip Pincus suggests, of being the only literary genre in which the dragon "finally kills St. George, runs off with the fairy princess, and they both live unhappily ever after."[1] There is something to be said for that conclusion when one considers the painful denouement of *Gulliver's Travels, Brave New World, Day of the Locust, The Loved One, 1984,* and *Don Quixote.*

Satirists who write novels usually subordinate the satire to the story. To sustain the reader's interest they use a number of devices. Some satirists string together a series of independent sections, achieving a tenuous cohesiveness by having one character involved in them, as in the picaresque tale or *Decline and Fall* or *Dead Souls* or *The Tin Drum;* or on a journey, as in *Don Juan* or Li Ju-chen's *Flowers in the Mirror.* Or they rely on a loose plot, as in Dickens or Thackeray or Lewis or Smollett; or a single setting, as in Norman Douglas and Peacock.

While idealists from Plato to modern social planners have dreamed of perfect societies, satirists from Aristophanes to modern skeptics have ridiculed utopias. When the satirist goes so far as to show an actual utopia (such as Eldorado in *Candide*), he implies that man is not ready to appreciate it. The satirist may exaggerate, as in *Brave New World,* or invert, as in *Erewhon,* but essentially it is reduction to absurdity that makes the satire of utopia effective. It is a particularly attractive device for the satirist, who often lacks imaginative power and is a commentator rather than a creator; the satiric utopia makes use of the structure of existing society as the model for distortion.

The satirist needs such devices to keep the satire moving. Ideas are not enough, dialogue is not enough. Action of some kind is necessary to interest the reader, to lull him into thinking that the story is the thing. The easiest kind of story to create is one based on a journey. Sometimes the satire is, or begins as, a parody of a particular popular book about a voyage; sometimes it is a broad burlesque of the whole genre of travel books.

Many satirists have used this device, recognizing, as Frances Russell says, that "fiction can do without satire much better than satire can do without fiction." The voyage is the basic means of sustaining narrative interest in *The Golden Ass, Jurgen, Gulliver's Travels, Candide, Simplicissimus, Rasselas, Erewhon, The Satyricon,* and many other satires.

Though it is heartening to find modern criticism acknowledging that satiric plot need not meet Aristotle's criteria, the efforts of scholars to find a uniform pattern in satiric plot have not proved satisfactory, being either too nebulous to be useful or proving applicable to some satires but not others. For example, one critic's description of satiric narrative as "really a compromise between the Shakespearean and Shandean techniques" is too ambiguous to be helpful.[2] Another scholar was much more persuasive when he contended that "pure" satires display a striking *absence* of plot than when he claimed in a later book that there are three kinds of satiric plot: "rising and falling" *(Volpone)*, "running in circles" (the early novels of Evelyn Waugh), and "everything and nothing" *(The Dunciad).*[3]

Still another approach is offered by J. L. Potts.[4] We must distinguish between "two kinds of plot: the tragic plot, in *time,* and the comic plot in *space.*" The proper pattern in a comedy is "a grouping of characters rather than a march of events." Beginning with this premise, Potts insists that the lack of logical sequence of events in comedy, far from being a weakness, is a demonstration of the writer's skill. We should apply this quite different criterion and applaud their achievements, admitting that Shakespeare's comic plots are careless, Congreve's improbable, Jane Austen's trivial, and Sterne's nonexistent. Actually, Potts suggests, the finest comic plot is *Don Quixote;* the whole significance of the story lies in the contrast between Quixote and Sancho. Other excellent comic plots appear in *Tristram Shandy,* with its "finely balanced quartet of central characters—Walter and Toby Shandy, Yorick and Corporal Trim"; *Tom Jones; A Midsummer-Night's Dream, As You Like It, The Tempest;* and Congreve's *Way of the World.*

There are, of course, some satiric narratives and dramas which do have neat plots and ironic climaxes. Coleridge thought that only Sophocles' *Oedipus* and Jonson's *Alchemist* were superior in plot to *Tom Jones*—and the latter two works are permeated with satire. Wilde's satires end in ironic twists, and so do Evelyn Waugh's and Huxley's. One could make a good case for excellence of plot in *The Inspector-General, Tartuffe,* Duerrenmatt, Camus, Jonson, and Christopher Fry. But most satires ignore the rules for tight plotting, as *Hudibras, The Dunciad, Penguin Island,* Gulliver's Third Voyage, *Rasselas,* and *Dead Souls* demonstrate.

Neither Aristotle's dictum (a good plot must be unified, causal, climactic, and consisting of a beginning, middle, and end) nor Henry James's strictures nor anyone else's arbitrary pronouncement applies to satire. The fact is that any arrangement of actions or statements or settings which successfully achieves the satirist's purpose constitutes an adequate satiric plot. The only relevant test is empirical: does the satire succeed in reaching the audience at which it is aiming? If it does, then the plot is satisfactory even if it violates every dogma concerning proper plotting.

 ## *Character*

THE BELIEF that satiric characters are "types" rather than individuals has long been accepted.

Although several modern critics offer convincing modifications, it is still almost an axiom that satire and comedy deal with types, tragedy deals with individuals.

The satirist tends to use types because he is usually concerned with Man rather than men, institutions rather than personalities, repeated behavior patterns rather than uncommon acts. The type is an aesthetic compromise between an abstraction (which is dull) and an individual (who is unique). The satirist observes representative qualities and creates representative characters.

Externality and typicality are appropriate for satire, introspection and individuality usually are not. Although both Candide and Raskalnikov have committed murder, we do not want anguished introspection from the former. Nor do we expect Tartuffe to soliloquize like Lear. The characters of a satirist serve a special purpose. They are not expected to search the soul of man or speculate on his relationship to God. They are intended to show man's behavior and to suggest that what is true for Volpone is true for thousands of other Volpones. It is not the unique but the typical, not the eccentric but the representative, that best serve the satirist's purpose. One of the reasons for the satirist's avoidance of deep insight into character is that such insight usually leads to sympathy. But the satirist does not want his reader to sympathize—he wants him to smile wryly.

In considering the achievements of satirists, it is well to remember that evaluating fictional characters is one of the most difficult tasks in literary criticism. Scholars have so blatantly contradicted each other in trying to determine whether an author has created a type or an individual, a shallow or a profound portrait, that perhaps the business of appraising fictional characters ought to be left to intrepid experts. A number of these have committed their judgments to print.

Hilaire Belloc admits that there is not a single "character" in all of Swift's work and that Swift was unique in his inability to portray the individual. Analyzing the characters in Oscar Wilde's *Importance of Being Earnest,* Louis Kronenberger notes that Lady Bracknell, Dr. Chasuble, and Miss Prism are not caricatures of *grande dame,* clergyman, governess. "Caricature goes to reality for a model; . . . but these people are devoutly unreal; . . . are not caricatures but originals or, at the very least, quite literally *reductiones ad absurdum.*"[5]

Lord Jeffrey thought that Byron's ultimate weakness as a poet and dramatist was due to the duplication of character in Harold, the Giaour, Conrad, Lara, Manfred, Cain, Lucifer: "There is the same varnish of voluptuousness on the surface, the same canker of misanthropy at the core, of all he touches." Other critics conclude that Aristophanes and W. S. Gilbert, like George S. Kaufman, give us "strokes so broad and sweeping, so grotesque, as to be irreconcilable with soundly human veracity"; that "Smollett could not draw characters in the round, only in the flat. . . . They are marionettes"; that Auden's favorite technique is the use of the satiric "portrait"—not of an individual but of a contemporary composite.

William Hazlitt called Shakespeare's characters "men" and Ben Jonson's "machines." But that, as Wyndham Lewis observed, is what both authors intended. Men are to some extent machines, and their machinations are often so transparent that they are comic. The satirist wants his audience to make a quick judgment of his characters; simplifying—often oversimplifying—helps achieve that effect. To create complex three-dimensional characters would interfere with the quick derision which the satirist wants to arouse on the part of the audience.

Far from apologizing for the use of types, many scholars consider the method indispensable. In his book on laughter Bergson maintains that the depiction of general types is precisely the object of high-class comedy, and that in providing this particular service comedy achieves something that no other art can successfully attain. Those elements of our personality which are mechanical are intrinsically comic; they force us to imitate ourselves, and to permit others to imitate us. In that sense every resemblance to a type is comical and every comic character is a type. The ideal qualities of the comic type, Bergson finds, are absentmindedness, vanity, and the rigidity of virtues (earnestness) as well as vices (greed). Alvin Kernan goes so far as to claim that we find *only* caricatures in satire, never characters; he cites Juvenal's Romans, Pope's Dunces, Swift's Yahoos, and Philip Wylie's Moms.

The comic character is often a man with an obsession, like Molière's Miser, Jonson's Volpone, Dickens' Pecksniff, or Goldsmith's Vicar. Brant in *Ship of Fools* made no attempt to use anything but caricatures. And Joseph Heller's *Catch-22* contains Dr. Daneeka, a hypochondriac physician; Dr. Sanderson, a neurotic psychoanalyst; and Colonel Cathcart, a cowardly commander.

Many modern satirists deliberately choose stereotypes instead of realistic characters. The theater of expressionism uses the type as its very basis—and much of that theater is satiric. The theater of the absurd is full of puppet characters pulled by flamboyantly exposed strings. Nathanael West admits that he wrote *Miss Lonelyhearts* in the literary form of the comic strip. And Genêt's characters, like Brecht's, do not even try to be types but instead symbolize ideas, attitudes, and passions.

Sometimes the mere names of characters indicate that the satirist is not attempting to portray rounded individuals. Thackeray uses names like William Dobbin, Judge Budge, Tom Eaves (a gossip), Lady Slowbore, Lord Cutts, and Lord Dozely. Huxley names a porcine character Stoyte, his mistress Virginia Maunciple, an impractical scientist Shearwater, and the character modeled on Middleton Murry, Burlap. Fielding has Allgood, Western, and Thwackum. And Joseph Heller crowds into *Catch-22* Major Major Major,

Hungry Joe, Generals Dreedle and Peckem, A. Fortiori, Lt. Scheisskopf, and a nymphomaniac named Dori Duz.

At times one suspects that the cantankerousness of satirists affects the students of satire, so that scholars disagree on almost every issue. Arthur Koestler rejects Bergson's claim that tragic art deals with individuals, comic art with generalized types. If "types" determined comedy, Koestler reasons, then Greek tragedy, Morality and Passion plays, and expressionistic drama would be comic whereas Shaw's and Wilde's characters would be tragic.

Other critics share Koestler's conviction that characterization does exist in comic and satiric literature. Frances Russell insists that the main road open to the writer of satirical intent is that of character. Eric Bentley suggests that the thoughtful comedy of Shaw, Wilde, Pirandello, and several other twentieth-century dramatists has presented convincing characters, a significant evolution from earlier types and caricatures. And James Hall, in *The Tragic Comedians,* maintains that a group of modern English novelists, including Huxley and Waugh, "have found their strongest tensions between the preexisting type and the individual or idiosyncratic."

Mary McCarthy goes further. She suggests that comic characters in fiction and drama are likely to seem more "real" than heroes and heroines; that these comic characters, instead of learning from experience and changing, remain incorrigible and unaltered; that this resistance to change is quite as accurate a reconstruction of reality as is the development of nobler characters; that we identify with comic characters because we share their defects; and that we admire them *more* than we admire heroes "because of their obstinate power to do-it-again, combined with a total lack of self-consciousness or shame." Miss McCarthy concludes: "Real characterization, I think, is seldom accomplished outside of comedy or without the fixative of comedy. . . . A comic character, contrary to accepted belief, is likely to be more enigmatic than a hero or a heroine, fuller of surprises and turnabouts."[6]

It is generally admitted that in depth of characterization Aristophanes, Swift, Rabelais, Voltaire, Jonson, Molière, and Juvenal are weak, intentionally or not. But a distinction must be made between pure satires and works in which the satiric spirit is only one of several elements. There are only types in the neoclassical comedies of Jonson. But as satire becomes a subordinate element, individuality of character appears. Addison's Sir Roger de Coverley is an early example of the break away from type. Fielding's Parson Adams is a delightful "character." Thackeray, Gogol, Dickens, Dos Passos, Lewis, Huxley, and Marquand have created individuals. Although satiric novelists have not produced many great characters, they have created enough to disprove the charge of incapacity.

The detachment which is indispensable for

satiric perspective limits the kind of character a satirist is likely to create; his emphasis is on seeing rather than feeling, and what one sees is the outside of things, the surface, the behavior—which is exactly what the satirist is criticized for showing. Ironically, the less detached a satirist is—and, consequently, the less satiric—the more likely he is to create memorable characters, as Fielding and Dickens were able to do.

It is a dilemma few satirists have been able to solve, and then always at the expense of satiric effect. As a general rule, the better the characterization, the more rounded the personality depicted, the less likely is the work to be pure satire. It may no longer be true, in the tragicomic context of twentieth-century satire, that all satiric characters must be types; but it is still true that the more profoundly a character is developed, the less likely he is to be a character suitable for pure satire. The people in Huxley's *Point Counterpoint* are far more credible than the puppets of *Brave New World*.

What satirists themselves say about characterization is interesting but not conclusive. Sinclair Lewis praised *Manhattan Transfer* because Dos Passos refused "to emblazon his characters by tricks of caricature, which, though they are considerably harder to achieve than is believed by the layman, yet are pathetically easier than authentic revelation of true personality."[7] And Evelyn Waugh, asked whether he considers his characters typical, replied that he emphatically did not. "A novelist has no business with types," he said, explaining that types are the property of politicians, economists, advertisers, and "other professional bores."[8] The artist, Waugh pontificated, is interested only in individuals.

Two extreme forms of satiric character—the ingenu and the sophisticate—serve similar purposes for the satirist. The naiveté of the ingenu and the ironic detachment of the sophisticate both provide entertaining contrast between appearance and reality.

The ingenu, such as Candide or Gulliver or Waugh's Paul Pennyfeather, is a naive, well-meaning person who travels through the world without understanding the hypocrisy, duplicity, and exploitation which he observes. He records the superficial data but fails to even suspect what is really going on. The reader, however, does see below the surface and does get the implications. He has the double pleasure of feeling superior to the ingenu and evading the censor by inferring what the satirist's critical intention is.

The ironic sophisticate provides a different satisfaction for the reader, who does not feel superior to Norman Douglas' Count Caloveglia or Oscar Wilde's Lord Henry but rather shares with them the detached, disillusioned view of a ludicrous spectacle. The reader likes the ingenu but cannot help laughing a little *at* him; the reader laughs *with* the ironic observer as the latter comments wittily on the pretensions of man and society.

The sophisticate appears as an ironic commentator in Anatole France, Pirandello, Gide's *Counterfeiters*, Huxley's *Point Counterpoint*, Wilde's *Picture of Dorian Gray*, Cabell's *Beyond Life*, in Shaw and Beerbohm and Nabokov and Edmund Wilson. Sometimes he is completely cynical, like Wilde's Lord Henry, sometimes philosophical like Mann's Settembrini, sometimes whimsical like Schnitzler's dilettantes.

In the long tradition of the ingenu a number of variations have appeared. The new element in twentieth-century use of the ingenu, David Worcester suggests, is that the device has become irony for its own sake; it serves no ulterior purpose, whereas Gulliver, Candide, and Rasselas did. No condemnation is intended, and the ingenu who was used in a positive way by Socrates, Swift, and Voltaire, serves a negative end in Anatole France, Huxley, and Waugh.

When a satirist uses the pastoral, he makes the shepherd a variant of the "fool" who hides his shrewdness beneath a mask of simplicity, as in La Fontaine. Lewis Carroll, as Edgar Johnson observes, uses "the naive symbolic dream of a child" to reveal "the shams of adult society." And the Socratic method is a form of pretended ignorance that exposes error and hypocrisy.

Among the many variations on the ingenu in satiric literature Don Quixote has been most popular. The naive, high-minded, ascetic idealist, contrasted with the practical sensualist Sancho Panza, is one of the glories of satire. Melville's intention was similar, though the result a failure, when he tried to make Pierre "the fool of Truth." Candide's name identifies his function in Voltaire's tale. *The Madwoman of Chaillot,* Paul Green's Johnny Johnson, Gumbril in Huxley's *Antic Hay,* Samuel Johnson's Rasselas, Ionesco's Beranger, *Jurgen,* Wilder's George Brush in *Heaven's My Destination,* Sir Oran Haut-ton in Peacock's *Melincourt,* and Hudibras all demonstrate, in one way or another, the ironic contrast between the real world and the naiveté of the simple idealist. Another way of communicating this information is through the letters of visitors to the Western world, as in Montesquieu's *Letters From a Persian in England* and Goldsmith's *Citizen of the World.*

In his "Essay on Comedy" Meredith pays tribute to two comic playwrights. "Menander and Molière have given the principal types to Comedy hitherto. . . . Tartuffe is the father of hypocrites; Orgon of the dupes; Thrace, of the braggadocios; Alceste of the "Manlys"; Davus and Syrus of the intriguing valets, the Scapins and Figaros. . . . The mordant women have the tongue of Celimene."[9]

Bernard Shaw's portrait gallery has also been examined by scholars. Arthur Nethercott classifies Shaw's protagonists (and claims that this is the way Shaw himself looked at them) as the Philistine, Idealist, Realist, Womanly Woman, New Man, and Artist Man. A. R. Thompson thinks that Shaw's characters, although intellectually mature, are (with the exception of a few women) "emotionally about twelve years old." Almost all of Shaw's characters are abnormal in the sense that they lack family feeling and are not interested in other people, except intellectually. David Daiches suggests that Shaw's revolutionary contribution was eliminating villains from his plays and "making his audience the true villain of his dramas."[10] Louis Kronenberger agrees and finds Shaw's inability to understand that there are wicked people a serious deficiency. Shaw exhibits "no awareness of evil . . . the lost, or damned, or guilt-gnawed"; instead he blames everything on "corrupt classes or intolerable social conditions or vicious laws."[11]

The major characters in Sinclair Lewis' best novels have been described as unique personalities by some critics, as "types" by others. But Carol Kennicott, Martin Arrowsmith, and Dodsworth are not really typical of any particular class. Babbitt has most of the attributes of a conventional businessman, but he endures the frustrations and exhibits the eccentricities of a particular human being. Many of the minor characters in Lewis' novels seem to be types because they are portrayed only when exhibiting the particular weakness that Lewis is satirizing through them.

Lewis' method of introducing his characters

is, at present, regarded as old-fashioned. He tells
the reader about them instead of letting the characters reveal themselves. Like Thackeray and
Dickens, Lewis discusses the appearance, temperament, and habits of the men and women he
creates. Minor characters he introduces briskly, in
a few pungent and withering phrases. If these
minor characters are objectionable, the phrases
are contemptuous, the adjectives disparaging. It is
characteristic of the satirist in Lewis that he de-
votes a great deal more time to characters whom
he criticizes than to those whom he admires.
While he was planning a novel, Lewis visualized
in great detail all of the characters in it, good and
bad; but as he wrote the novel, he found himself
preferring to work on satirizable characters and
to ignore the "good" people such as Guy Pollock
in *Main Street,* Seneca Doane in *Babbitt,* and the
Catholic priest in *Elmer Gantry.* Critics of Lewis
say that his characters are largely adolescents,
overgrown boys like Babbitt and Gantry, shallow
girls like Carol Kennicott; the mature individuals
in his world are likely to be Europeans.

Lewis himself claimed that nowhere in the
world are there such exaggerated types as in the
United States. Americans, he said, are so ludi-
crously intense that realism—not satire—is sufficient to portray the grotesqueness. Lewis insisted
that the characters of satirists are convincing; he
once offered to name fifty characters in Dickens'
novels who are credible and memorable. In
reference to his own work he observed that no

fascist in *It Can't Happen Here* was as vicious as actual fascists, at the Nuremburg Trials, were proved to have been; that Sharon Falconer in *Elmer Gantry* was a virtuous lady in comparison with Aimee Semple MacPherson; and that he did not dare put Senator Bilbo of Mississippi into a novel, because he would be charged with ludicrous exaggeration.

It is true that the characters in satire are handled differently than in other genres. But it is not necessarily true that they are inferior. The purposes of the satirist in creating character are special. For one thing, as Pirandello said, "The humorist does not recognize heroes." So he is likely to delete heroic attributes in his characters. Furthermore, the satirist shares the French attitude toward politics—"Always changing, always the same"—and extends it to other areas of human activity. For that reason his characters rarely grow, develop, or change. Unlike the tragic hero who supposedly attains inspiring "perception," the satiric protagonist remains essentially the same. He may become resigned to a frustrating world, as Candide and Babbitt do, or intensify his misanthropy, as Gulliver does, but he does not really change.

The characters of successful satire achieve the purpose of the satirist. But he is castigated more than other writers for the inadequacy of his characterization, in spite of the fact that his purpose is often quite different from that of other writers. To create realistic characters like those of

Tolstoy, Mann, and Proust would interfere with his satiric objective. The unique intention of the satirist determines to an enormous degree the kind of characters he creates; satirists utilize certain personae and certain types because they have found, empirically, that they work, regardless of what scholars may or may not recommend.

Monologue

THE MONOLOGUE is used by satirists in two quite different ways: (1) The speaker unintentionally reveals his own defects, prejudices, and motivations while he thinks he is impressing his audience with his talents, wit, and magnanimity. (2) The speaker is intentionally satiric about the objects of his satire.

Sinclair Lewis uses the monologue very effectively for unintentional self-condemnation on the part of the speaker, and a close look at Lewis' method reveals most of the potentialities of this device. Lewis makes it a special kind of burlesque. The Lewis monologue is effective only when it is used as a subordinate device, in a narrative carried along by other methods. (Lewis' single attempt at a novel consisting entirely of a series of long monologues—*The Man Who Knew Coolidge*—was not successful.) The monologue is spoken by a victim of Lewis' satire, and the speaker quickly but unintentionally reveals that he is pompous, ignorant, stupid, verbose, trite, and confused. Proudly and confidently, he gushes an endless stream of platitudes, absurdities, and prejudices. The speaker often divulges in a few minutes his philosophy, politics, and intimate biographical details and expresses dogmatic opinions on the subjects Lewis is satirizing. The monologue is delivered in such realistic idiom that the mimicry becomes a kind of superrealism. Everything is said exactly as the speaker would have said it, if he had actually had occasion to say all of it at one time.

At its best the Lewis monologue convinces the reader that he is seeing a compression of truth rather than a perversion of it. That there is need to concentrate this kind of material is evident when one contrasts these satiric monologues with the serious soliloquies that Lewis' characters also indulge in. The soliloquies are realistic, credible, and dull. They parallel accurately the meanderings of a superficial mind and result in prosaic, trivial reflections.

The Lewis monologist consistently employs certain stock devices. He invariably speaks in euphemisms; he quotes overfamiliar proverbs; he constantly misrepresents the position of an imaginary opponent by stating it in obviously absurd terms—then refutes it; he digresses on any provocation; he discusses irrelevant minutiae interminably; he insists on explaining the obvious in stultifying detail; he proudly discloses "inside" information—which is patently incorrect. He makes confidential prophecies—which are ridiculous.

He soberly tells anecdotes about famous men; the anecdotes are pointless. He dramatically asks rhetorical questions and answers them—the answers are childish truisms. He makes a number of deprecatingly self-complimentary remarks—they prove contradictory. He repeats a curious scientific fact, the only inference he reaches from it being, "Now isn't that interesting." He implies with transparent modesty that the friends he mentions are important people, who rely heavily on his advice. He is proud of his cheap "cultural" and "artistic" tastes. He regards himself as religious, law-abiding, tolerant, and sensitive—and immediately displays his callousness, dishonesty, prejudice, and crudeness. In sentences full of abysmal grammatical errors he laments the misuse of language by the younger generation. He protests too much his lack of social ambition and his indifference to public opinion. And he likes to challenge an imaginary or absent opponent to stand up instantly and reply to devastating charges—as Lewis himself challenged God to prove His existence.

The comic monologue is a familiar device in American folk humor. Twain used it often, particularly in the person of Colonel Sellers in *The Gilded Age*—a forerunner of Babbitt—and in the diatribes of Huckleberry Finn's father. Ring Lardner employs the monologue for satiric purposes in a number of his most successful stories, particularly "Haircut." John O'Hara, Finley Dunne, and Arthur Kober make use of the device, emphasizing mimicry, burlesque, and exaggeration.

Robert Browning often utilizes the dramatic monologue for satiric purposes, as in "Soliloquy of the Spanish Cloister," "The Bishop Orders His Tomb," "Bishop Blougram's Apology," and "Mr. Sludge, the Medium." Evelyn Waugh's characters continually reveal their inadequacies and sometimes their asininity, as Lady Stitch does with her chatter in *Scoop*. The Chancellor in Lewis Carroll's *Sylvie and Bruno* begins a speech with "Ahem, ahem, ahem," and soon finds himself demanding less bread and more taxes. The female goddess takes an entire book to defend her position in Erasmus' *The Praise of Folly*. And Jules Feiffer presents brief cartoon dialogues in which both speakers rationalize and posture and reveal their hypocrisy while smugly assuming that they have fooled everyone.

There are of course many levels of subtlety. The monologues of Snoopy, the introspective dog in Schulz's "Peanuts," are likely to be fairly transparent. J. Alfred Prufrock conveys his love song at a slightly more complex level of self-revelation. John P. Marquand develops a number of ingenious variations in *The Late George Apley*. And Beranger, Ionesco's protagonist in *The Killer*, at the end of the play addresses to the one-eyed dwarf a long monologue in which modern philosophical concepts, science, politics, and Christianity are satirized.

The other kind of satiric monologue is de-

livered by a speaker who knows what he is doing—
satirizing individuals, institutions, or the cosmos.
Sometimes an entire book or play is built on this
device, as in Camus' *The Fall,* Fielding's *Jonathan
Wild,* or Beckett's *Krapp's Last Tape.* Beckett
also gives Lucky a ghoulish monologue in the
middle of *Waiting for Godot.* And Finley Dunne
let Mr. Dooley use this method frequently and
pungently. Sometimes the satirist uses dialogues,
as J. K. Bangs did in *A House-boat on the Styx,*
C. E. S. Wood in *Heavenly Discourses,* Landor in
Imaginary Conversations, and Lucian in *The
Dialogues of the Dead.*

Several contemporary entertainers use the
satiric monologue in nightclubs, and on radio and
television. Usually, the larger the audience the
more censored the entertainers are, either for political reasons in totalitarian countries, or by social
pressures and advertisers' restrictions in democracies. In spite of these handicaps such American
monologists as Mort Sahl, Will Rogers, Bob Newhart, Lenny Bruce, and Dick Gregory have managed to express a limited amount of social satire.

For each of these devices—plot, characterization, and monologue—the test should be pragmatic: Does it help the satirist achieve his purpose?
If it does, then it is proper for satire even though
it may contradict academic dicta, or ignore rules of
logic, or be inappropriate for other genres. There
are so many varieties of successful satire that no

latter-day Aristotle can impose his personal preferences as objective criteria. Satirists work out their
techniques and practice their craft, largely indifferent to all scholarly discussions of the nature
of satire.

PART FOUR

The Results of Satire

CHAPTER ELEVEN

Effects

MEN HAVE long considered satire a significant social force. The Roman emperor Augustus passed a law against satires and lampoons, the punishment for offenders being death by whipping. In some early societies, such as the Celtic and Arabian, satirists were taken into battle to shout insults and curses at the enemy.[1] In 1599 an edict in England forebade the publication of satire. Plato proposed laws against magicians and satirists.

Among the ancient Celts the writing of abusive and slanderous poems was considered an important part of the tribal poet's work, and specific provisions about the maledictions of satirists appeared in ancient Celtic laws. American Pueblo Indians use satire to help control and discipline the community. In each tribe there is an organization of religious clowns whose duties include entertaining the crowds during the intervals between ritual dances. These clowns ridicule white men, tourists, Indian women who imitate white women, and offending members of their own group whom they identify publicly.[2]

✳ *Effect on Society*

Proponents of the theory that satire is a powerful social force tend to be enthusiasts like Gilbert Cannan who says, "No tyrant, no tyrannous idea ever came crashing to earth but it was first wounded with the shafts of satire: no free man, no free idea ever rose to the heights but it endured them."[3] It has been suggested that the satirist is needed because he expresses what Dr. Otto Rank calls the "disjunctive process": the universal and ceaseless attempt of maturing individuals to liberate themselves from current moral, social, and aesthetic ideologies. Or, satire may serve a quite different psychoanalytic purpose: if Freud was right when he said that mental aggression is the modern form of the death wish, satire may be providing a socially acceptable release for a great many potential suicides.

Among satiric works which have been credited with important social or political results are Erasmus' *In Praise of Folly,* Swift's *Modest Proposal* and "Tracts," Sydney Smith's "Plymley Letters," the letters of Junius, the works of Philip Freneau and the Hartford Wits, and the satires of Charles Churchill and Peter Pindar and George Canning. Because he was so persistent, so prolific, and so long-lived, Voltaire probably had more influence on society than any other Western satirist. By the nineteenth century in France when the press became especially vehement, the custom had grown of saying, "It's Voltaire's fault."

In spite of these claims, the notion that satire has played an important part in reforming society is probably a delusion. Satirists themselves know better. Swift said that mankind accepts satire because every man sees in it his fellow's failings, never his own; a few months after the publication of *Gulliver's Travels* Swift wrote a letter pretending to be amazed that society had not already reformed itself. *Don Quixote* did not kill chivalry; it was dying already. Sinclair Lewis admitted that *Main Street* did not have the slightest effect on American provincialism, nor *Babbitt* on Babbitts. When Ring Lardner told a friend that he was going to crusade in his *New Yorker* radio column against vulgar jokes and stupid songs, he did not expect to succeed. "It won't do any good," he admitted, "except to my disposition." And John Donne doubted that satire would reform readers:

> To teach by painting drunkards, doth not last
> Now; Aretines pictures have made few chast.

It is wise of satirists to recognize their ineffectuality, for satire has had no more influence on society than other forms of literature. Swift's *Drapier's Letters* were less influential than *Uncle Tom's Cabin*. Juvenal's *Satires* disturbed Rome as little as Samuel Butler's *Erewhon* disturbed England. With great vigor Sinclair Lewis exposed fascism, prisons, lobbying, conformity, and provincialism without changing the normal course of events at all. Katherine Lever thinks that Aristophanes knew his limitations and, toward the end of the Peloponnesian War, "realized that the comic poet was powerless to alter conditions; all he could do for his fellow-sufferers was offer them escape through the imagination."[4]

The Pooh Perplex is delightful satire of modern literary critics, but the stream of absurd mythological, psychoanalytic, and religious interpretations keeps pouring out, unabated. *Mad* magazine has long ridiculed the excessive claims of American advertisers, without appreciable effect. Nor did *A Modest Proposal* convince a single English landlord to modify his policies in Ireland.

One reason for satirists' failure to achieve important results is that they rarely attack the basic problems of their societies. They tend to criticize hypocrisy, dullness, snobbishness, and folly and to avoid such issues as the political and economic structure of their specific society. But even when they do express themselves openly on contemporary issues, as Daumier and H. L. Mencken and Goya have done, they do not have any appreciable effect on war, injustice, and brutality, *except when they are expressing attitudes already strongly held by large numbers of people.* When a satirist is in tune with his time and expresses popular dissatisfaction, he may give the impression that he is influencing events. Usually, however, he is a symptom, not a cause.

When people already hold the opinions which satire expresses, those opinions are reinforced. But man's action is rarely initiated merely by aesthetic pleasure. When social change follows satiric protest, it is dangerous to conclude that the satire caused the change. What is far more likely is that society is ready for the change, the old institution has decayed and only its form remains, rigid and obsolescent. This principle also applies to new institutions which satire attacks, as conservative satirists often attack innovations; if the new institution is rejected, it will be because it is genuinely inadequate or premature, not because satirists opposed it. Significant satire deals with reality, not wishfulness, and it cannot successfully or permanently pervert the truth. The satirist who expresses unpopular views has no social effect, no matter how entertaining he may be. The unacknowledged legislators of the world are, like Congress, considerably behind the times.

Satirists rarely attack the fundamental political or economic structures of their specific society. Gogol satirizes politicians but praises the czar. Juvenal complains about the quality of emperors but accepts the principle of monarchy. Thackeray concentrates on snobbishness, scarcely a subject profound or dangerous. Dickens is concerned with hypocrisy and folly. But both Victorians accept the artificial morality of their time. Both pretend to take seriously the standards of their England. Francisco Quevedo ridicules types and vices but accepts the Inquisition and tyranny. In American satire Bierce and Mencken have ridiculed democracy; but Twain, Lewis, and John P. Marquand limit themselves to criticism of social conditions rather than of their causes. Modern Communist satirists accept the principle of communism.

Literature may have been influenced by certain characteristics of satire. Walter Blair suggests that in the burlesques of the late nineteenth century, "these irreverent comic men battled against the sentimental literature which became so popular."[5] But at the same time, other American comic men were deriding the new realistic and antisentimental literature. The modern American humorist may be, as Norris Yates describes him, "the conscience of the twentieth century." But it has proved to be a fairly genteel conscience.

Summarizing the influence of satire on English literature, John Peter concludes that "its function has been catalytic, its virtue to interpenetrate and refine the prose or poetry of other forms." The general effect, he thinks, has been to curb extravagance in style and promote discernment. Aesthetic effect satire has had, as every literary form should have. But hardly more than that.

Significant satire is concerned with the nature of reality. The reality which satire unveils proves to be always imperfect, often hypocritical, sometimes horrible. It is natural for an idealistic or naive reader to assume that the satirist is not only showing what is wrong but recommending what is right. The assumption is magnanimous but not necessarily correct. Often the satirist is telling us two truths: (1) There are many things wrong in the world and (2) nothing much is likely to be done about it.

Satire has not caused any major reorganization of society, which is probably just as well. The satirist rarely knows how to remodel society. To the extent that all literature has some effect, satire has influence. But it is doubtful that the influence of satire is as significant as its proponents claim. Also, since much satire is conservative, it cannot have any great influence, for its implied alternative is not very different from what it is criticizing.

Effect on the Individual

INSTITUTIONS, then, are not likely to be influenced by satire. But individuals are. Being exposed to public ridicule is generally regarded as one of the less desirable forms of recognition. Some people, deeply hurt as the result of satire, withdraw from activities which may expose them to further attack. Some strike back. Others try to camouflage their behavior to prevent future attacks. Still others pretend to share in the merriment at their own expense and thus minimize the sting. But no one really enjoys being satirized.

The effects of derision are sometimes tragic. Anthropologists have gathered from primitive cultures many examples of individuals who responded to public ridicule by killing themselves. Paul Radin, for example, lists in his *Primitive Man As Philosopher* some early societies in which the fear of ridicule was so strong that men would commit suicide rather than be exposed to it. Radin suggests that the need for prestige is so strongly felt that ridicule becomes a powerful instrument of social force. At this very early stage ridicule was doing what satire, more subtly and perhaps less effectively, would be attempting later.

A startling number of Japanese who committed what we would consider trivial *faux pas* felt that they had no recourse except suicide. In the United States too there have been excessive reactions to mockery. A Florida shrimp fisherman abandoned his family and pretended to have drowned. His reason: he was afraid of being teased unmercifully for falling overboard. Another instance is less amusing. When an earnest but naive high school student was asked in his high school English class, "What is in *Walden?*" he replied, "Water." The class laughed, and that evening the boy shot himself.

Professional satirists are credited with a long list of victims. Historians cite Archilochus, who twenty-six centuries ago revenged himself on a treacherous woman by writing such a devastating satire that she and her father hanged themselves. Scholars still point with pride to this literary achievement. A little later Hipponax, another Greek satirist, drove two sculptors to suicide by composing uncomplimentary verses about them.

Modern satirists have less lethal effects. When Swift prophesied the death of Partridge and then pretended that the astrologer had died, he made a laughingstock of the charlatan but did not cause his death. It was the kind of prank Augustan wits enjoyed. Nor did their Restoration predecessors practice moderation in attacking their enemies. Other satirists who named names include Juvenal and Aristophanes, Mencken and Twain, St. Jerome and Quevedo, Marston and Bierce, Hugo and Byron.

Not all scholars agree that satiric attack is particularly effective, even with individuals. A. R. Thompson makes the reasonable point that the persons most likely to understand and appreciate irony are "of the self-indulgent, ironic type" who are highly unlikely to put into practice the lessons it teaches. A *New Yorker* profile on a presidential candidate coined the remark "It's impossible to dislike X until you know him well," but there were better reasons for X's defeat. And there is no evidence that the anti-Walpole satire of John Gay, Henry Fielding, and Samuel Johnson had the slightest effect on Walpole's political activities.

The chief effect of satire is pleasure. That pleasure may consist of relief from dullness, as in Charlie Chaplin's definition: "Slapstick is a break in the monotony of normal conduct." It may be relief from "the tyranny of reason," as Schopenhauer suggested. Or, in Freud's view, it may be relief from authority. Satire offers the consolation of superiority, which is useful even if it is ephemeral; for many people even a momentary feeling of superiority is rare. Satire may also provide a fresh perspective, detachment, or balance. But essentially it offers aesthetic pleasure.

The direct effects of satire are less than momentous. It does have the indirect effect of influencing young writers and the intellectually curious—such as college students, still interested in ideals and susceptible to objective truth rather than purely selfish motivation. Satire affects the thinking and the styles of minds which have not yet frozen into rigid patterns. Some of these men and women eventually reach positions where they can influence social action. But satire is not unique in this potentiality. Every other form of literature does as much—or as little.

CHAPTER TWELVE

Limitations

SATIRE BEARS a bad name. Even writers interested in it have made disparaging remarks about it. Meredith's famous essay distinguished sharply between humor, which he admired, and satire, which he called venomous and disreputable.[1] The author of the only history of English satire, Hugh Walker, concluded that "satire at its best is a second-rate type of literature."[2] And Joseph Conrad dismissed satire as an inadequate art form.

Satiric books appear on publishers' remainder shelves soon after publication. George S. Kaufman, a successful playwright, when asked why he did not write significant satire, replied, "Satire is what opens on Monday and closes on Saturday." Frances Russell concluded that satire is "confined to the middle plane of life, shut out alike from its sublime heights and tragic depths."[3] The attempt to make Bernard Shaw's house a shrine, supported by public subscription, failed; people do not donate money for satirists, even the greatest satirists. They may respect them, but they do not love them.

There are several good reasons for the unpopularity of satire. One of its basic disadvantages is that *good satire appeals more to the intellect than to the emotions*. It does not appeal completely to the intellect, as Henri Bergson claimed, but to the degree that it requires the reader to think, it limits the satirist's audience; and to the degree that satire fails to offer emotional satisfaction, it loses popular appeal. Few magazines which are predominantly satiric remain in circulation very long. Satiric entertainers, like Henry Morgan, Mort Sahl, Bob Newhart, and Lenny Bruce, have never been able to keep a sponsor very long.

The detachment of the satiric method minimizes emotional involvement on the part of the spectator or reader, and to that extent limits the amount of empathy that he can experience. Without empathy there can be little catharsis. This is true not only in satiric literature but also in humor. Groucho Marx had to temper the sharpness of his wit and become a more "genial" commentator before he could achieve popularity on his television program.

It is a serious defect of satire, this inability to satisfy the fundamental drives and repressed desires of men. Myths satisfy these needs but when satire uses a myth it distorts or perverts it, instead of pretending that the myth is worthy of reverent treatment. Love, fear, sex, excitement—other forms of literature try to describe these emotions, but satire teases them, plays with them, creates a mood in which conventional attitudes are inverted.

A second limitation, related to its intellectual emphasis, is the fact that *satire is often puzzling.*

For millions of literal-minded readers any kind of indirection is mystifying, and any attempt to infer is uncomfortable. Even intelligent readers of satire sometimes reach conflicting interpretations. Daniel Defoe's *Shortest Way With the Dissenters* was at first approved by the Anglican church as propaganda for its position; when his real intention was recognzed, Defoe was put in the pillory. Herman Melville's *Confidence-Man* has been interpreted both as a cynical repudiation of the text from Corinthians and is a subtle affirmation of faith in that text. Exen Artemus Ward, who did not specialize in innuendos, sometimes found it necessary to add the postscript: "This is wrote Sarcastikul." When satire is most successful in achieving indirection and subtlety, it is least likely to be popular. There is always the chance, especially with understatement and dry humor, of being taken in—and nobody likes to be taken in. So the satire most likely to be widely understood is the poorest kind of satire—obvious, blunt, and oversimplified.

Still another handicap, stemming from the previous two, is the fact that *pure satire is rarely able to hold a reader's interest for a prolonged period of time.* Being witty is not enough. "Wit is the salt of conversation, not the food," said William Hazlitt, and Swift surprises us with: "But as for comic Aristophanes, the dog too witty and too profane is." Satire works most effectively in brief episodes; perhaps, as with sermons, few souls are saved after the first twenty minutes. There may, it has been suggested, be a feeling of guilt about laughing too long in a world which is not wholly suitable for that sort of activity. Montaigne's laughing philosopher, Democritus, could justify an eight-hour laughing day only as an alternative to constant weeping. But neither alternative is really practical.

Another disadvantage of satire is that *some truths are simply too uncomfortable to admit*, or to live with for more than a brief period at a time. The best-selling books are sentimental or historical or religious or sex-filled novels; the public knows what it wants. It is true that much of this popular literature also contains unpleasant material. But unlike popular literature and tragedy, both of which provide a natural emotional relief—tears— satire offers only the "unnatural" (socially conditioned) relief of laughter.

But life is not that funny, and satire remains an artificial technique for adapting to existence. Though Dr. Edmund Bergler overstates his case as usual when he says that men joke not because they are in a gay mood but only because they are "furnishing inner defenses in reply to a monster, conscience," nevertheless it is true that significant satire offers much more than gaiety.[4] Satire that survives is likely to deal with serious subjects and to emphasize the unpleasant aspects of those subjects. Most readers do not like to be exposed to unpleasantness—or, if they are, they want to be comforted and reassured about the unpleasantness. Satire, far from comforting or reassuring, exaggerates the disagreeable elements to a distressing degree, as in Mencken's remark: "The meek shall inherit the earth—and the strong will take it away from them."

A fifth limitation on its popularity is the fact that *satire is, or is generally regarded as being, cruel.* Caustic people are not popular, for even those who laugh at the satirist's quips are uncomfortably aware that his next jibe may be at their expense. They prefer to avoid him. Since superiority and aggression are basic elements in the satiric process, there is much that is cruel in the satirist's method. And to the extent that cruelty is repugnant, satire is objectionable.

This attitude is not new. Almost three centuries ago William Congreve's *Love for Love* was advertised in these words:

> There's humor, which for cheerful friends we got,
> And for the thinking party there's a plot,
> We've something too, to gratify ill-nature,
> (If there be any here,) and that is satire.

Satire offers considerable evidence that the good often suffer, the wicked often prosper, and lions prefer eating lambs to lying down with them. The well-meaning ingenus of Voltaire, Petronius, Swift, and Evelyn Waugh are mistreated, taunted, and defeated, with a minimum of sympathy expressed by the authors. Readers have perhaps felt justified in suspecting that satirists devote an inordinate amount of space to the brutal abuse of man by other men, by society, and by the universe. It is surprising how many characters are killed off by such humorous writers as Evelyn Waugh, Mark Twain, Gogol, and Rabelais. The Yahoos thrive and Hollywood mobs riot and Winston Smith surrenders to Big Brother. In all but one of Sinclair Lewis' successful satires, the sympathetic characters are defeated by society, and even Martin Arrowsmith can survive only by retreating to a research laboratory. The Elmer Gantrys win and the Savage kills himself in the Brave New World and Don Quixote dies.

Why men enjoy reading material such as this has long been debated. Some critics think sadism is the answer. Others, more subtle though not necessarily more correct, suggest that man transmutes his self-contempt—the awareness of his own failures and weaknesses and guilt—into the hatred of somebody else. Fictional characters serve this purpose almost as well as colored men in Mississippi, Jews in Germany, white men in the Congo, or Christians in ancient Rome. Freud identified repressed aggression as a common neurosis; satire permits the spectator to share in an attack on specified individuals and identified institutions, to take vicarious pleasure in punishing and ridiculing and scolding—all within the safety of a library or a theater.

So men sometimes enjoy cruelty, especially if the cruelty is displayed in socially approved form (gladiators in Rome, professional wrestlers in the United States, clowns beating one another, animals in Walt Disney cartoons committing mayhem). But even while men enjoy it they feel guilty about it, and aggression becomes annoying after awhile. A little of it goes a long way with people who are not abnormal, or who have not been made abnormal by war, hatred, or conditioning. So there is revulsion as well as pleasure in satire which exploits cruelty—either the cruelty of events or the cruelty of the satirist.

Emphasizing criticism rather than constructive solutions, *satire is accused of being negative*, still another limitation. Most people assume that positive motivations are healthier than negative ones, that it is more useful to do something right than to point out what is being done wrong. The "booster" psychology is not limited to Babbitts; most people dislike criticism. The fact that this virtuous attitude completely contradicts the pleasure the same people get out of released aggressions and expressions of superiority does not disturb them in the least. Most of them never become aware of the contradiction and resent Swift's comment: "We have just religion enough to make us hate, but not enough to make us love."

The satirist criticizes because he is skeptical of utopias, altruism, sincerity. Through careful observation he has compiled a long list of hypocrisies and imperfections, and he complains about them. But no one likes a complainer, even when he is right. So there is resentment against satire on this count.

As usual, psychoanalysts offer a different explanation. In this case it is Dr. Edmund Bergler who radiates light. People do not like satire, he says, because they know subconsciously that satire is not a genuine attack upon evil or weakness, but is, instead, a pseudoaggressive mechanism by means of which the neurotic satirist works off some of the conflicts within his masochistic personality.

From a very different source and at a conspicuously different level of sophistication comes another answer to the same question. In *Seven Days to Lomaland* Esther Warner quotes the remarks of her illiterate African houseboy: "White people tell stories just to give each other belly-laughs. That is a wrong-thing to do with a story. . . . The reason to tell stories is to say a true true thing that you do not know any other way to say. . . . I like on my tongue the taste of stories I can swallow down."[5]

Still another disadvantage, and a very important one, is that *satire dispels illusions.* Man needs illusions, even the illusions of fan clubs and intercollegiate athletics and aphrodisiac hair creams. Satire often points to the truth, and the truth is sometimes unpalatable. When persons whom we admire or attitudes which we share are derided by the satirist, we feel an irritation or shame, partly because we ourselves are disappointed and partly because our idols and ideas have been made to appear ridiculous. There are genuine rewards for accepting conformity, for being "well-deceived," which help account for the unpopularity of satire. A status quo which is wrong but socially approved gives more security than a truth which is not accepted. The stories which are most popular all over the world are, for children and adults, those with happy endings. Satire usually provides an unhappy ending.

Because it is an art specializing in exposure rather than praise, satire does not stress human yearnings for perfectibility and immortality. Consequently, it loses the attraction those aspirations hold for readers. Freud mentions a form of satire he called "skeptical wit," in which the writer "attacks not a person or an institution, but the certainty of our knowledge." Obviously no one who attacks the certainty of our knowledge is going to be very popular, or for very long. Everyone some of the time, and most people all of the time, read or watch or listen for sheer relaxation. Satire does not provide it.

Pragmatism is a universal and perennial philosophy, not merely a modern American one; the inhabitants of each society accept, or pretend to accept, whatever ideas are dominant in their society. But ironically, as the satirist sees it, men tend to exaggerate the virtues in their society (loyalty, honesty, kindness) and minimize the vices (murder, theft, corruption). The satirist suspects that, except in science, what men really want is not merely truth but a convenient truth—that is ,a statement which supports the attitude they already have. Modern American wits know that only their superficial criticism and innocuous humor are wanted on television; there is no market for the penetrating social commentary of which they are capable, or for Ambrose Bierce's definitions: "Immoral: inexpedient" and "Really: apparently."

Satire suffers from an eighth deficiency—*satire*

has a short life. Part of the problem is the purely technical difficulty of changes in language, which make puns pointless and witticisms perplexing. But far more responsible is selection by satire of material which is topical and quickly forgotten. Depending as it usually does on transient social conditions and values, on external manifestations of behavior rather than depth psychology, and on man's conflict with society rather than with destiny, satire tends to become dated much more quickly than does literature depending for its effect on universal emotions and lasting conditions. Very few satires written before 1800 provide pleasure today for readers outside the classroom. Mencken's books on philology have already outlived his satire. And Dorothy Parker remarked recently in an interview, "Let's face it, honey, my verse is terribly dated."

A final limitation is that *satire provides neither the catharsis of tragedy nor the escapism of romantic literature.* The effect of satire is ambivalent and ambiguous. It arouses conflicting emotions but does not quite satisfy them. It leaves the reader feeling simultaneously entertained and disturbed, pleased and annoyed. The resolution is not satisfying; no orderly pattern is offered, no harmonious unity imposed. Things simply come to an end, with a bang or a whimper. The reader feels, on the basis of his experience with other arts, that he is entitled to more than that.

In Defense of Satire

THERE ARE MANY JUSTIFICATIONS for satire. It makes criticism more palatable. It often reveals the truth, and knowledge of the truth is generally regarded as desirable. Satire is a gadfly to society, provoking a reevaluation of its attitudes, though not necessarily prompting any action to change those attitudes.

Satire entertains—that is its basic appeal. Its business, as Mencken says, is diagnostic, not therapeutic. It is not responsible for alternatives, nor should it be. It offers new perspectives to old problems. Like a plane spotter the satirist lets us know of the presence of an enemy whom radar has failed to observe; but the satirist does not himself fly the counterattacking plane, nor man the antiaircraft battery.

Many of the objections made against the satirist are unfair, because they criticize satire for failing to achieve objectives which satire is not trying to achieve. The purposes of satire often make indispensable such traits as unfair exaggeration, inadequate alternative, portrayal of an unpleasant world, and lack of beauty and sensitivity. Also, the use of types rather than characters, the lack of emotional richness, and the one-sided view of society are characteristic of satire and often necessary for successful achievement of the satirist's purpose.

Different kinds of minds make great criticism and great societies. It is absurd to attack satirists for not suggesting solutions for the world's problems. Satirists have a talent for seeing what is wrong; they have no special ability for seeing how it should be corrected.

By reading satire, one can see the ubiquity of social problems and the continuity of social criticism. He may develop a sensitivity to subtlety. He will be constantly reminded that the conventional picture of the world is, to varying degrees, a false picture. Such reappraisal is refreshing and stimulating and healthy. These things good satire achieves. They are not mean achievements.

Notes

CHAPTER ONE

Characteristics of Satire

1. David Worcester, *The Art of Satire* (Cambridge: Harvard Univ. Press, 1940), p. 37.
2. The satiric personality is discussed in: Leonard Feinberg, *The Satirist* (Ames: Iowa State Univ. Press, 1963).
3. Louis I. Bredvold, "A Note in Defense of Satire," *English Literary History*, 7 (Dec. 1940), 250–62.
4. John Dryden, "A Discourse Concerning the Original and Progress of Satire," *Essays of John Dryden*, ed. W. P. Ker, 2 (Oxford: Clarendon Press, 1926), 15–114.
5. See "Symposium on Norms in Satire," *Satire Newsletter*, 2, No. 1 (Fall, 1964), 2–25.
6. Robert C. Elliott, "The Definition of Satire," *Yearbook of Comparative and General Literature*, No. 2 B (1962), 19–23.

CHAPTER TWO

Sources

1. Kimball Young, *Social Psychology* (New York: F. S. Crofts, 1930), p. 130.
2. Bonaro Overstreet, quoted in newspaper interview.
3. Herbert J. Müller, *Uses of the Past* (New York: Mentor, 1954), p. 208.
4. J. Delancey Ferguson, *Mark Twain: Man and Legend* (New York: Bobbs-Merrill, 1943), p. 69.
5. Heinrich Heine, *Works of Prose* (New York: Secker & Warburg, 1943), p. 120.
6. V. K. Whittaker, "The Humorless Indian," *Pacific Spectator*, 1 (Autumn, 1947), 460.
7. Francis Bacon, "Of Discourse," *Essays* (New York: Charles Scribner's Sons, 1908), p. 152.
8. Molière, *L' Impromptu de Versailles, Dramatic Works*, 1 (London: George Bell & Sons, 1891), 407.

9. Bernard Shaw, *Quintessence of G.B.S.*, ed. Stephen Winsten (New York: Creative Age Press, 1949), p. 25.

10. Heinrich Heine, *Works of Prose* (New York: Secker & Warburg, 1943), p. 177.

CHAPTER THREE

Image of the World

1. Ruby Cohn, *Samuel Beckett: The Comic Gamut* (New Brunswick: Rutgers Univ. Press, 1964), p. 299.

2. Sven Armens, *John Gay: Social Critic* (New York: Kings Crown Press, Columbia Univ., 1954), p. 183.

CHAPTER FOUR

The Bitter and the Sweet

1. Ernst Kris, "Ego Development and the Comic," *International Journal of Psychoanalysis*, 19 (1938), 88.

2. Arthur Koestler, *Insight and Outlook* (New York: Macmillan, 1949), p. 71.

3. David Worcester, *The Art of Satire* (Cambridge: Harvard Univ. Press, 1940), pp. 60–70.

4. Sidney Tarachow, "Clowns and Circuses," *Psychoanalysis and Social Sciences*, 3 (1951), 181.

5. Wolfgang M. Zucker, "The Image of the Clown," *Journal of Aesthetics*, 12 (1954), 312.

6. M. J. Rudwin, *The Devil in Legend and Literature* (London: Open Court Publ. Co., 1931), p. 279.

7. Francis M. Cornford, *Attic Comedy* (London: E. Arnold, 1914), p. 68.

8. Phyllis Greenacre, *Swift and Carroll* (New York: Int. Univ. Press, 1955), p. 115.

9. John Dryden, "A Discourse Concerning the Original and Progress of Satire," *Essays of John Dryden*, ed. W. P. Ker, 2 (Oxford: Clarendon Press, 1926), 65.

10. Mary Claire Randolph, "The Structural Design of Formal Verse Satire," *Philological Quarterly*, 21 (1942), 373.

CHAPTER FIVE

Theory of Satiric Technique

1. John Dryden, "A Discourse Concerning the Original and Progress of Satire," *Essays of John Dryden*, ed. W. P. Ker, 2 (Oxford: Clarendon Press, 1926), 102.

CHAPTER SIX

The Technique of Incongruity

1. Edmund Bergler, *Laughter and the Sense of Humor* (New York: Intercontinental Medical Book Corp., 1956), p. 65.
2. H. L. Mencken, *Notes on Democracy* (New York: Knopf, 1926), pp. 55–56.
3. Northrop Frye, *Anatomy of Criticism* (Princeton: Princeton Uni. Press, 1957), p. 224.
4. Arthur Koestler, *Insight and Outlook* (New York: Macmillan, 1949), p. 78.
5. Harold E. Pagliaro, "Paradox . . . ," *PMLA*, 79 (Mar., 1964), 42–50.

CHAPTER SEVEN

The Technique of Surprise

1. Joseph Shipley, "Types of Irony," *Dictionary of World Literature* (New York: Philosophical Library, 1943), pp. 330–332.

CHAPTER EIGHT

The Technique of Pretense

1. Aldous Huxley, "Young Archimedes," *Literature for Our Time*, ed. H. O. Waite and B. P. Atkinson (New York: Holt, 1958), p. 27.
2. Walter Blair, *Native American Humor* (San Francisco: Chandler Publ. Co., 1960), p. 104.
3. Maynard Mack, "The Muse of Satire," *Yale Review*, 41 (1951), 80–92.
4. See "Symposium on Persona in Satire," *Satire Newsletter*, 3, No. 2 (Spring, 1966), 89–153.

CHAPTER NINE

The Technique of Superiority

1. Horace Beck, "Indian Humor," *Pennsylvania Archeologist*, 19 (1949), 54–60.

CHAPTER TEN

Beams and Studs

1. Philip Pincus, "St. George and the Dragon," *Queen's Quarterly*, 70 (Spring, 1963), 36.

2. W. O. Sutherland, *The Art of the Satirist* (Austin: Univ. of Texas Press, 1965), p. 93.
3. Alvin Kernan, *The Cankered Muse* (New Haven: Yale Univ. Press, 1959), pp. 31–34; and Alvin Kernan, *The Plot of Satire* (New Haven: Yale Univ. Press, 1965), pp. 95 ff.
4. J. L. Potts, *Comedy* (London: Hutchinson's Univ. Library, 1948), pp. 130–40.
5. Louis Kronenberger, *The Thread of Laughter* (New York: Knopf, 1952), p. 223.
6. Mary McCarthy, *On the Contrary* (New York: Farrar, Straus, and Cudahy, 1961), pp. 88–89.
7. Sinclair Lewis, review in *Saturday Review of Literature*, 8 (Dec. 5, 1925), 361.
8. Evelyn Waugh, "Fanfare," *Life*, 20 (Apr. 8, 1946), 56.
9. George Meredith, *An Essay on Comedy* (London: Scribner's Sons, 1913), p. 53.
10. David Daiches, "GBS," *Saturday Review*, 39 (July 21, 1956), 10.
11. Louis Kronenberger, *The Republic of Letters* (New York: Knopf, 1955), p. 176.

CHAPTER ELEVEN

Effects

1. Robert Elliott, *The Power of Satire* (Princeton: Princeton Univ. Press, 1960), p. 18.
2. V. K. Whittaker, "The Humorless Indian," *Pacific Spectator*, 1 (Autumn, 1947), 458.
3. Gilbert Cannan, *Satire* (London: G. H. Doran, 1914), p. 13.
4. Katherine Lever, *The Art of Greek Comedy* (London: Methuen, 1956), p. viii.
5. Walter Blair, *Native American Humor* (San Francisco: Chandler Publ. Co., 1960), p. 123.

CHAPTER TWELVE

Limitations

1. George Meredith, *An Essay on Comedy* (London: Scribner's Sons, 1913).
2. Hugh Walker, *English Satire and Satirists* (London: E. P. Dutton and Co., 1925), p. 143.
3. Frances Russell, *Satire in the Victorian Novel* (New York: Macmillan, 1920), p. 38.

4. Edmund Bergler, "Dislike for Satire at Length," *Psychoanalytic Quarterly*, 26 (1957), 195.
5. Esther Warner, *Seven Days to Lomaland* (Boston: Houghton Mifflin, 1954), p. 49.

Bibliography

AUDEN, W. H. *The Dyer's Hand*. New York: Random House, 1962.

BENTLEY, ERIC. *The Playwright As Thinker*. New York: Meridian Press, 1955.

BERGLER, EDMUND. *Laughter and the Sense of Humor*. New York: International Medical Book Corp., 1956.

BERGSON, HENRI. *Laughter*. London: Macmillan, 1911.

BLAIR, WALTER. *Native American Humor*. San Francisco: Chandler, 1960.

BOND, RICHMOND P. *English Burlesque Poetry (1700–1750)*. Cambridge: Harvard Univ. Press, 1932.

BREDVOLD, LOUIS I. "A Note in Defense of Satire," *ELH*, 7 (1940), 253–64.

BULLITT, JOHN. *Jonathan Swift and the Anatomy of Satire*. Cambridge: Harvard Univ. Press, 1953.

CAMPBELL, OSCAR J. *Shakespeare's Satire*. New York: Oxford Univ. Press, 1943.

CANNAN, GILBERT. *Satire*. London: G. H. Doran, 1914.

CHEVALIER, HAAKON. *The Ironic Temper*. New York: Oxford Univ. Press, 1932.

CLAYBOROUGH, ARTHUR. *The Grotesque in English Literature*. Oxford: Clarendon Press, 1965.

DRYDEN, JOHN. "A Discourse Concerning . . . Satire," *Essays of John Dryden*, ed. W. P. Ker. Vol. 2. Oxford: Clarendon Press, 1926.

DYSON, A. E. *The Crazy Fabric*. London: Macmillan, 1965.

EHRENPREIS, IRVIN. *Swift, the Man, His Works and the Age*. Vol. 1. Cambridge: Harvard Univ. Press, 1962.

ELLIOTT, ROBERT C. *The Power of Satire: Magic, Ritual, Art.* Princeton: Princeton Univ. Press, 1960.

ESSLIN, MARTIN. *Theater of the Absurd.* New York: Doubleday, 1961.

EWALD, W. B. *The Masks of Swift.* Cambridge: Harvard Univ. Press, 1954.

FALK, ROBERT P. *American Literature in Parody.* New York: Twayne, 1955.

FEIBLEMAN, JAMES. *In Praise of Comedy.* New York: Macmillan, 1939.

FEINBERG, LEONARD. *The Satirist.* Ames: Iowa State Univ. Press, 1963.

FREUD, SIGMUND. *Wit and Its Relation to the Unconscious.* London: Moffatt, Yard & Co., n.d.

FRYE, NORTHROP. *The Anatomy of Criticism.* Princeton: Princeton Univ. Press, 1957.

GROTJAHN, MARTIN. *Beyond Laughter.* New York: McGraw-Hill, 1957.

HALL, JAMES B. *The Tragic Comedians.* Bloomington: Ind. Univ. Press, 1963.

HERZBERG, MAX. *Insults.* New York: Greystone Press, 1941.

HIGHET, GILBERT. *The Anatomy of Satire.* Princeton: Princeton Univ. Press, 1962.

JACK, IAN. *Augustan Satire.* Oxford: Clarendon Press, 1957.

JOHNSON, EDGAR. *A Treasury of Satire.* New York: Simon & Schuster, 1945.

KAYSER, WOLFGANG. *The Grotesque in Art and Literature.* Bloomington: Ind. Univ. Press, 1963.

KERNAN, ALVIN B. *The Cankered Muse.* New Haven: Yale Univ. Press, 1959.

————. *The Plot of Satire.* New Haven: Yale Univ. Press, 1965.

KNOX, NORMAN. *The Word Irony and Its Context, 1500–1700.* Durham: Univ. of N.C. Press, 1961.

KOESTLER, ARTHUR. *Insight and Outlook.* New York: Macmillan, 1949.

————. *The Act of Creation.* London: Hutchinson, 1964.

KRIS, ERNST, AND GOMBRICH, ERNST. *Psychoanalytic Explorations in Art.* New York: Int. Univ. Press, 1952.

KRONENBERGER, LOUIS. *The Thread of Laughter.* New York: Knopf, 1952.

LANGER, SUZANNE. *Feeling and Form.* New York: Scribner, 1957.

LAUTER, PAUL. *Theories of Comedy.* New York: Doubleday, 1964.

LEVER, KATHERINE. *The Art of Greek Comedy.* London: Methuen, 1956.

LEWIS, WYNDHAM. *Men Without Art.* London: McClelland, 1934.

LEYBURN, ELLEN. *Satiric Allegory: Mirror of Man.* New Haven: Yale Univ. Press, 1956.

LOWREY, BURLING. *Parody.* New York: Harcourt, Brace, 1960.

MACDONALD, DWIGHT. *Parodies.* New York: Random House, 1960.

MACK, MAYNARD. "The Muse of Satire," *Yale Review,* 41 (1951), 80–92.

McCARTHY, MARY. *On the Contrary.* New York: Farrar, Strauss & Cudahy, 1961.

MEREDITH, GEORGE. *An Essay on Comedy.* London: Scribner's Sons, 1913.

MONRO, D. H. *Argument of Laughter.* Melbourne: Melbourne Univ. Press, 1951.

O'CONNOR, WILLIAM VAN. *The Grotesque: An American Genre and Other Essays.* Carbondale: S. Ill. Univ. Press, 1962.

PAGLIARO, HAROLD E. "Paradox. . . ." *PMLA,* 79 (March, 1964), 42–50.

PETER, JOHN. *Complaint and Satire in Early English Literature.* New York: Oxford Univ. Press, 1956.

PINCUS, PHILIP. "St. George and the Dragon," *Queen's Quarterly,* 70 (Spring, 1963), 30–49.

POTTS, J. L. *Comedy*. London: Hutchinson's Univ. Lib., 1948.

QUINTANA, RICARDO. *The Mind and Art of Swift*. New York: Oxford Univ. Press, 1936.

RANDOLPH, MARY CLAIRE. "The Structural Design of Formal Verse Satire," *Philological Quarterly*, 21 (1942), 368–84.

RAPP, ALBERT. *The Origins of Wit and Humor*. New York: Dutton, 1951.

ROSENBERRY, EDWIN. *Melville and the Comic Spirit*. Cambridge: Harvard Univ. Press, 1955.

ROSENHEIM, EDWARD. *Swift and the Satirist's Art*. Chicago: Univ. of Chicago Press, 1963.

ROURKE, CONSTANCE. *American Humor*. New York: Harcourt Brace, 1931.

RUDWIN, MAXIMILIAN. *The Devil in Legend and Literature*. London: Open Court Publ. Co., 1931.

RUSSELL, FRANCES. *Satire in the Victorian Novel*. New York: Macmillan, 1920.

SUTHERLAND, JAMES. *English Satire*. Cambridge: Cambridge Univ. Press, 1958.

SUTHERLAND, W. O. S. *The Art of the Satirist*. Austin: Univ. of Tex. Press, 1965.

TAVE, STUART. *The Amiable Humorist*. Chicago: Univ. of Chicago Press, 1960.

THOMPSON, ALAN R. *The Dry Mock*. Berkeley: Univ. of Calif. Press, 1948.

WALKER, HUGH. *English Satire and Satirists*. London: E. P. Dutton, 1925.

WELSFORD, ENID. *The Fool: His Social and Literary History*. New York: Farrar & Rinehart, n.d.

WORCESTER, DAVID. *The Art of Satire*. Cambridge: Harvard Univ. Press. 1940.

YATES, NORRIS. *The American Humorist*. Ames: Iowa State Univ. Press, 1964.

Index

ADDAMS, Charles: cosmic irony, 40; use of grotesque, 66–67

Aggression: appeal of, 5, 6, 10

Allegory: relation of satire to, 3; satiric technique, 201–5

Alternatives: failure to offer, 14–15; of Huxley, Lewis, 15

Amis, Kingsley: social satire, 27; unexpected honesty, 147

Amorality: in Mencken, Douglas, West, *et al.*, 9, 10; pleasure in satire, 7

Animal fable, 51–55

Anticlimax, 156–57

Apuleius, Lucius: references to sex, 75

—*Golden Ass:* satiric journey, 229

Aristophanes: attacks individuals and types, 29; effect, 255–56; hostile to his milieu, 43; hypocrisy, 25; insult, 225; misfortunes, 211; parody, 188; references to sex, 75; unexpected logic, 153; unexpected truth, 149; unmasking, 215

—*Lysistrata:* dramatic irony, 170

Austen, Jane: contrast, 128; use of fools, 48–49; verbal irony, 181

Ausubel, Nathan: "schlemiel" and "schlimazel," 49

BANALITY: satiric device, 218–20

Beckett, Samuel: contrast, 128–29; dramatic irony, 161; in-congruity, 103; monologue, 249; use of fools, 50; use of grotesque, 69–70; world as puppet show, 47

—*Waiting for Godot:* banality, 220; cosmic irony, 42; use of elementary devices, 89

Beerbohm, Max: indirection, 91

Bernard, Tristan: unexpected logic, 154–55

Bierce, Ambrose: animal fable, 52; attacked individuals and types, 29; insult, 209; verbal irony, 182

Big Mac: satiric allegory, 204

Bitterness: image of world, 58–60

Brant, Sebastian: world as fools' carnival, 48

Brecht, Bertold: use of knaves, 51; world as madhouse, 45

—*Good Woman of Setzuan:* cosmic irony, 42

Brevity: psychoanalysis for need, 96; technique of satire, 95–98

Browning, Robert: monologue, 248

Bruce, Lenny: monologue, 249

Burlesque: defined, 185–86

Burns, Robert: mixture of content, 79

Byron, George: characterization, 233; mixture of content, 79; unexpected honesty, 149

CAMUS, Albert: dramatic irony, 170

Capek, Karel: satiric allegory, 203; symbols, 199; unexpected logic, 152–53; use of animals, 54; use of realism, 62–63

Caricature, 116–19; art and painting, 118, 199; individuals, 118

Carroll, Lewis: banality, 219–20; parody, 190–91; unexpected honesty, 148; unexpected logic, 152; use of animals, 54

—*Alice in Wonderland:* world as madhouse, 44

Catcher in the Rye: hypocrisy, 23

Censor: evasion of, 8, 176–77

Cervantes, Miguel: dramatic irony, 160; subjectivity, 95; symbols, 199

—*Don Quixote:* characterization, 240–41; chivalry, 16; misfortunes, 211

Chaplin, Charles: use of sentiment, 77

Characteristics: appeal to intellect, 4; derision, 6; exposé, 3; freshness, 15–17; mixture of humor and criticism, 4; pleasure, 7, 8; pretense, 3, 4; stimulation, 17–18; superiority and aggression, 5; unfairness, 13–15

Characterization, 231–45

Chekhov, Anton: realistic satire, 100

Chesterton, Gilbert: Catholic satire, 9

Cliché twisting: technique for satire, 135–36

Comparison: disparaging, 130–33

Concentration: satiric technique, 99

Confidence-Man: use of devil, 73

Contrast, 124–30; theory, 124–26

Cosmic irony, 160–68 *passim*

Cosmos: source of satire, 39–43

Country Wife: deception, 193

Crane, Stephen: dramatic irony, 167–68; verbal irony, 182

Criticism: amount in satire, 4, 58–60

Cuppy, Will: understatement, 123–24; verbal irony, 179

Cynical wit, 138–39

DANTE: satire in censored society, 43

Daumier, Honoré, 39

Definition, 18–19

Derision, 6

Devil: function as critic, 72–73

Dickens, Charles: banality, 219; characterization, 235; mixture of content, 79; realistic satire, 61; subjectivity, 95

Disguise and deception, 192–93

Disparaging comparison, 130–33; theory, 130–31

Dissimulation: cosmos, 39–43; individual, 24–31; reasons for, 23–24; society, 32–39; source of satire in general, 23–24

Distortion, 4, 90–91; dialogue. 99–100

Dr. Strangelove: dramatic irony, 163, 171; references to sex, 76; world as madhouse, 45

Donne, John: effect, 255

Dramatic irony, 157–75; cosmic, 160–68 *passim;* social, 168–75; theory, 157–60; types, 159

Dryden, John: indirection, 93; insult, 225; preferred Juvenal, 7; satiric allegory, 202

Dunne, Finley Peter: monologue, 247, 249

EDUCATION: object of satire, 36

Effects: on individual, 259–62; on literature, 258; on society, 254–59

Egoist: dramatic irony, 160

Eisenhower, Dwight: parodied, 189–90

Endings: plot in satire, 227–28

Epigram, 133–42; theory, 133–35

Erasmus, Desiderius: monologue, 248

Erewhon: effect, 255; *reductio ad absurdum,* 112; satiric allegory, 203; satiric journey, 229; satiric utopia, 56–57

Erskine, John: realistic satire, 62; unexpected honesty, 147

—*Helen of Troy:* dramatic irony, 161

Exaggeration, 105–19

Expressionism, 100; satiric allegory, 47, 205

Externality, 93–95

FABLE: use of by satirists, 51–55

Feiffer, Jules: monologue, 248

Fielding, Henry: characterization, 235, 237; mixture of content, 79

—*Jonathan Wild:* pseudo detachment, 95; verbal irony, 179

Fool, 48–51

Fools' carnival: image of the world, 48–51

France, Anatole: characterization, 240; dramatic irony, 160; mixture of content, 79; unexpected truth, 149–50; use of animals, 53; verbal irony, 179, 183

Freshness, 15–17

Function: stimulus of satire, 17–18, 273–74

GAY, John: animal fable, 52

Genêt, Jean: characterization, 235; incongruity, 103; personae, 195; satiric allegory, 204; satirized law, 39; world as madhouse, 45

—*Balcony:* disguise, 193

Gide, André: subtlety, 92

Gilbert, W. S.: attacked individuals and types, 29

Giles Goat-Boy: satiric allegory, 204

Giradoux, Jean: satire in free society, 42; social satires, 27

Goethe, Johann: world as madhouse, 46

Gogol, Nikolai: satire in censored society, 42; satire in unstable society, 42; use of fools, 50

—*Dead Souls:* dramatic irony, 169; unfinished, 227

—*Inspector-General:* deception, 193; dramatic irony, 173; misfortunes, 211

Golden, Harry: *reductio ad absurdum,* 113–14

Golding, William: social satire, 28

Graham, Harry: understatement, 121

Grass, Günter: references to sex, 76; world as madhouse, 44

—*Tin Drum:* comparison, 131; dramatic irony, 164; *reductio ad absurdum,* 115; satiric allegory, 203–4; symbols, 200–201; use of grotesque, 68–69; use of realistic detail, 63

Gregory, Dick: monologue, 249

Grotesque, 63–72; historical context, 64–65; use in painting, 67–68

Guareschi, Giovanni: realistic satire, 61; social satire, 27

HARDY, Thomas: dramatic irony, 163

Heine, Heinrich, 6; contrast, 126; insult, 223, 224; irony of racial prejudice, 34, 35; mixture of content, 78

Heller, Joseph: characterization, 235; references to sex, 76; social satire, 27

—*Catch-22:* comic irony, 174–75; exaggeration, 107–8; mixture of content and techniques, 80; parody, 189; *reductio ad absurdum,* 115; unexpected honesty, 147–48; unexpected logic, 155; world as madhouse, 45

Hemingway, Ernest: contrast, 125

Horace, 7; attacks individuals and types, 29; Horatian satire, 4

Honesty, unexpected: satiric technique, 144–50

Hudibras: satiric allegory, 202; unfinished, 227

Humor: amount in satire, 4

Huxley, Aldous: characterization, 235, 236, 240; dramatic irony, 165; insult, 224; parody, 187; references to sex, 75; unexpected logic, 153; verbal irony, 183

—*Brave New World:* contrast, 128; imaginative richness, 8; pretensions of science, 16; *reductio ad absurdum,* 112, 113; satiric allegory, 203; satiric utopia, 56; use of realistic detail, 63

—*Point Counterpoint:* dramatic irony, 169; satirized individuals, 31

Hypocrisy: social reasons for, 26–29; source of satire, 23–43 *passim*

IBSEN, Henrik: realistic satire, 100

Ignorance, 215–18

Image of the world: animal fable, 51–55; criticism, 58–60; fools' carnival, 48–51; madhouse, 44–46; puppet show, 46–48; utopia manqué, 55–58

Immorality: in satire of Machiavelli, 13

Incongruity, 8; theory, 101–4

Incongruous groupings: technique for satire, 129–30

Indignation: moral indignation in relation to satire, 6

Indirection, 91–93

Individual: object of satire, 29–31; source of satire, 24–31

Ingenu: satiric type, 239–41

Intellect: source of satiric appeal, 4

Intention: means of distinguishing satire from humor, 4

Insult, 220–25

Invective, 8, 108–12; insults listed, 109

Ionesco, Eugene: banality, 219; dramatic irony, 171–72; exaggeration, 107; incongruity, 103; monologue, 248; satiric allegory, 205; world as puppet show, 47

Irony: dramatic, 157–75; verbal, 178–83

JACKSON, Shirley: dramatic irony, 168

Jerrold, Douglas: insult, 223

Johnny Johnson: world as madhouse, 45

Johnson, Samuel: need for brevity, 96

—*Rasselas:* characterization, 240; satiric journey, 229

Jonson, Ben: banality, 219; characterization, 234; hypocrisy, 25; misfortunes, 211; unmasking, 215; use of fools and knaves, 51

—*Alchemist:* deception, 193; greed and hypocrisy, 30

Joyce, James: impressionistic satire, 100; symbols, 200

Juno and the Paycock: use of elementary devices, 88

Jurgen: evasion of censor, 8; satiric journey, 229

Juvenal, 7; characterization, 235; effect, 255; hostile to his milieu, 43; invective, 8; realistic satire, 61; references to sex, 75; satirized law, 39; subjectivity, 95; Juvenalian satire, 4

—*Satires:* unfinished, 227

KAFKA, Franz: contrast, 128; cosmic irony, 42; dramatic irony,

161; satiric allegory, 204; symbols, 200; unexpected logic, 151–52; use of animals, 54; use of grotesque, 70
—*Castle:* dramatic irony, 165–66

LA FONTAINE, Jean: animal fable, 52
Lagerkvist, Pär, 100; dramatic irony, 165; satiric allegory, 204
Lamb, Charles, 72
Lardner, Ring: banality, 219; dramatic irony, 169–70; monologue, 247; realistic satire, 61; unmasking, 214
La Rochefoucauld, 3, 138
Law: object of satire, 38–39
Lehrer, Tom: use of grotesque, 68
Letdown: unexpected, satiric technique, 156–57
Lewis, C. S.: use of indirection, 91
—*Screwtape Letters:* verbal irony, 179
Lewis, Sinclair: alternation of direct satire, 92; banality, 219; characterization, 242–44; conformity as puppet show, 47; contrast, 127; criticized for distortion, 18; effect, 255; mixture of content, 78; monologue, 245–47; realistic satire, 61, 62, 99; social satire, 26; unmasking, 215; verbal irony, 180
Limitations: ambivalent, 272; cruel, 267–69; disturbing, 266–67; iconoclastic, 270–71; intellectual, 263–64; negative, 269–70; puzzling, 264–65; short interest span, 265–66; short-lived, 271–72
Li'l Abner: incongruous characters, 8
Logic, unexpected: satiric technique, 150–55

McCARTHY, Mary: subtlety, 92
—*A Charmed Life:* dramatic irony, 169
Madhouse: image of the world, 44–46
Maltz, Albert: dramatic irony, 168–69
Mandragola: deception, 193
March, William: animal fable, 52
Marquand, John P.: characterization, 237; monologue, 248; realistic satire, 61, 62; social satire, 27
Marquis, Don: understatement, 122–23; use of animals, 54
Marx, Groucho: evasion of censor, 8
Mask-persona: satiric technique, 194–98
Maugham, Somerset: cosmic irony, 41
Maupassant, Guy de: cosmic irony, 41; dramatic irony, 163–64
Menander: characterization, 241
Mencken, H. L.: 15, 16; attacks individuals, 29; insult, 209; invective, 108; *reductio ad absurdum*, 112; unexpected logic, 151; verbal irony, 181, 182
Menon, Aubrey: subtlety, 92
Misfortunes: satiric device, 209–12
Mixture: materials by satirists, 78–81
Mizner, Wilson: grotesque, 66
Moby-Dick: comic irony, 173; comparison, 131; dramatic irony, 166–67
Molière: banality, 219; characterization, 235, 241; criticized for characterization, 18; dramatic irony, 172–73; hypocrisy, 25; misfortunes, 211; overblunt satire, 93; satire in stable society, 42; unexpected logic, 153–54; unmasking, 215; use of fools and knaves, 51

Molière *(cont.)*
—*Tartuffe:* lust and hypocrisy, 30
Mondo Cane: use of animals, 54
Monologue, 245–50
Morality: difficulty of defining moral norms, 9; excessive morality of Alceste, 11
Mrozek, Slawomir: *reductio ad absurdum*, 115–16; use of animals, 54
—*Elephant:* satiric allegory, 204

NABOKOV, Vladimir: characterization, 240; subtlety, 92
Newhart, Bob: contrast, 125; monologue, 249; personae, 198
New Yorker: contrast, 125
Nietzsche, Friedrich, 16
Norms: reliance of satire on, 9–13; social, violated, 33; social norm base of satire, 11–13

O'NEILL, Eugene: social satire, 28
Orwell, George: cliché twisting, 136; parody, 187–88; satiric allegory, 203; social satire, 27; use of animals, 53
—*Animal Farm:* satiric utopia, 56
—*1984:* reductio ad absurdum, 113; satiric utopia, 56; use of realistic detail, 63; verbal irony, 182

PARADOX, 139–42; theory, 139–40
Parker, Dorothy: anticlimax, 143; insult, 222, 224
Parody: evidence of social norm, 11; literary genres, 188–89; religious, 186–88; satiric technique, 184–92; theory, 184–86
Peacock, T. L.: use of animals, 53

"Peanuts": exposé of pretenses, 31; incongruous characters, 8
Petronius, Gaius: references to sex, 75
—*Satyricon:* dramatic irony, 160; satiric journey, 229
Pirandello, Luigi: contrast, 129; cosmic irony, 42; dramatic irony, 162; unexpected truth, 150; verbal irony, 183
Plautus: use of fools and knaves, 51
Pleasure: element in satire, 7, 8
Plot, 226–31; types, 229–30; in time, in space, 230
Politics: conflict of Dryden, Marvell, and Rochester; Johnson and Charles Churchill; Roy Campbell and W. H. Auden, 9; object of satire, 37
Pooh Perplex: effect, 256; parody, 11
Pope, Alexander: attacks fools, 11; attacks individuals and types, 29; characterization, 235; insult, 225; satire in stable society, 42; world as fools' carnival, 48
—*Rape of the Lock:* contrast, 125
Porter, Katherine Ann: world as fools' carnival, 48
Practical joke: satiric device, 211–12
Psychology: hypocrisy, 24–25
Puppet show: image of the world, 46–48

RABELAIS, François: characterization, 237; invective, 8; references to sex, 75; satiric utopia, 55; subjectivity, 95
Realism: use of by satirists, 61–63
Realistic satire: characteristics, 98–99
Reality: relation of satire to, 3
Reductio ad absurdum, 112–16
Religion: object of satire, 38
Rogers, Will, 4; monologue, 249
Romantic satire, 98

SAHL, Mort: monologue, 249
St. Jerome: insult, 225
Saki (H. H. Munro): understatement, 121; verbal irony, 182
Sartre, Jean Paul: dramatic
irony, 161, 164, 165
Satiric allegory, 201–5
Satiric definition, 137–38
Schopenhauer, Arthur: incongruity theory, 101; "tyranny of
reason," 5
Sentiment: use of by satirists,
76–77
Sex: reference to by satirists, 74–
76
Shakespeare, William: use of
fool, 50; verbal irony, 181–82
—*Hamlet:* dramatic irony, 163
Shaw, Bernard, 17; anticlimax,
156; attacks conventional morality, 10; characterization,
236, 241–42; dramatic irony,
172; mixture of content, 79;
no shrine, 263; satire in free
society, 42; social satire, 26; socialist satire, 9; understatement, 122; unexpected honesty, 147, 149; unexpected
logic, 152; verbal irony, 182;
vulgarity, 105
—*Androcles and the Lion:* use of
elementary devices, 88
—*Devil's Disciple:* contrast, 126–
27
Simplicissimus: satiric journey,
229
Sinet, Maurice: use of grotesque,
67
Skepticism, 5
Smith, Sydney, 12
Socratic irony: hypocrisy, 25
Society: irony of hypocrisy, 33–
36; relationship of society to
satire, 42–43; source of satire,
32–39
Sophisticate: satiric type, 239–41
Sot Weed Factor: disguise, 193
Style: "rough" and "smooth," 92
Superiority: appeal of, 5, 6; the-
ory, 206–9
Surprise: theory, 143–44

Swift, Jonathan: characterization, 233, 240; contrast 124,
125, 126; effect, 255; invective,
110–11; mixture of images of
world, 58; personae, 194; satire
in censored society, 42; satiric
allegory, 202, 203; symbols,
199; unexpected logic, 151; use
of animals, 53; use of grotesque, 71; use of realistic detail, 63; verbal irony, 183
—*Gulliver's Travels:* imaginative
richness, 8; misunderstood, 3;
satiric journey, 229; symbols,
199–200; world as madhouse,
45
—*Modest Proposal:* effect, 256;
evasion of censor, 8; *reductio
ad absurdum,* 113; verbal
irony, 179
Symbol: satiric technique, 198–
201

TAINE, Hippolyte: satire in tune
with society, 43
Technique: impression of infallibility, 86; mixture of content
and techniques, 88; nastiness
without irritation, 86; problem
of holding interest, 85; use of
elementary devices, 88–89; variation, 89
Thackeray, William: characterization, 235; mixture of content, 79; subjectivity, 95
Theater of the absurd: caricature, 119; cosmic irony, 42; incongruity, 103; satiric allegory,
205
Theater of expressionism: world
as puppet show, 47
Thurber, James: animal fable,
52; anticlimax, 157; subtlety,
93; understatement, 122; verbal irony, 179
Travesty: defined, 185–86
Twain, Mark: attacks conventional morality, 10; dramatic
irony, 160, 165; insult, 209;
mixture of content, 79; mono-

Twain *(cont.)*
logue, 247; personae, 198; pseudo detachment, 95; satire in free society, 42; social satire, 26; unexpected logic, 154; use of animals, 54; use of devil, 73; use of fools, 51; verbal irony, 183
—*Huckleberry Finn:* dramatic irony, 169; unmasking, 214–15
—*Mysterious Stranger:* cosmic irony, 41
Types: characterization, 231–45 *passim*

UBIQUITY: satirists in all kinds of society, 43
Ubu Roi: world as puppet show, 47
Understatement, 119–24; theory, 119–20
Unfairness: reasons for, 13–14
Ungerer, Tomi: use of grotesque, 67
Unmasking, 212–15
Utopia manqué: image of the world, 55–58

VARIETIES: types of satire, 98–99
Varronian satire, 79
Verbal irony, 178–183
Vercors: dramatic irony, 168; realistic satire, 61; satirized law, 39
Verse satire: mixture of content, 81
Victims: no restrictions, 36–37
Voltaire, François: characterization, 237, 240; contrast, 125; effect, 254; references to sex, 75; satire in unstable society, 42; satirized law; unmasking, 215
—*Candide:* misfortunes, 210–11; satiric journey, 229; sustained mockery, 8

WAUGH, Evelyn: characterization, 236, 237–38, 240; contrast, 126; dramatic irony, 165; exaggeration, 106–7; hostile to his milieu, 43; incongruity, 103–4; references to sex, 75; unexpected logic, 154; unexpected truth, 149; use of grotesque, 69
—*Decline and Fall:* satirized individuals, 31
—*Loved One:* contrast, 125
Wells, H. G.: realistic satire, 62
West, Nathanael: banality, 219; characterization, 235; cosmic irony, 40; dramatic irony, 162; use of grotesque, 69; world as madhouse, 45
—*Miss Lonelyhearts:* dramatic irony, 164–65
White, E. B., subtlety, 93
Wilde, Oscar, 5; bohemian satire, 9; characterization, 233, 236; dramatic irony, 164; unexpected logic, 150–51, 152; unexpected truth, 149
—*Importance of Being Earnest:* contrast, 126; deception, 193; mixture of content and techniques, 80; use of elementary devices, 89

ZAMIATIN, Eugene: social satire, 57

Acknowledgments

Grove Press, Inc., for permission to quote from *Waiting for Godot,* by Samuel Beckett, translated from the French by the author, copyright 1954 by Grove Press.

Faber and Faber, Ltd., for permission to quote from *Waiting for Godot,* by Samuel Beckett. (English language rights outside the United States.)

The Viking Press, Inc., for permission to quote a two-line poem by Dorothy Parker, from the *Portable Dorothy Parker,* 1944.

Satire Newsletter, for permission to reprint in altered form two of my articles which first appeared in *Satire Newsletter,* Vol. 2, No. 1, and Vol. 3, No. 2.

Iowa State University Press, for permission to reprint several paragraphs from my book *The Satirist,* 1963.

The Public Trustee and The Society of Authors, London, England, for permission to quote from George Bernard Shaw's *The Devil's Disciple.*